Nam Vo has commendably dug deep into the Christian theological traditions to weave the different strands together into a coherent thesis that can be applied to the digital milieu, in particular, to the reality and the issue of discipling today's youth. One noteworthy aspect of this book is Vo's effort to contextualize the theological discussions in his personal experiences with Vietnamese young people with whom he ministered. The situation of Vietnamese youth depicted in the book demonstrates that the digital culture has permeated every geographic, social, and cultural reality, and presents similar concerns for the global church. Thus Vo's work is a valuable and unique contribution to the conversation that addresses the religious, spiritual, and moral development and well-being of the youth in the contemporary age – not in the least for the advancement of a theology of the youth in the author's home country of Vietnam.

Anthony Le Duc, PhD
Executive Director,
Asian Research Center for Religion and Social Communication,
St John's University, Thailand

Asian cultures have a reputation for embracing the internet with great enthusiasm. But what happens to people – to the church – when this momentous cultural change washes over a whole society? The first answers to this question are written in the lives of youth. Nam Vo's burning desire for the church to disciple the next generation well yields an impressive book that asks how social media use changes us. To ask this question well demands asking in fine-grained detail how youth are having their attention, lives, and relationships to their elders reshaped in "wired" age. Vo's careful engagement with these practical questions leads into a theologically rich response that offers a cutting-edge theological analysis of our social media culture and its effects. It should be mandatory reading for youth pastors in every nation in which having a smartphone is a rite of passage.

Brian Brock, PhD
Professor of Moral and Practical Theology,
School of Divinity, History and Philosophy,
University of Aberdeen, UK

Many churches seem to be fighting a losing battle to retain their youth in the digital age. This book addresses the problem head-on and offers a concrete proposal on how to help young people be faithful disciples of Christ. But it is not merely a how-to book; its unique strength lies in the solidly theological perspectives on which the praxis of youth discipleship is based. Perhaps more importantly, Vo shows that his practical proposals are doable by locating them in the context of Vietnam.

Simon Chan, PhD
Editor, Asia Journal of Theology
Formerly Professor of Theology,
Trinity Theological College, Singapore

Vo Nam moves us through and then beyond the tribal arguments of the evils or benefits of digital culture for young people and for the church. He leads the reader and the whole church to a place where we have a robust theological foundation for understanding discipleship that includes and uses the digital world. If you are reading this book, be prepared to be inspired to take your ministries of discipleship to new places and depths.

Rev. Steven Emery-Wright, PhD
Formerly Executive Committee Member,
International Association for Study of Youth Ministry
Former Lecturer,
Hyupsung Methodist University, South Korea

Fifty-two percent of the world's population is under thirty years of age and almost every one of them a digital native. Effectively communicating the gospel with people of this generation, and facilitating their discipleship, presents the greatest challenge to cross-cultural missions since the apostolic era when the Jewish story of the Messiah had to be mediated to a gentile world.

The global disconnect between the church and millennials has not only distanced Christianity from unreached youth, it has led to staggering numbers of christianized young people exiting church communities at speed. Vo Huong Nam's groundbreaking exploration of the relationship between digital media, youth, and discipleship could not therefore have been more exquisitely timed. Through his book, Dr. Vo expertly walks the reader through the complexities of ministering to young people immersed in the dynamic environment of the digital world. His Vietnamese heritage, research in Western Europe, and hands-on experience of youth ministry – together with deep insights into the theologies of formation of practitioners as diverse as Calvin, Bonhoeffer, and Nouwen – combine to ensure that *Digital Media and Youth Discipleship* will long remain an invaluable resource for this new frontier of missions for churches and seminaries worldwide.

Ivor Poobalan, PhD
Principal, Colombo Theological Seminary, Sri Lanka
Co-Chair, Lausanne Theology Working Group

Young people will be served well when leaders in the church listen well to the challenges they face, respond wisely with deep theological reflection, and seek above all things to present them with the good news of Jesus. Nam has served youth well in this work, and serves the church well, by bringing together a careful consideration of Christian spiritual formation with the challenges and opportunities of the digital age.

Graham Stanton, PhD
Lecturer, Practical Theology,
Director, Ridley Centre for Children's and Youth Ministry,
Ridley College, Australia

Digital technology is here with us to stay. But it is an ambiguous medium. On the one hand, it opens up new possibilities for networking and innovative community building. On the other hand, it opens up space for abuse, misinformation, and an attack on the nature of truth that should not be underestimated. This book begins with the premise that it is the responsibility of the church to guide young people through the complexities of digital technology and to help them utilize it faithfully as they work to participate in God's mission to the world. In wrestling with the question of what it means for young people to be disciples in a digital age, the book draws on theology as a dialogue partner and a guiding light, which can enable digital technology to fulfill its theological potential and to become a useful and valued aspect of the church's ministry. This book is both fascinating and timely.

Rev. John Swinton, PhD
Professor, Practical Theology and Pastoral Care,
King's College, University of Aberdeen, UK

Digital Media and Youth Discipleship

Pitfalls and Promise

Vo Huong Nam

© 2023 Vo Huong Nam

Published 2023 by Langham Monographs
An imprint of Langham Publishing
www.langhampublishing.org

Langham Publishing and its imprints are a ministry of Langham Partnership

Langham Partnership
PO Box 296, Carlisle, Cumbria, CA3 9WZ, UK
www.langham.org

ISBNs:
978-1-83973-663-6 Print
978-1-83973-881-4 ePub
978-1-83973-882-1 PDF

Vo Huong Nam has asserted his right under the Copyright, Designs and Patents Act, 1988 to be identified as the Author of this work.

All rights reserved. No part of this publication may be reproduced, stored in a retrieval system or transmitted, in any form or by any means, electronic, mechanical, photocopying, recording or otherwise, without the prior written permission of the publisher or the Copyright Licensing Agency.

Requests to reuse content from Langham Publishing are processed through PLSclear. Please visit www.plsclear.com to complete your request.

Scriptures taken from the Holy Bible, New International Version®, NIV®. Copyright © 1973, 1978, 1984, 2011 by Biblica, Inc.™ Used by permission of Zondervan.

British Library Cataloguing-in-Publication Data
A catalogue record for this book is available from the British Library

ISBN: 978-1-83973-663-6

Cover & Book Design: projectluz.com

Langham Partnership actively supports theological dialogue and an author's right to publish but does not necessarily endorse the views and opinions set forth here or in works referenced within this publication, nor can we guarantee technical and grammatical correctness. Langham Partnership does not accept any responsibility or liability to persons or property as a consequence of the reading, use or interpretation of its published content.

Contents

Summary xiii

Acknowledgments xv

Introduction 1
    The Importance of This Project for the Church in Vietnam 2
    Methodology, Context, and Audience 2
    Definitions 3
    My Church Tradition 4
    Evangelical Spirituality 5
    Approach to Spiritual Development 10
    Thesis Introduction 13
    The Path of the Thesis 15

Chapter 1 19
    The Time of Digital Media
    1. Description of the Emerging Connected Society 20
        a. Optimistic 20
        b. Balanced 21
        c. Pessimistic 23
    2. Christian Response 30
        a. Early Calls for Christian Response to Digital Media 30
        b. Mid-stage Engagement 33
        c. Digital Theology 39
    3. Theology of Youth Work 46
        a. God at the Mall 46
        b. Starting Right 50
        c. Bonhoeffer as Youth Worker 52
        d. Networks for Faith Formation 55
        e. Faith for Exiles 57

Chapter 2 61
    The Impacts of Digital Media
    1. The Impacts of Digital Media on Society 62
        a. A Brief History of Communication 62
        b. Characteristics of the Digital Age 63
    2. The Impacts of Digital Media on Youth 66
        a. Dumber or Smarter? 67
        b. More Self-Absorbed or Better at Collaboration? 72

    3. Youth Identity in the Digital Age 74
        a. Theories of Identity 74
        b. The Influence of Digital Media on Identity Formation
           of the Youth of Gens Y and Z 81
    4. Mentoring Youth 91
        a. Education 92
        b. Family 98

Chapter 3 101

Theology of Spiritual Formation

    1. The History of the Term "Spiritual Formation" 101
    2. Theology of Spiritual Formation 104
        a. John Calvin 105
        b. Dietrich Bonhoeffer 121
        c. Henri Nouwen 130
    3. The Practice of Solitude 141

Chapter 4 145

The Theologies Needed for Youth Discipleship Given by Dietrich Bonhoeffer

    1. Digital Media and the Gospel 148
    2. Theology of Self-Identity 152
        a. Type 1: Sculpture or Painting 156
        b. Type 2: Mirror 156
    3. Theology of Discipleship 164
    4. Theology of Community 172
        a. A True Community 173
        b. Participation 176
        c. Virtual Church 179
    5. Theology of Youth 188
        a. The Divinization of Youth 188
        b. First Thing First 190
        c. View of Youth in the Bible 192
        d. Prophetic Voice 194

Chapter 5 199

Youth Discipleship in the Digital Age

    1. What Aspects of Digital Technology Are Really Helpful? 201
    2. Youth Ministry 205
        a. Relationship 205
        b. Central Concern 209
        c. Participation 210

    d. Balance 210
  3. Implications for the Church's Practice of Discipling the
    Youth of the Digital Age 211
    a. Being "All Things to All People" 211
    b. Practical Applications 215
  4. Contextualizing the Theology of Spiritual Formation for
    Youth Ministry in Vietnam 225
    a. In the Faith Community 227
    b. In Personal Daily Life 231

Conclusion 239
Appendix 249
  Definitions of Spiritual Formation
Bibliography 257

List of Figures

Figure 0.1. The convergence of digital media, youth, and discipleship 15

Figure 2.1. The convergence of digital media and youth 61

Figure 4.1. The convergence of digital media, youth, and discipleship 147

Figure 5.1. The convergence of digital media, youth, and discipleship 200

Figure 5.2. Mapping the themes of spiritual formation with practical
    applications 227

Summary

Digital technology has permeated our everyday lives, especially the lives of the youth of Generations Y and Z who grew up immersed in it. Recent studies in the West have shown the downsides of this immersion in digital technology: the displacement of real community, cyber addiction, and the hypertrophy of self-publication. How should the church theologically and practically respond to this contextual challenge? This research will engage these problems as well as the positive sides of digital technology in the lives of youth in the digital age, focusing particularly on how youth ministry might understand the task of discipleship today. The thesis of this project is that the church that faithfully undertakes its Great Commission call to make disciples must minister to youth who are immersed in the internet culture. This project aims to be both critical and constructive; the church should neither just embrace nor just deny digital culture. Youth discipleship, as argued and proposed in this project, aims to help youth to encounter Christ in Christian community and personal daily life. Part of this task is to help them to understand what it means to be Christian in the world today surrounded, as it is, by digital media.

First, this research discusses the social and theological context for discipling youth in the digital age by surveying the best insights from various types of literature on the impact of digital media, concentrating on the topics of youth and discipleship. After investigating the impacts of digital media on society in general and on the youth of the digital age in particular, this project discusses a theology of spiritual formation by proceeding through main themes on this topic proposed by John Calvin, Dietrich Bonhoeffer, and Henri Nouwen, supplemented by several modern authors. Then it develops a constructive theology of discipleship by exploring the theologies needed for this task of discipleship such as a theology of identity and "self," communication, community, and youth. The concluding discussion reflects on the ecclesiological and cultural implications of this theology for church practice, and it issues a call to be "all things to all people," engaging practically in discipling the youth of the digital age. It also contextualizes the theology of discipleship among young people in Vietnam, suggesting spiritual disciplines in the digital age, particularly the practice of solitude, silence, and prayer.

Acknowledgments

This project is dedicated as an offering to God, who makes this project possible. I am also thankful to the many people and institutions who supported me with guidance, companionship, encouragement, finance, and prayers during the completion of this project. Some are specially mentioned as followed:

Prof. Brian Brock, my lead supervisor, who guided me throughout the whole project with great knowledge, patience, and encouragement.

Dr. Kenneth Jeffrey, my second supervisor, who guided me in writing one core theological chapter with wisdom, care, and attention, and gave helpful feedback on the whole thesis.

Prof. John Swinton and Dr. Eric Stoddart for examining this thesis.

Dr. John Jeacocke for proofreading this thesis.

Rev. Dr. Thai Phuoc Truong and Rev. Phan Quang Thieu, Principal and Vice Principal of the Institute of Bible and Theology (Ho Chi Minh City) for the endorsement to pursue a PhD in Divinity at University of Aberdeen.

Langham Partnership for the scholarship and its staff – especially Malcolm and Liz McGregor, Elizabeth Hitchcock, Dr. Danny Crowther, Dr. Parush Parushev, and Dr. Riad Kassis – for their wonderful care, support, guidance, and prayers.

Lecturers from Trinity Theological College – Rev. Dr. Simon Chan, Rev. Dr. Daniel Koh, Rev. Dr. Tan Yak Hwee, and Rev. Dr. Steven Emery-Wright – for encouraging me to pursue this study.

Lecturers from University of Aberdeen – Dr. Michael Mawson, Dr. Michael Laffin, Prof. John Swinton, Dr. Léon Van Ommen, Prof. Paul Nimmo, Prof. Tom Greggs, and Dr. Robert W. Heimburger – for imparting knowledge and giving guidance.

School mates from the University of Aberdeen – Emily Stevens, Juheon, Aleks, Kevin, Phil, Oscar Hyde, Samyeol Kim, Xam Murillo, Jiseung, and Sung Bin – for great companionship and support.

Aberdeen Chinese Christian Church for the accommodation, job, care, and ministry experience. Faithful leaders Maureen, Yuk Chun, Dick, Nga Lai, David, Jenny; all the children and youth in Sunday school; students in Friday Fellowship; and wonderful friends Man and Yvonne, Kayla, Fung, Qin, Elaine, June, Annie Wong, Annie Chan, Alice, Teresa and Kit, Grace, Allan, (Big) James, Sunny, Leo, Kate, Holly, Joyce, (Small) Yvonne, Jo, and Oscar Siu. Special thanks to Samuel and Faith, who have accompanied me closely since my first day in Aberdeen, worked together with me in children and student ministry, and shared with me wonderful meals, food recipes, and many things in life.

Friends from Bon Accord Free Church, especially Pastor David and Martha; Auntie Moira; Eugene, Carol, and the kids; Anthony and Enid; Alex and Thaisa; Lean; Richard; John; and JB.

The Vietnamese community in Aberdeen who made me feel less homesick by sharing Vietnamese food and having conversations in my mother tongue.

My home church in Ho Chi Minh City, all the youth who inspired this project, and all the youth workers who have journeysed with me during my time serving in youth ministry: Chị Bích Trang, Mỹ Phước, Bảo Toàn, Bảo Quốc, Tố Trinh, Bích Nga, Hồng Vân, Vĩnh Phước 85, Vĩnh Phước 88, Nguyên Ái, Đức Huy.

Wonderful friends – especially Bà Mục Sư Thiều, Cô Diệp, Anh Thiên Ân và Chị Thiên Âu, Anh Nhân Từ, Chị Kim Châu, Chị Kim Thoa, Chú Thắng and Cô Bích, Chị Hải Vân, Anh Việt Anh, Thanh Nhãn, Anthony Lee, Gloria, Abdiel, Mục sư Đỗ Đăng Khoa, Cô Thiên Hương, Anh Lê Vi, Anh Vũ Lê from BSV, Phước Thiên, Bảo Sơn, Hồng Trinh, Chị Tuyết Mai, Chị Xuân Thủy, Chị Huyền Thy, Trần Nguyên Ái, Ngọc Lý, Khánh Loan, Thiên Phong, Steven Hamilton, and Andrew and Marjory – for friendship, prayers, and support.

My uncles, aunts, and cousins for their love and care, especially my cousin Tâm Phương for giving feedback on some parts of this thesis.

And most importantly my parents and sisters for their unconditional love and endless support.

Introduction

Digital media, especially the internet, has permeated our everyday lives. The youth of today's generation, being the first to grow up surrounded by digital media, are eager to adopt modern technology for both convenience and entertainment. Most of them are very familiar with email, Google, YouTube, Facebook, Instagram, Snapchat, online games, etc. However, it seems that the church either has missed the importance of digital media in the lives of the youth or does not know what to do about it. As a result, churches are hemorrhaging their youth. How should the church of Christ respond to the dynamics of this digital culture and disciple the youth of this generation? Should the contemporary Christian church use digital media in discipling their youth?

As one who has been ministering to young people for quite a number of years, I understand the struggles they are going through as they try to make sense of this new world that is crashing down on them. Fascinated by the newfound freedom and access the internet allows them, they also have a hard time sifting through the good and the bad, discerning what to keep and what to discard, and avoiding the temptations so tantalizingly present at every click of the mouse. More importantly, the youth are not equipped to recognize and handle the moral implications that digital media has on their spiritual lives. Among older Christians, fear and feelings of inadequacy in addressing the issue are also understandable. The aggressive pace of technology makes it tremendously hard for the leaders of the church, mostly several generations removed from the youth, to keep up, let alone to utilize its impact for the good of the youth. Their seeming lack of concern is thus also best sympathized with rather than criticized. We need to come alongside the church to encourage and assist Christians in their effort to disciple youth in this digital age.[1]

After initially indicating the relevance of this thesis for my home church context in Vietnam, this introduction will briefly present the methodology, context, and audience of this project and give definitions of some key terms. The focus of my analysis is on my church tradition, evangelical spirituality, with its characteristic approach to spiritual development. The introduction ends with an outline of the argument of the thesis as a whole as well as a survey of the arguments of the thesis chapters.

The Importance of This Project for the Church in Vietnam

In my home country, Vietnam, the church has not built a theology for discipling youth in the digital age. The principal aim of this thesis is creating a theology of discipleship for young people in today's digital age. This thesis is an exercise in pastoral and practical theology, and it aims to assist churches in the task of discipling young people more adequately as well as empowering them to participate in and to bless the church through their gifts. It serves the church's pastoral work of helping youth to be at home in an authentic community where real living for Christ is shared face to face and beyond. A better understanding of the effects that modern technology has on youth will help the church disciple this generation with discernment, authenticity, and faithfulness.

Methodology, Context, and Audience

This research will be a study of written sources to construct an inductive understanding of how young people receive and communicate the gospel digitally. At the same time, it will also examine various approaches in discipleship in this particular context of digital culture. At last, as one who belongs to Gen Y and has been ministering to young people for quite a number of years, I will suggest practical applications to disciple the youth of the digital

---

1. These opening paragraphs previously appeared in my article: Vo, "What is Good about Digital Technology," 212–237.

age. These applications came from my personal experience, observations, and ministry encounters.

I grew up in a local church, under the denomination called the Evangelical Church of Vietnam, and served there for a few years as a youth worker. Briefly setting out the constraints and questions that arose in this context will clarify why I emphasize certain theological threads in the thesis. Normally our church meets for Sunday school and a corporate worship service on Sunday morning and a youth worship service on Sunday afternoon with a mid-week youth Bible study in addition. This is where the youth are divided into smaller groups, and they have the opportunity not only to study the Bible through discussion, but also to encourage one another to grow in their spiritual lives through worshipping, having meal fellowship, evangelizing, visiting one another, and sharing their life experiences. In addition, we also have various activities to help the youth grow in their spiritual life such as games, movies, Bible quizzes, outdoor activities, home visitations, counseling, vocation training, social work, corporate prayer, and silent meditation. A Bible camp is organized once a year so that the youth can stay together for a few days to meditate on God's words and strengthen their relationships with God and with one another.

My home context is Vietnam, but since the world has become a "global village"[2] in the digital age, the theology for discipling the youth of this age and the practical applications suggested in this research can contribute to the knowledge of how to disciple youth in the larger context of the world. The main audiences of this project are pastors, church leaders, Sunday school teachers, youth workers, youth's parents, and those who are interested in mentoring the youth of the digital age. This audience is not limited to those in Vietnam but is applicable worldwide.

Definitions

The term *youth* used in this project mainly refers to adolescents but can be extended to refer to emerging adults since the context of the modern day has

---

2. McLuhan, *Understanding Media*. The term "global village" was coined by McLuhan to describe a world in which communication is instantaneous and distances are annulled by technological evolution.

prolonged the transition from adolescence to adulthood. *Emerging adulthood* encompasses late adolescence and early adulthood (typically between eighteen and roughly twenty-five years of age) where youth become more independent and explore various life possibilities.[3] The term *Generation Y*, or *Gen Y* for short, refers to those – also known as millennials – whose birth years are typically from the early 1980s to the mid-1990s.[4] *Generation Z*, or *Gen Z* for short, the demographic cohort of people succeeding Gen Y, are those whose birth years are typically from mid-1990s to the early 2010s.[5] The *Net Generation*, or the *Net Gen* for short, as Don Tapscott defines it, is the cohort of young people aged 13 to 30 who have grown up in an environment in which they were constantly exposed to computer-based technology.[6] Since the Net Gen and the youth of Gens Y and Z are quite close, in this project, I will use the terms interchangeably.

My Church Tradition

I come from the Evangelical Church of Vietnam (ECV, *Hội Thánh Tin Lành Việt Nam*), the largest registered and oldest Protestant church in Vietnam. It was founded by missionaries of the Christian and Missionary Alliance (C&MA).[7] This mission to Vietnam was founded by A. B. Simpson, a Presbyterian pastor, who "believed that Christ was not only his Savior, but also his Sanctifier, Healer, and Coming King."[8] This belief is the core "theology" of the C&MA:

> As we seek to know Jesus personally, being one with Him, He will reveal Himself as our Savior, Sanctifier, Healer, and Coming King. Simpson called this theology the Fourfold Gospel, the Christological summary on which the spiritual DNA of The Christian and Missionary Alliance is built.[9]

---

3. Arnett, "Emerging Adulthood," 469.
4. Rauch, "Generation Next."
5. Williams, "Move Over, Millennials."
6. Tapscott, "The Net Generation."
7. Reimer, *Vietnam's Christians*, 26–27, 52; Nguyen, *Cultural Integration and the Gospel*, 11.
8. "History: Then and Now," TheAlliance. Walle, *Heart of the Gospel*, 21.
9. "Beliefs: What We Do believe?" TheAlliance, The Christian and Missionary Alliance, accessed October 14, 2020, https://www.cmalliance.org/about/beliefs.

Simpson's initial idea was to form a missionary society and not a denomination. Therefore, in the early years of the denomination (1887–1919), members of the C&MA's congregations came from various Protestant denominations.[10] C&MA missionaries established the first permanent mission station in 1911 and the first full-time Bible school in 1921 in Danang, a central city in Vietnam.[11] The Vietnamese national church called the Evangelical Church of Indochina (*Hội Tin Lành Đông Pháp*) was established in 1927 and later changed its name to the Evangelical Church of Vietnam in 1950.[12]

Given this church background, when I discuss the "church" in this thesis, I mean primarily the evangelical Protestant church in my Vietnamese context, though one constitutive belief of these Christians is that they are part of a much longer history of Christians who worship the Trinitarian God and confess Jesus Christ as their personal Savior. Continuing in the interdenominational spirit set by the founder of my denomination, A. B. Simpson, this thesis will engage eclectically with theologians from other traditions. I understand my own rooting in the evangelical Protestant tradition to warrant extended engagement with the magisterial reformers, such as John Calvin, a key theologian of the Protestant Reformation. I will also reach beyond but, in the spirit of my own tradition, will do so by drawing on and theologically engaging with the theology of Dietrich Bonhoeffer, a Lutheran pastor and theologian, and Henri Nouwen, a Catholic priest and theologian, as both theologians present arguments that fit with and helpfully extend my theological account.[13] The reasons for engaging these three theologians will be discussed in more detail in the thesis introduction. What I am doing in this thesis is reading theologians from other traditions, such as Nouwen and Bonhoeffer, from the perspective of Evangelicalism, as explained in the next section discussing evangelical spirituality.

---

10. "History: Then and Now," TheAlliance.
11. Reimer, *Vietnam's Christians*, Timeline.
12. Nguyen, *Cultural Integration and the Gospel*, 12.
13. My church tradition does not relate much to Puritans. Therefore, I will not engage with them since they do not fit my theological account.

Evangelical Spirituality

Dallas Willard, a renowned contemporary theologian, has called for a renewal of spiritual disciplines among evangelical circles. He observes that in recent years there has been a rediscovery in the evangelical church of the Christian tradition, that aims to engage more intentionally with the spiritual life of its members in response to the decay of any meaningful "discipleship" programs in a contemporary evangelical church that has become obsessed with preparation for soul winning.[14] Defining spiritual formation as "shaping our spirit toward union and action with a triune God,"[15] he points out eight reasons why the renewal of spirituality should be a main concern for evangelical Christians:

> The first of my eight points was that life in Christ, and therefore *biblical* spirituality, has to do with obedience to Christ. My second point was that life in Christ is a matter of the "spirit." My third point was that spiritual life is a matter of living our lives *from* the reality of God. My fourth point is that Christian spirituality is supernatural *because* obedience to Christ is supernatural and cannot be accomplished except in the power of a "life from above" . . . The fifth point concerns *spiritual formation*. "Spiritual formation" refers to the *process* of shaping our spirit and giving it a definite character. It means the formation of our spirit in conformity with the Spirit of Christ . . . Now, my sixth point is that such a process is not a matter of the human spirit or heart *only* . . . Rather, spiritual formation is a whole life process dealing with change in every essential part of the person.[16]

The seventh point relates to the effect of transformation of all parts of the person, and the final point discusses some issues such as the relationship between grace and works, or perfectionism.[17] Willard's eight points highlight important themes such as grace, empowerment by the Holy Spirit, the process

---

14. "Spiritual Formation: What It Is, and How It Is Done," Dallas Willard (website), Dallas Willard, accessed June 4, 2018, http://www.dwillard.org/articles/individual/spiritual-formation-what-it-is-and-how-it-is-done. See also: Willard, "Spiritual Formation," 45.
15. Willard, 39, 45.
16. Willard, 44–46.
17. Willard, 49–50.

of transformation, and being conformed to the image of Christ. These themes are commonly discussed in contemporary writings on spiritual formation among evangelical writers such as James C. Wilhoit, Michael Burer, Kenneth Boa, Jeffrey P. Greenman, Diane J. Chandler, Paul Petit, Richard Foster, and Nathan Foster. As compared to Christian literature that responds to social changes caused by digital media, and which will be discussed in chapter 1, the literature on spiritual formation has a longer history and is much more developed. The importance of spiritual formation is widely agreed upon by Christian churches. Modern Christian writers have defined spiritual formation in various ways but mostly agreed with one another in main themes. Therefore, I will not do a literature review on spiritual formation but will list, in the appendix, key definitions of spiritual formation proposed by contemporary authors and then show the occurrence of nine common themes of spiritual formation in these definitions. The purpose of this survey is to secure a clearer picture of the definition of spiritual formation. This also provides detailed information for the discussion of a theology of spiritual formation in chapter 3.

Willard places strong emphasis on obedience to Christ: "The missing note in evangelical life today is not in the first instance *spirituality* but rather *obedience*."[18] Obedience is expressed in the Great Commandments as well as the small words, "Bless those that curse you," "Go the second mile," and so forth.[19] Willard points out that many Christians have turned "spirituality" into another aspect of "Christian consumerism" as they consume Christian services rather than show obedience to Christ.[20] However, obedience is not based on our effort but God's grace. Therefore, spiritual disciplines are needed to "enable us to do what we cannot do by direct effort."[21] Tom Schwanda traces spiritual disciplines back to the eighteenth century among evangelical circles:

> Early evangelicals referred to spiritual disciplines as the means of grace. John Wesley (1703–1791) defined these means as "outward signs, words, or actions ordained by God, and appointed for this end—to be the ordinary channels whereby he might

---

18. Willard, 40.
19. Willard, 40.
20. Willard, 45.
21. Willard, 41.

convey to men preventing, justifying, or sanctifying grace" . . . Wesley affirmed the essential role of the Holy Spirit, for there is no profit in engaging the means without depending on the Spirit's guidance.[22]

It is significant to practice spiritual disciplines "under the umbrella of God's grace."[23] Schwanda also highlights that spiritual disciplines must be practiced in the context of Christian communities with guidance from spiritual directors or mentors in order to avoid turning them into individualistic pursuits.[24]

Schwanda defends the spiritual practice of "contemplation" which has played a significant role in the history of Christian spirituality regardless of tradition – whether Roman Catholic, Orthodox, or Protestant – due to the recent evangelical concern that contemplation can tend to devalue Jesus Christ and his atonement, marginalize Scripture, and not witness to the gospel in the world.[25] He argues:

> Contemplation was common among eighteenth-century American Evangelicals. Regardless of gender, both men and women; regardless of theological tradition; both Reformed and Arminian reveals ample appreciation for contemplation. Further, each person recognized the centrality of Jesus Christ and the role of Scripture. None of them sought to achieve these deep spiritual experiences by their own efforts apart from God's enabling grace . . . Union with Christ is always the foundation for deeper communion with God. Solitude was a common denominator among them all, but like Jesus (Mark 1:35; Luke 5:16, 6:12; etc.) it was a temporary withdrawal from the busy demands of life to cultivate a deeper intimacy with God and not a permanent isolation from foe world. [26]

These Christians also engaged in spiritual practices such reading and meditating on Scripture, journaling, praying and fasting, maintaining spiritual

---

22. Schwanda, "Evangelical Spiritual Disciplines," 221–222.
23. Schwanda, 235.
24. Schwanda, 235.
25. Schwanda, "'To Gaze on the Beauty,'" 62.
26. Schwanda, 83.

friendship, and walking in the woods and enjoying creation. These practices are done in solitude with the "sensitivity to notice God's presence in the world and in our lives."[27] Gordon T. Smith gives a call for appreciating the historic monasticism that the Protestant Reformation chose to discard and suggests that evangelical Christians should "find ways of incorporating ancient monastic practices into the routines and rhythms of our days and weeks."[28] Therefore, this thesis will explore the practice of spiritual disciplines, especially solitude, in the context of Christian community and daily life.

One spiritual practice that can be beneficial for evangelical Christians in engaging with God's Word is *lectio divina* which means "divine reading" in Latin.[29] According to Evan B. Howard, this spiritual practice is very familiar to the evangelical tradition:

> Indeed, a tracing of evangelical use of Scripture from its Reformation roots through the twentieth century (through Puritans, early Anglicans, Pietists, revivalists, Holiness supporters, Fundamentalists, and so on) suggests that a formative approach to the reading of Scripture bearing great similarity to what we call lectio divina today was a common, if not normal practice.[30]

Howard points out that one key characteristic feature of evangelicalism is a reverence for or devotion to the Scriptures.[31] Indeed, devotional Bible reading found in the broad history of evangelicalism from the sixteenth through the nineteenth centuries is very similar to *lectio divina*.[32] Therefore, this thesis will also explore this practice for youth discipleship.

Willard also adds that another reason for the renewed interest in spiritual formation is the "break down of the significance of denominational differences."[33] Most people, especially the youth, do not care about denominational identity. This led to the need of a new common language for all

---

27. Schwanda, 83.
28. Smith, "Restoring Historic Monasticism?" 271.
29. Howard, "Lectio Divina," 57.
30. Howard, 57.
31. Howard, 59.
32. Howard, 76.
33. Willard, 45.

denominations, and this is where the term "spiritual formation" can fill in to express the common commitment to Christ. Therefore, since this thesis discusses spiritual formation for youth in the digital age, it is relevant for me to engage with writers who are beyond my tradition, such as Bonhoeffer and Henri Nouwen, and who can provide a strong theological backup for contemporary accounts of spiritual formation. Because this thesis focuses on youth, it is significant to discuss my approach to youths' identities and spiritual development in the next section.

Approach to Spiritual Development

Catherine Stonehouse helpfully summarizes the foundational assumptions underlying the evangelical Protestant understanding of the work of spiritually nurturing young people.[34] Since the sixteenth century, Protestant Christians and leaders have invested much effort in nurturing children and youth spiritually through Sunday schools for children and through youth groups in which adolescents can explore their faith together.[35] In the synoptic gospels, Jesus affirmed the spiritual potential of children: "the kingdom of God belongs" to the children. This provides the church with the theological foundation and motivation to disciple young people.[36] Stonehouse describes the process of spiritual growth in children:

> It is important to note that spirituality is not explainable in terms of human development. However, the spiritual interfaces with and is influenced by all facets of human development. During the first years of life, children construct their initial image or understanding of God. Drawing from important relationships with parents and other significant adults, the words they have heard about God, and rituals they have experienced, children are putting together their understanding of the great "Other" [whose] presence they have sensed.[37]

---

34. Stonehouse, "After a Child's First Dance," 95.
35. Stonehouse, 95.
36. Stonehouse, 96.
37. Stonehouse, 99–100.

As children grow into adolescents and face developmental changes, they feel the need to explore the meaning of life and examine their faith on a deeper level.[38] This involves not just knowing God but having a personal relationship with him.[39] Stonehouse highlights the significance of the Bible in this process: "For Christians the Bible contains the Master Story of their faith, the story that make sense of life. It is important to the spiritual life of children and youth that they know and value the Master Story."[40] Stonehouse does well in setting the stage for exploring a possible approach to youths' identities and spiritual development.

James W. Fowler presents the growth of faith as a holistic, staged development in his 1981 book, *Stages of Faith*.[41] Following Jean Piaget and Lawrence Kohlberg, he understands children to develop ideas about God and religion in general across their lifespan. Fowler's account of faith development is composed of six stages.[42] These are well encapsulated by Jeff Astley:

> *Stage 0: Primal faith.* This stage may be described as *nursed faith, foundation faith* (age: 0–4 approximately). This is not so much a stage as a 'pre-stage' . . .
>
> *Stage 1: Intuitive-projective faith.* This stage may be described as *impressionistic faith, imaginative faith, unordered faith* (age: 3/4–7/8 approximately). At this stage the child's relatively uninhibited imagination yields a chaos of powerful images . . .
>
> Stage 2: *mythic-literal faith.* This stage may be described as *ordering faith, narrative faith* (age: 6/7–11/12 approximately, and some adults). At this stage an individual's power to think logically, to unify experience, and to trace patterns of cause and effect enables that person to order his or her experience . . .
>
> *Stage 3: Synthetic-conventional faith.* This stage may be described as *conforming faith* (age: 11/12–17/18 approximately, and many adults). The ability to think abstractly develops in

---

38. Stonehouse, 100.
39. Stonehouse, 101.
40. Stonehouse, 103.
41. Fowler, *Stages of Faith*.
42. Fowler, 117–214.

this stage and there is a new capacity for mutual, interpersonal perspective-taking...

Stage 4: Individuative-reflective faith. This stage may be described as *choosing faith, either/or faith* (age: from approximately 17/18 onwards, or from the 30s or 40s onwards). I am now able to take a 'third person' perspective, 'a transcending standpoint' from which I can evaluate my beliefs and relationships...

Stage 5: Conjunctive faith. This stage may be described as *balanced faith, inclusive faith, both/and faith* (age: rare before 40)... The stage may emerge through coping with failure and living with the consequences of earlier decisions...

Stage 6: Universalizing faith. This is a very rare stage and something of an extrapolation from stage 5. It may be described as *selfless faith* (age: very rare and usually only in later life). This way of being in faith is essentially a relinquishing and transcending of the self...[43]

Though Fowler's framework elaborates the "cognitive developmental psychology" or "cognitive structural approach" of Piaget and Kohlberg,[44] he does add many conceptual, theological, and empirical nuances.[45] That said, Fowler's account is not sufficiently aware of the insights of depth psychology,[46] and it is overly normative about the sequence of stages. As a result, Fowler's scientific research has been criticized for conceptual and empirical weaknesses.[47] Therefore, in this thesis I will not follow Fowler's approach but will follow the other approach called "depth psychology," "psychoanalysis," or "psychotherapy," which has strongly influenced much Christian pastoral work. This approached is associated with Sigmund Freud and Erik Erikson.[48] These authors will be mentioned in chapter 2 where I will discuss the topic of youth identity in the digital age. Karen-Marie Yust explains why this

---

43. Astley, "Faith Development," xx-xxii.
44. Astley, xvii.
45. Astley, xxiii.
46. Astley, xviii.
47. Astley, xix.
48. Astley, xvii.

approach, when engaging the experiences of the majority of young people in the world, is insightful regarding the implications of the fact that more and more of them can access the internet and cannot imagine their world apart from social networking and gaming activities:

> This fast-paced change in the modes and dynamics of human interaction calls for careful research into the ways in which digital culture and its various components exert a growing power over the identity formation and relationships of children and youth, and thus over the spiritual development of young people. Who children imagine themselves to be, how they perceive other young people, and what they understand and experience to be the nature and goal of relationships is and will continue to be shaped by their online and gaming activities.[49]

This thesis will discuss this topic in dialogue with contemporary authors such as David Buckingham, Rob Cover, Jesse Rice, Shoshana Zuboff, Hal Niedzviecki, Howard Gardner, Katie Davis, Sandra Weber, and Claudia Mitchell. This will be followed by "Theology of Self-Identity" in chapter 4, which will show that identity is defined in a worshipping relationship with God. It will then propose ways to help youth build an intimate relationship with the relational God in this digital age.

Thesis Introduction

The thesis of this project is that the church that faithfully undertakes its Great Commission call to make disciples must minister to youth who are immersed in the internet culture. This thesis will provide a robust theology of discipleship for the youth of Gens Y and Z in the midst of the digital age. This Christian theology of discipleship will situate the practices of engaging and criticizing the habits of youth in this age. The approach of this project is critical and constructive; the church should neither just embrace nor just deny digital culture. Youth discipleship, as argued and proposed in this project, aims to help youth to encounter Christ in Christian community and personal daily life. Part of this task is to help them to understand what it means

---

49. Yust, "Digital Power," 141.

to be Christian in the world today surrounded, as it is, by digital media. Discipleship must be the central concern of the church, for it undergirds all the other tasks of the church – worship, fellowship, mission, and evangelism. Discipleship is most effective when it leads to youth partaking in the total life of the church.

First, this research will survey the best insights from various types of literature related to the impacts of digital media, especially on youth and discipleship. Then this project will discuss a theology of spiritual formation by proceeding through main themes on this topic proposed by John Calvin, Dietrich Bonhoeffer, Henri Nouwen, and modern authors. Reformed theologian John Calvin helpfully offers a developed theology of spiritual formation. Bonhoeffer adds a solid theology of the Word of God and the Christian community as the loci of spiritual formation. Nouwen's contribution is to draw these themes together with significant writings on spiritual practices and especially the practice of solitude dated back to the Desert Fathers.

Then, with the purpose of building a solid theology for discipleship to youth in the digital age, an understanding of how digital media affects the communication of the gospel to youth will be thoroughly examined. This project will continue to study the writings of Dietrich Bonhoeffer on self-identity, discipleship, community, and youth in order to construct a workable digital theology applicable to the current youth culture.[50] Bonhoeffer is focused on here because he is a master of reimagining Christian orthodox faith for the new era. His theology of youth was prompted and construed by his own context. With a strong emphasis on Christ and the Word, Bonhoeffer's theology of youth is still very helpful for theologians, pastors, and youth workers to reflect upon and apply in today's context of digital culture. More importantly, Bonhoeffer seeks to maintain traditional creedal Christianity – but in a way that evolves as society evolves. Rather than reconstructing what Bonhoeffer says, a deployment of his thoughts on self-identity, discipleship, community, and youth will be employed to serve as a good premise for theological reflections on discipling youth in the digital age. In conclusion, this research will reflect on the theological implications ecclesiologically and culturally. Finally,

---

50. Digital theology is the term best defined by the CODEC Research Centre for Digital Theology from Durham University as a "thoughtful response, as Christians, to digital media" or a "theology done digitally, using insights found in digital media to inspire us to think differently about faith." Hutchings, "On Digital Theology."

this research will suggest ways in which the church can practically disciple youth in the digital age.

The Path of the Thesis

Chapter 1 will survey the best insights from various types of literature related to social study of cultural changes in the digital age as well as Christian responses to these changes and the theology of youth work. Scholars are divided in their views of the effect of digital media on society. Some view digital media as more negative while some see more positive effects. Tracking the divide between social-scientific analyses of digital culture, Christian responses to social changes caused by digital media also range from pessimistic, to more balanced, to optimistic. This project will take from these Christian responses the call to develop a digital theology that takes into consideration both positive and negative influences of digital technologies as well as the need to find ways to communicate the gospel to youth where they are, both online and off-line. The literature on youth ministry and theology of youth work will be helpful for this work of communicating the gospel to youth in digital culture. Despite all this good work, there remains a need to construct a theology for discipling youth in the digital age, which will be the central task undertaken here. The subsequent chapters will discuss the three topics of digital media, discipleship, and youth – and the convergence between them.

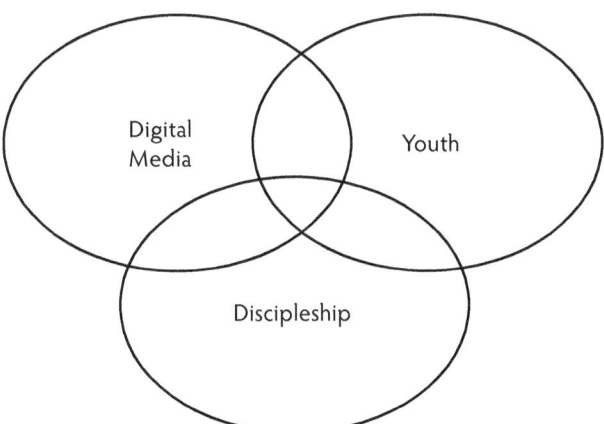

Figure 0.1. The convergence of digital media, youth, and discipleship

Chapter 2 will investigate the impacts of digital media on society in general and on the youth of the digital age in particular. This chapter will focus on the topics of digital media and youth, especially the convergence between them (see the chart above). It will be proposed that the Net Generation is not smarter or dumber than the previous generations since each generation has its own set of challenges and opportunities. It is understandable that their facility with technology is born out of accessibility and familiarity. However, there is a need to teach them to morally engage with digital media with responsibility and discernment. In order to journey with them and bring out the best in them, it is necessary for us to think of ways to reorganize school, family, or church in order to acclimatize them to the changing time.

Chapter 3 will discuss the theology of discipleship or spiritual formation. It will discuss the history of the term "spiritual formation" followed by the theology of spiritual formation drawn from modern writers in Western literature, who propose nine common emphases in the definitions of spiritual formation, to be surveyed in the appendix. The study of spiritual formation shows that spiritual formation is the sole work of God; it is by His grace and not human tasks. It also reminds us of the biblical standards of spiritual formation and that we should not neglect the context of the faith community and its influence on others and the world. Most of these modern authors mention the inner person, the Holy Spirit, and the process of transformation, and all these authors mention that spiritual formation is conforming to Christ's image, which is the ultimate goal of spiritual formation. However, most of the writing on spiritual formation in recent years does not seem strong in theology and tradition. This thesis remedies that deficit by drawing on the theologies of Calvin and Bonhoeffer as well as the Desert Fathers as presented by Henri Nouwen. Finally, this chapter will explore the significance of solitude, examining the practice of solitude in the Christian tradition beginning with the Desert Fathers. This chapter will conclude that spiritual formation is encountering Christ or conforming to Christ. This is done by the Spirit who engrafts us into a mystical union with Christ. This process requires solitude, which means opening ourselves before God in the context of the faith community or in personal daily life.

Chapter 4 will elaborate the theologies needed for youth discipleship suggested by Bonhoeffer. It will analyze the impacts of digital media on discipleship and construct a subsequent theology of discipleship to youth in the Christian community. It will focus on the convergence between the topics of digital media and discipleship and then on the convergence between the topics of discipleship and youth. The main point presented here is that the arrival of the digital age has profound implications for culture, self-identity, and the gospel. There is a need for listening to and understanding the world's viewpoints, beliefs, and needs; contextualizing the message; presenting Scripture in the language of the youth; and finally bridging the generational gaps arising in digital culture. To disciple youth in the digital age, the church should be prepared to build a theology of identity and "self" which enables this generation to respond adequately to the negative impacts of digital media and to come to know Christ as his/her personal Savior. The theology of communication and the theology of incarnation are equally important in discipling youth in the digital age because God is by nature a communicator who has been communicating with humans from the creation of the world, with the final words culminating in the birth of Jesus into the world. The gospel of Jesus Christ is always incarnate and thus, requires the dynamic interaction with the Christian community. This will then lead to a theology of community rooted in the persons of the Trinitarian God and manifested through the Christian community where the authentic gospel is communicated. It is necessary to build the theology of youth in the digital age that is appropriate to the place of the youth in the church. The church should proclaim the Word to the youth, and their youthfulness should be fully embraced and engaged. It is important for the church to be humble in listening to the youth and letting them bring their gifts to the table. As young people learn new ways of communicating and inhabiting community, the church and family, in turn, should be prepared to learn how the digital world relates to young people's faith in order to engage with them.

Chapter 5 will contextualize the theology of discipleship in the setting of youth ministry in the digital age. It will focus on the convergence between the three topics of digital media, discipleship, and youth. It will discuss the helpful aspects of digital technology and the theology of youth ministry. It will also draw implications of the whole project together and issue a call to be "all things to all people," engaging practically in discipling the youth of the digital age. Finally, it will contextualize the theology of discipleship among young people in Vietnam, by showing how spiritual disciplines in the digital age – particularly the practices of solitude, silence, and prayer – have been practiced in a local church setting.

CHAPTER 1

The Time of Digital Media

Digital technology, with its distinctive characteristics, presents a radical shift in culture. Digital communication technologies are deeply embedded into our daily lives and shape the lives of the people of our time in an unprecedented way. The literature on this topic that has emerged so far tends to fall on one of two extremes: it either argues that digital media dumbs young people down and makes them more disconnected from everyday life, or it proposes that digital media makes them smarter and better at collaboration. Both approaches tend to assume a separation between the virtual life and the physical life as well as the virtual self and the "real" self. This project seeks to find a balanced and holistic approach in discipling youth, both theologically and practically. Theologically, it argues that the self cannot, should not, and is not to be divided – not even by the new dimension of cyberspace – and that embracing the whole self is the key to living out the life of Christ. Practically, digital media, with its positive and negative influences, shapes youth in distinctive ways, and thus, in acknowledging both, we can provide both acceptance and approval of their world while providing the necessary teachings and guidance to help youth better navigate life in the digital age. This chapter is devoted to a review of literature that is relevant for understanding the cultural context in which we discuss the ethics and theology of social media use. First, this chapter reviews the social-scientific research on the cultural movements afoot in the domain of social media, then Christian responses to this context. Finally, it surveys various attempts to grapple with these issues by those writing on youth ministry and on the use of social media. This chapter will be grouped into three sections discussing the description of the emerging connected society, Christian response to these changes, and a theology of youth work. This chapter is not a comprehensive literature review but a more focused review that explores those texts that are clearly related to the central question of the thesis. This literature review describes what related research has already been conducted, how it informs the thesis, and how the thesis fits into the research in the field.

1. Description of the Emerging Connected Society

This section surveys some of the more important lines of analysis of the social changes reshaping the culture of the digital age. Scholars' views range from optimistic to balanced to pessimistic.

a. Optimistic

In his 2009 book *Growing Up Digital*,[1] Don Tapscott presents a comprehensive profile of the Net Generation, the first generation to grow up fully immersed in digital technologies. They seem to live doing many things at the same time: checking Facebook or Instagram, texting friends, watching YouTube, downloading music, uploading videos. Tapscott's social-scientific study leads to the conclusion that people of the Net Gen are not dumber, nor do they have shorter attention spans. Rather, they are brighter and exhibit new ways of thinking, interacting, working, and socializing. He points out:

> For the first time in history, children are more comfortable, knowledgeable, and literate than their parents with an innovation central to society. And it is through the use of the digital media that the Net Generation will develop and superimpose its culture on the rest of the society.[2]

He offers a strong defense against the negative impacts of digital media on youth, arguing that youth relate to technology in a different way than their parents' generation does.

Tapscott identifies eight characteristics of the Net Generation: freedom of choice, customization, collaboration, skepticism, integrity, entertainment, speed, and innovation. The Net Generation is "smarter" than their parents'

---

1. Tapscott, *Growing Up Digital*.
2. Tapscott, 2.

generation and better at collaboration.³ Youth seek freedom in everything they do, from freedom of choice to freedom of expression. They want to have fun in their work, education, family, and social lives. They are very collaborative through the practice of playing multi-user video games; texting each other instantly; and sharing files for school, for work, or just for fun. They also influence each other through online discussion. They seek innovative environments and are constantly looking for innovative ways to collaborate, entertain themselves, learn, and work.⁴ Through the book's thirteen chapters, Tapscott presents how the brain of the Net Generation processes information. He proposes ways to attract and engage young talent in the workforce and guidelines for educators and parents to mentor the Net Generation. He also shows how young people and the internet are transforming democracy.

Tapscott may well be overoptimistic about the impacts of digital media on youth, especially when saying that today's youth are smarter and better at collaboration than previous generations. However, his view of the positive effects of digital media on youth provides a helpful counterbalance to the predominantly negative early analyses. This is helpful for adults walking with youth in starting from a will to accept youth and their involvement with digital media and then in seeking to reform school, family, and church to bring the best benefits to youth. This notion of digital impacts on youth and how to mentor youth will be further discussed in chapter 2.

b. Balanced

In *The Rise of the Network Society*, Manuel Castells explores the relationship of information technology with economy, society, and culture under the overarching concept of the "Network Society."⁵ Information technologies led to the rise of a new form of social organization called the "Network Society." As Castells describes, "a technological revolution, centered around information technologies, began to reshape, at accelerated pace, the material basis of society."⁶ Because of its ubiquity, the information technology revolution is the entry point for Castells to analyze the complexity of the new economy,

---

3. Tapscott, 6.
4. Tapscott, 34–35.
5. Castells, *The Rise of the Network Society*.
6. Castells, 1.

society, politics, and culture brought by the new digital media.[7] In the late 1990s, the internet, together with new telecommunication and computing technologies, brought about a paradigm shift from decentralized to pervasive network computing.[8] New information technologies influence all areas of human activity by making it possible to establish boundless connections between different domains, elements, and agents to carry out such activities.[9] The book gives a compressive picture of the rise of the "Network Society," but this picture is not sharp and up to date enough since it was written during the early stage of this phenomenon.

Holding a pretty neutral view, like Castells, Robert Hassan describes, in his 2008 book *The Information Society*, that modern people are immersed in an information environment.[10] Digital technology constantly connects us with others in an unprecedented way regardless of our location and time zone. Digital technology speeds up our lives by enabling us to multitask and by "shrinking" our space as it allows us to communicate with people across the globe much more easily than ever.[11] This immersion reshapes our relationships, our cultural forms, and our individual identities.[12] Hassan suggests that two interdependent processes are decisively shaping our present-day world; together, neoliberal globalization and the revolution in information technology are producing a "speeding-up" of time and a "shrinking" of space.[13] As the logic of *The Information Society* stems from the conjunction of neoliberal globalization and the revolution in digital technologies, applications and gadgets are developed, not primarily to meet human need, but as commodities for sale. An unnoticed but significant conflict is set up between what can be marketed and sold and what sorts of digital technologies are actually useful.[14] Therefore, it is important to evaluate the usefulness of digital technologies and their influences on our lives. Digital technologies demand deeper thinking about the lifestyles they demand of us.

---

7. Castells, 5.
8. Castells, 51–52.
9. Castells, 78.
10. Hassan, *The Information Society*.
11. Hassan, x.
12. Hassan, vii.
13. Hassan, ix.
14. Hassan, 218–219.

c. Pessimistic

With a little more pessimism than optimism, Howard Gardner and Katie Davis, two Harvard educators, published *The App Generation: How Today's Youth Navigate Identity, Intimacy, and Imagination in a Digital World*[15] in 2013. The book paints a pessimistic picture of the young people, called the "app generation," who are surrounded by smart devices. The authors categorized the impact of apps into two kinds: app-enabling and app-dependent. App-enabling allows users to pursue new possibilities while the other restricts users' procedures, choices, and goals.[16] According to Gardner and Davis, as we use apps, "we encounter the paradox of action and restriction," since apps are created by some authors with their own ideas to enable certain actions and, at the same time, restrict other actions.[17] Though apps enable people to join various online communities, people tend to communicate with "similarly oriented people." The range of self-expression is restricted as designed by the app.[18] People can either have a stronger identity enabled by some apps or they can become "someone else's avatar," formulated by some app producer. Apps are good at problem solving but have negative effect on young people who rely on them rather than using their brains.[19] As a result, apps lead to changes, not only in identity formation, but also intimacy and imagination in the app generation. The book concludes that, as humans, we face a choice to take up apps with control or to let them control us. However, throughout the book, it seems that the authors present more negative influences of apps on the app generation and do not suggest constructive ways to avoid those negative influences other than escaping from the digital world. The most important point of their analysis is to highlight the impacts of apps on youths' identity formations – a topic that will receive sustained attention in chapter 2 in the section *Youth Identity in the Digital Age*.

As compared to Gardner and Davis, who hold just a bit of pessimism, Mark Bauerlein depicts an extremely pessimistic picture of the young people of the digital age, whom he calls the "dumbest generation," in his 2009 book

---

15. Gardner and Davis, *App Generation*.
16. Gardner and Davis, 10.
17. Gardner and Davis, 24.
18. Gardner and Davis, 60.
19. Gardner and Davis, 34.

The Dumbest Generation: How the Digital Age Stupefies Young Americans and Jeopardizes Our Future (Or, Don't Trust Anyone Under 30).[20] The book depicts an extremely negative picture of the young people growing up in the digital age whom the author calls the "dumbest generation." He asserts that the intellect of Americans under-30-year-olds is lower that of previous generations.[21] His main claim is that it is much more convenient for young Americans today to access knowledge and information, especially via the internet.[22] They enjoy "access to first-rate culture and vital facts that earlier cohorts couldn't even imagine. Consider how many more opportunities the youth of today's generation have for compiling knowledge, elevating taste, and cultivating skills."[23] However, they are:

> no more learned or skillful than their predecessors, no more knowledgeable, fluent, up-to-date, or inquisitive, except in the materials of youth culture. They don't know any more history or civics, economics or science, literature or current events. They read less on their own, both books and newspapers.[24]

However, his claim that this generation is the dumbest as compared to previous generations is debatable. He has offered some proof of reduction in knowledge and skills – especially of academic skills of young people today as compared to previous generations – but this needs to be surveyed and analyzed in the long-term and on bigger scales. His account focuses on some traditional forms of knowledge and skill that he thinks are important, but the new age presents new kinds of intellect that previous ages do not have. Even if his proofs that young people today have less knowledge and skills are correct, it is not because they are dumber but because educational institutions and families have not educated them in their digital involvement or imparted the knowledge to them in a way that is interesting and relevant to their culture.

Similar to Bauerlein, Hal Niedzviecki presents a depressing portrait of the people in the "Peep culture," fostered by digital media. Niedzvieckis 2009

---

20. Bauerlein, *Dumbest Generation*.
21. Bauerlein, 7.
22. Bauerlein, 8.
23. Bauerlein, 30.
24. Bauerlein, 8–9.

book *The Peep Diaries: How We're Learning to Love Watching Ourselves and Our Neighbors* defines "Peep culture" thus: [25]

> Peep culture is reality TV, YouTube, Twitter, Flickr, MySpace and Facebook. It's blogs, chat rooms, amateur porn sites, virally spread digital movies of a fat kid pretending to be a Jedi Knight, cell phone photos—posted online—of your drunk friend making out with her ex-boyfriend, and citizen surveillance. Peep is the backbone of Web 2.0 and the engine of corporate and government data mining. It's like the famous line about pornography: you know it when you see it. And you do see it. All the time, every day, everywhere.[26]

"Peep culture" is embedded in social media and has a pervasive influence. Niedzviecki observes both the negative and positive influences of this "Peep culture." The negative aspects of this culture are that it makes people waste so much time on looking at posts from other people on social media. Niedzviecki observes, "It's about wanting to know everything about everyone and, in turn, wanting to make sure that everyone knows everything about you."[27] However, social media causes addiction, not just because of curiosity, but because of the lack of community living fostered by city life. People feel the need to connect to like-minded people.[28] There is a risk of oversharing online because what we share online can be used against us. We also search other people's information out of curiosity or another intention.[29] Niedzviecki observes that society is negatively changed with the use of more instant judgments, stolen innocence, and mass delusion. People are trading every secret, scandal, and crime. However, in a positive way, there is a possibility for enhanced democracy and equality.[30]

Niedzviecki presents well the "Peep culture" with all its negative influence in people's lives. To prove his points, he filled his book with extreme or unethical cases of people producing amateur porn or watching others

---

25. Niedzviecki, *Peep Diaries*.
26. Niedzviecki, 1–2.
27. Niedzviecki, 8.
28. Niedzviecki, 8.
29. Niedzviecki, 10.
30. Niedzviecki, 20.

excessively. He is undoubtedly onto something when he observes that the main cause of the rise of "Peep culture" is a lack of community life. It is fair to say that most of us are affected by "Peep culture." The book reminds us that we should be careful with what we share online and not to be obsessed with watching other people's private lives. However, the author seems to go too far when equating the digital age and digital media with "Peep culture," especially when he says, "Peep is the backbone of Web 2.0 and the engine of corporate and government data mining."[31] Digital media gives rise to "Peep culture," but "Peep culture" is not the whole of digital media. Regardless of its negative influence, in this thesis, I will assume that there are positive aspects of digital media – or at least some positive ways of using digital media which a faithful contemporary church should further explore.

Continuing on the dark picture of lives in the digital age, in his 2017 book *Radical Technologies: The Design of Everyday Life*, Adam Greenfield offers a comprehensive manual for navigating our daily lives in the world surrounded by radical technologies:[32] the smartphone and the Internet of Things; augmented and virtual reality; 3D printing and other technologies of digital fabrication; cryptocurrency and the blockchain; and the dense complex of ideas surrounding algorithms, machine learning, automation, and artificial intelligence.[33] He observes the effect of these radical technologies:

> Networked digital information technology has become the dominant mode through which we experience the everyday. In some important sense this class of technology now mediates just about everything we do. It is simultaneously the conduit through which our choices are delivered to us, the mirror by which we see ourselves reflected, and the lens that lets others see us on a level previously unimagined.[34]

These radical technologies are deeply reshaping the social landscape and our daily lives. Because Greenfield's book does more to raise questions than to encourage readers to embrace digital technology, it helpfully raises several warning flags as we navigate our lives in the digital age. If we deny that any

---

31. Niedzviecki, 2.
32. Greenfield, *Radical Technologies*.
33. Greenfield, 8.
34. Greenfield, 6.

technology can provide a perfect solution for our life, we begin to gain the critical distance from familiar devices, such as smartphones and the Internet of Things, that promise much convenience but also implicate huge risks such as data security, addiction, and attention deficit. Greenfield's warning questions are not the end of the story, however, as technology is also having a positive impact on the lives of the young people born in the digital age.

As compared to the pessimistic views presented above, Shoshana Zuboff presents the latest and also darkest picture of life in the digital age, which is controlled by surveillance capitalism. In her 2019 book *The Age of Surveillance Capitalism: The Fight for a Human Future at the New Frontier of Power*, she presents a comprehensive account of the new form of economic and technological tyranny named surveillance capitalism carried out by big technological companies which seek to control our lives.[35] She starts the book with the big question, "Can the digital future be our home?"[36] Her answer dwells on the dark side of "ubiquitous computing," which makes it possible for technology companies to harvest data about human experience. Surveillance capitalism harvests human experience for translation into behavioral data, then this data is processed by machine intelligence in order to predict future behavior. This data is traded for benefits. In order to make more benefits from yielding more predictive behavior data, these automated processes not only harvest or predict the data but also shape our behavior. Zuboff calls this process instrumentarianism, and it works through ubiquitous computational architecture to predict and shape human behavior toward some commercial outcome.[37] Commercial activities have now saturated the internet and behind them is commercial surveillance.[38]

Zuboff points out that instrumentarianism aims to tune our society toward a similar "social confluence" where individual behaviors are modified to conform to social norms created by group pressure and computer algorithm. The obvious evidence of this is the effect of social media on Gens Y and Z,

---

35. Zuboff, *Age of Surveillance Capitalism*.
36. Zuboff, 4.
37. Zuboff, 8.
38. Zuboff, 11.

which are the first generations living in the "hive" with no exit created by surveillance capital.[39] She describes this phenomenon:

> Adolescence and emerging adulthood in the hive are a human first, meticulously crafted by the science of behavioral engineering; institutionalized in the vast and complex architectures of computer-mediated means of behavior modification; overseen by Big Other; directed toward economies of scale, scope, and action in the capture of behavioral surplus; and funded by the surveillance capital that accrues from unprecedented concentrations of knowledge and power. Our children endeavor to come of age in a hive that is owned and operated by the applied utopianists of surveillance capitalism and is continuously monitored and shaped by the gathering force of instrumentarianism power.[40]

In such an emerging cultural context, the need for a sanctuary or a space for inviolable refuge is much more urgent than ever.[41]

Zuboff's observations about the developing surveillance capitalism are a very important addition to the critical discourse about the emerging connected society. Though surveillance capitalism has a huge impact on our lives in this digital age, especially the lives of young people, it may not cover each and every aspect of our lives in the digital age. At this stage, it is still too early to observe the full impacts of surveillance capitalism in our world. Zuboff does not suggest how to get into the sanctuary except by destroying the walls of the "hive" created by surveillance capitalism. The increasing necessity of finding a place of refuge from this digital environment is one of the main constructive interests of this thesis.

This section has surveyed some of the more important lines of analysis of the social changes reshaping the culture of the digital age. Scholars' views range from optimistic to balanced to pessimistic. Tapscott presents an optimistic view of youth, whom he says are smarter and better at collaboration.

---

39. Zuboff, 21.

40. Zuboff, 448–449. On page 376, Zuboff defines Big Other as the "the sensate, computational, connected puppet that renders, monitors, computes, and modifies human behavior" and surveillance capitalism is its puppet master.

41. Zuboff, 21.

Taking a more neutral view, Castells describes the complexity of the new economy, society, politics, and culture brought by the new digital media – and in a way that provides a contrast with Hassan's depiction of the information society that springs from neoliberal globalization and the information technology revolution, which drives a "speeding-up" of time and a "shrinking" of space. Thus each, in their own way, calls for deeper thinking about the lifestyles that digital media demands of us. With a little more pessimism than optimism, Gardner and Davis add to the negative picture of digital technologies in their discussion of the app generation, whose identity, creativity, and imagination are shaped by apps in a more negative way than positive unless they choose to resist its negative influences. Bauerlein depicts an extremely pessimistic picture of the young people of the digital age, whom he calls the "dumbest generation," but his claim that the youth of today's generation are dumber than previous generations is questionable. Niedzviecki presents a depressing portrait of the people in the "Peep culture" fostered by digital media. Most recent and in-depth studies by Greenfield and Zuboff agree with Niedzviecki on the dark picture of lives in the digital age. Greenfield provides a comprehensive manual for navigating our daily lives in the world surrounded by radical technologies, which change the social landscape and our daily lives tremendously in mostly negative ways. Zuboff presents the darkest picture of surveillance capitalism.

It is clear that the earlier social-scientific studies of digital technology are more focused on forecasting the impacts of this rising technological phenomenon, while later studies of the topic arrive at very different and sometimes diametrically contradicting views. The most recent developments in this field of study provide the sharpest picture of the powerful influence on the shape of human identity that has come with the dominance of radical digital technologies. These scholars are highlighting out a complex set of competing and contradictory cultural trajectories: digital media is clearly having *both* good and bad effects on the minds, identities, and relationships of contemporary youth. This suggests that the task for the contemporary church is to help them learn to navigate these challenges in a discerning way, rather than to wholly embrace or wholly reject digital media use. This literature review has depicted the social changes afoot in the digital age, helpfully revealing the work context in which Christians must learn to respond to these phenomena.

2. Christian Response

In this section, we will survey Christian literature that responds to social changes caused by digital media.

a. Early Calls for Christian Response to Digital Media

Christian authors such and William F. Fore, Robert S. Fortner, and Shane A. Hipps offered the first wave of Christian responses to the influence of digital media.

In *Mythmakers: Gospel, Culture and the Media*, published in 1990, William F. Fore presents the effects of communication approaches such as oral, handwritten, printed, and electronic on cultural values throughout human history.[42] He suggests that communication technology has had a major effect on the evolution of cultures with the emergence of new technologies being incorporated into cultures and daily life. He equates the history of communication technology with the history of our cultures.[43] He invites us to watch the effect of digital media wisely through the lens of the gospel and to live faithfully in a world where news is managed, violence entertains, and religion is in competition with other forms of entertainment and information. Fore suggests that the great themes of the Bible – the creation story, the fall, and salvation – provide a basis to construct a digital theology for discipling the youth of this digital age.[44] He gives the call to interpret the gospel, which always comes wrapped in a cultural context, and to proclaim it to people in the digital age.[45] Though the book is outdated in terms of the study on digital technology, Fore's study of the history of communication and his call to proclaim the gospel in digital culture remains relevant in reminding contemporary Christians of the necessity of assessing both the values of contemporary culture and the contemporary meaning of the gospel in order to bridge the gap to communicate a gospel message that is relevant and meaningful to the people in contemporary culture.[46]

---

42. Fore, *Mythmakers*.
43. Fore, 29.
44. Fore, 56–59.
45. Fore, 16–17.
46. Fore, 3, 8–11.

In 1999, Robert S. Fortner published the article "The Gospel in a Digital Age,"[47] in which he observes that the distinctive characteristic of the digital age is its breaking the link between communication and information.[48] In this new context, Christians should be promoting values of the gospel where human beings are respected and celebrated. This includes identifying those elements in the media that are points of contact with gospel values, and teaching true personhood and wholeness of spirit to this generation which is living in fragmented and incoherent societies caused by digital media. The gospel of wholeness, or "oneness" is needed to make connection with the heart and soul in an age of multiple selves of the digital age.[49] Fortner suggests that to disciple youth in the digital age, it is helpful to build a theology of "self" which assists this generation to respond adequately to the negative impacts of digital media in their lives of discipleship.[50]

Fortner's presentation is insightful in the following respects. He usefully highlights the different characteristics of the electronic age and digital age in order to draw attention to the unique effects of digital culture.[51] His call to look fairly at digital technologies and their effects on culture, rather than zooming in on the negative effects, is also a useful warning to those Christians and churches who think that the way to deal with the negative effects of digital technologies is to ban them.[52] He is thus a forerunner of the important challenge to effectively bring the gospel to the inhabitants of this digital age.[53] Yet he does not himself offer a constructive theology for discipling youth in the digital age. Fortner's study of the digital age's profound implications for culture, self-identity, and the gospel was written at a time when digital technology was new, and thus his analysis was underdeveloped. His article does not attempt to construct a digital theology. Though he highlights the need to develop a theology of "self" in order to communicate the gospel in the digital age, he does not develop this theology.[54] He does not propose a

---

47. Fortner, "Gospel in a Digital Age."
48. Fortner, 9.
49. Fortner, 4, 14.
50. Fortner, 14.
51. Fortner, 3–5.
52. Fortner, 8.
53. Fortner, 15.
54. Fortner, 15.

theology of discipleship or how to communicate the gospel to youth who are mostly influenced by digital culture.

In the 2005 book *The Hidden Power of Electronic Culture: How Media Shapes Faith, the Gospel, and the Church*, Shane A. Hipps observes that there is a reduction of rational discussion caused by image-based communication and the increase of concrete and intuitive thoughts.[55] In the digital age, there is a shift from a modern, individualistic, and highly rational concept of the gospel to a postmodern, communal, holistic, and experiential one. The gospel message is no longer an abstract, fixed idea but rather an unfolding, incarnational drama in which God is working to bring the world back into a reconciled relationship with himself. Young people need to be part of a community where they encounter redemptive relationships that involve engaging one another with the hope of the gospel – but this is threatened by the virtual community with its disembodied interactions and emotional promiscuity.[56] Hipps's observations about the effects of digital media and the call to communicate the gospel in a relevant way and include youth in the Christian community are helpful. Yet, again, the question that remains is how to do it.

Though their works are outdated in terms of digital technology, Fore, Fortner, and Hipps offered early calls to respond to the effects of digital media, which are helpful in highlighting the need for a constructive and developed theology for discipling youth that takes account of the developments of the technological and life-experience of contemporary youth. In pursuit of that project, they confirm important insights affirmed and further developed by this thesis. First, digital technologies have an unprecedented impact on culture. Thus, second, there is a need to look both into the values of contemporary culture and the meaning of the gospel in order to conduct a proper contextualization of the gospel. We turn now to the later literature on digital theology to secure a better view of digital culture as well as its effects on society and communication of the gospel.

---

55. Hipps, *Hidden Power*.
56. Hipps, 88–89.

b. Mid-stage Engagement

Other authors such as Jesse Rice, Elizabeth Drescher, Tim Challies, Adam Thomas, and Leonard Sweet offered the second wave of Christian responses to the influence of digital media.

In his 2009 book, *The Church of Facebook: How the Hyperconnected Are Redefining Community*, Jesse Rice describes how the social network Facebook attracts many millions of users and impacts their ways of life, identities, and relationships with others.[57] Attracting us with online communities and connections with many online friends, Facebook uncovers our deepest need: connection.[58] The question to ask is whether these communities and connections are really authentic and helpful. Overloading us with new posts from thousands of online friends, Facebook makes us feel compelled to check and try to keep from "missing out" on anything. As a result, we feel overstimulated and unfulfilled. This also affects our attention and leads to addiction.[59] With the growing number of relationships on Facebook, we then have less time for each one. As a result, friendship becomes superficial, with just enough time for a quick wall posting, a link, a short status update, or a like or comment rather than long emails, shared meals, or face-to-face conversations.[60] Facebook has redefined friendship. A friend on Facebook can be someone we have only met once, have never met before, or have no intention to meet in the future.[61] In causing us to feel compulsively online constantly and not fully present in the moment, Facebook negatively affects our self-confidence and the clarity of self-concept.[62]

Even though he presents many negative impacts of Facebook on authentic connections and community, Rice does not reject Facebook but suggests practical ways of using it that can enable authentic connections: the practicing of regular check-ins, which means focusing our attention on the here and now; not going online immediately before bed and after waking up, but praying to God; practicing mindful Facebooking, such as paying attention to how much time we spend on Facebook; practicing authentic Facebooking, such as

---

57. Rice, *Church of Facebook*.
58. Rice, 45.
59. Rice, 102–104.
60. Rice, 110.
61. Rice, 138.
62. Rice, 146–49.

checking whether the information we have shared on Facebook reflects our God-given nature; and adopting one or two Facebook friends for a month with whom to have an in-depth interaction.[63] Even though Rice has not developed a theology of community, his call for an authentic connection in the digital age is insightful. Though not in-depth or up-to-date, his observation of the impacts of social networking on personal identity is also informative. Therefore, this thesis will later engage more deeply these aspects of digital media on youths' identity formation and the theology of community.

In the 2011 book *Tweet If You Love Jesus: Practicing Church in the Digital Reformation*, Elizabeth Drescher observes the effects of the digital reformation on human consciousness, relatedness, communication, community, and leadership.[64] Social media such as Facebook, Twitter, and YouTube create new modes of access, participation, co-creativity, etc.[65] Digital technology with its mobility is integrated into the fabric of our daily lives and blurs the boundary between virtual and physical reality.[66] In her view, social media are transforming the contemporary church in the same way that the printing press transformed the medieval church.[67] Increasing numbers of apps for spiritual guidance as well as websites/blogs of scholars in theology and religious studies are becoming available. Social media create opportunities to connect with other people of similar religious affiliation.[68]

The call of this book for the church to utilize social media to build healthy, interactive connections with people and minister to them is helpful since one of the deepest desires of humans is connection – which is one of the central promises of digital media. What the book does not do, however, is ask whether digital media enable meaningful connection and interaction or hinder it. The book draws an analogy with the late-medieval church's embrace of the printing press to call the contemporary church to embrace digital media. Yet digital media have their own unique characteristics requiring much in-depth study before the church can consider embracing or rejecting it. It is also debatable that social media such as Facebook, YouTube, and Twitter are

---

63. Rice, 211–215.
64. Drescher, *Tweet If You*.
65. Drescher, 1.
66. Drescher, 4.
67. Drescher, 2–3.
68. Drescher, 5–6.

adequate channels for discussing theology or providing spiritual nurturing. Therefore, this research will study the pitfalls and promise of digital media for discipleship and construct a theology for this task.

In *The Next Story: Life and Faith after the Digital* (2011), Tim Challies begins from the digital explosion.[69] He compares digital technologies' influences with the effect of the biggest nuclear bomb, Tsar Bomba, in reshaping the landscape of our lives: destroying, creating, splitting things apart, and bringing them together in new ways. Since the invention of the microprocessor in 1971 and its integration into calculators, computers, televisions, mobile phones, automobiles, and toys, digital technologies have powerfully changed our lives.[70] He calls for Christian discernment on its effect. The book explores how God intended technology to function in the world he created. The author starts with *imago Dei* as he suggests the mandate of technology: "If bearing the image of God is what gives us our ability to create, God's mandate – his commanded purpose for human beings – is what drives our desire to create."[71] Challies claims that "obedience to God requires that we create technology. This tells us that there is some inherent good in the technology we create . . . In other words, it is not the technology itself that is good or evil; it is the human application of that technology."[72] However, this view is questionable since the fall corrupted the whole world including the technology we create. Technology is not neutral, and digital technology is not simply a tool that we can just take it up and put it down easily. Challies, in fact, grants this when noting that technology can become an idol, concluding: "Our task, then, is not to avoid technology but to carefully evaluate it, redeem it, and ensure that we are using it with the right motives and for the right goals."[73]

Challies offers a valid starting point with the discussion of *imago Dei*, a theme to which this thesis will return. His book provides a valid Christian response to the influence of digital media. His theory of digital technology is helpful, and his applications are relevant and clear, but his view of technology as neutral is debatable. Technology is not neutral, and digital technology is not

---

69. Challies, *The Next Story*.
70. Challies, Calibre pages 6–7/211.
71. Challies, Calibre page 18/211.
72. Challies, Calibre page 20/211.
73. Challies, Calibre page 28/211.

simply a tool that we can just take it up and put it down easily. His book seems to suggest more evil than good of digital technology, and the applications are more about escaping from the virtual world. My project will take from Challies's book the explosive impacts of digital media, its possible negative influences, and the need for face-to-face contacts, but it will explore ways to disciple youth where they are, regardless of the negative online and off-line impacts of digital media. There is still space to reach out to youth who are lonely and lost in cyberspace.

As a millennial, one of the vanguard of the generation whose first members were born in 1982, Adam Thomas presents a more positive approach to digital media in his 2011 book *Digital Disciple: Real Christianity in a Virtual World*.[74] His premise is that God is with us while we are in digital space, even in World of Warcraft.[75] He feels that God moves in both his virtual and real lives (Psalms 139).[76] He asks the following questions: "Is it possible that Jesus might find me and I might find him on those virtual paths? Is it possible that God can use the Tech to create better followers of Jesus Christ?"[77] His answer is yes – but with a warning label. Unlike Christians before us, Christians today are now digital disciples since digital technology has added a new dimension to our lives. Yet God continues to move through every facet of our existence, including our virtual lives.[78] Thomas moves very quickly to assert that God is present in the virtual realm, leaving aside any in-depth probing of the question of what is meant by the claim that God is present in a virtual realm. Of course, God can be with a person and communicate with him when he is playing a game, but it seems rather quick to move to assert that God is present in the game. We cannot just make a box and say that God is present in the box that we have created even if we affirm God's omniscience.

Close examination reveals that Thomas has a compartmentalized view of the online and off-line worlds, even though he strongly highlights the presence of God in both "compartments" of the digital native's life. He shares that God encountered him on more than one occasion in the virtual World

---

74. Thomas, *Digital Disciple*.
75. Thomas, Calibre page 21/110.
76. Thomas, Calibre pages 89–90/110.
77. Thomas, Calibre page 14/110.
78. Thomas, Calibre page 14/110.

of Warcraft. With regards to in-game experience, he asserts that the "virtual world and the physical world can coexist, but one can't permeate the other."[79] While it is true that the virtual aspects of a game do not directly escape into the physical world, the virtual world clearly does have physical and psychological effects on the players. Young people spend real money to buy items for online games or earn money by playing games. In similar ways, social media also affects real-life relationships. Virtual and physical life are more intertwined with each other than Thomas assumes, though his claim is much more theologically defensible when he claims that God is with all his children while they live their life off-line and online.

Besides calling Christians to practice communion to tackle the negative effects of digital technology, Thomas also challenges us to practice spiritual disciplines such as reflection based on St. Ignatius's "Examen," breath prayer, *lectio divina*, and Tech Sabbath.[80] As compared to Tim Challies's book, which focuses more on the risks rather than the opportunity of digital technology, this book is more positive regarding digital media since Thomas is a digital native. Though Thomas is optimistic at certain points, it is true that youth can encounter God when they are online or off-line. However, overall, the book finally does not offer a developed digital theology capable of orienting the contemporary church as it seeks faithfully to disciple its youth.

In his 2012 book *Viral: How Social Networking Is Poised to Ignite Revival*, Leonard Sweet presents an optimistic picture of the current "Google Generation," which is driven by "God-given" desire to connect with people.[81] As God invites us into relationship with Him and with other people, this generation is using digital media to go "viral," staying connected with others. Older Christians can learn from them to befriend people. The author starts by stating that faith is not static or regimented but that it is viral and dynamic. People can experience God in different ways, but we all share the basics needs of nourishment, shelter, and networks of companions. These biological and relational needs shape us. The author asserts that "connection is one of the absolutes of life. We don't choose it; it is hard-wired within."[82]

---

79. Thomas, Calibre page 21/110.

80. Thomas, Calibre pages 71–91/110.

81. Leonard Sweet, *Viral: How Social Networking Is Poised to Ignite Revival* (Colorado Springs: WaterBrook Press, 2012).

82. Sweet, 1.

We long for self-expression and sharing of life. These needs shape us as human beings as God created us. Our faith is shaped not only by nature and nurture, destiny and design, but also by the culture in which we live. Research on neuroplasticity argues that the structure of the human brain is shaped by our experiences, technologies, and culture. Cultures can shape our behavior and faith's expression.[83]

The author seems quick to uphold all the strengths of the "Googlers" without investigating their weaknesses as compared to the "Gutenbergers."[84] The main point of the book is that "Googlers" are good at connections and community lives, but the latest research shows otherwise. "Peep culture" and surveillance capitalism discussed above show that while youth are yearning for connections, the connections they find online are shallow and not satisfying. This book does not establish a theology of incarnation and community as it should be. The valid point of the book is pointing to the deeper need of the human being, in the digital age, that is seeking for real connections and meaningful life sharing. This thesis, therefore, will discuss the theology of community in chapter 4.

In short, as compared to early calls for a substantively Christian response to digital media, mid-stage treatments of this topic articulate a more nuanced view of digital culture, its effects on society, and the communication of the gospel. Rice called for authentic connections and community, which Facebook seems to promise to provide but fails to do in reality. Sweet is overly optimistic about the "Googlers," saying that they are good at connections and community lives, but he is right in pointing to the deeper needs of human beings in the digital age for real connections and meaningful life sharing. Neither Sweet nor Rice provides a theology of community. As a digital optimist, Drescher suggests that the church should utilize social media to build healthy, interactive connections with people and minister to them, but he does not explore whether digital media enables meaningful connection and interaction or hinder it. Challies provides a valid Christian response to the influence of digital media, but his theology of digital media is underdeveloped.

---

83. Sweet, 2.

84. The "Googlers" are the generation born in the internet age and familiar with using Google, whereas without "Gutenbergers" are the previous generation born in the age of printing press.

He seems to suggest more evil than good of digital technology, and the applications proposed in his book are more about escaping from the virtual world than navigating it wisely. Being an optimist, Thomas sees negative effects of digital technology as a call to spiritual disciplines. However, much like Challies, Thomas has not proposed a solid digital theology for disciplining youth. The mid-stage engagement with this topic, therefore, remains in need of a digital theology to substantiate it.

c. Digital Theology

In agreement with Hassan's view that virtual reality is now weaved into real life, Philip R. Meadows, in his article "Mission and Discipleship in a Digital Culture" (2012), begins with the presumption that we are experiencing a convergence of cyberspace and physical life by way of our constant connection to the internet via digital devices.[85] Digital media is becoming an inextricable aspect of everyday life. Young people especially are immersed in a world in which cyberspace is folded into the flow of everyday life. Given this convergence of cyberspace and physical life through the immersion of youth in digital technology, Meadows suggests that virtual relationships can also become a means of spiritual formation.[86] In important respects, Meadows's view is close to the one taken in this thesis, and it will be revisited later. However, the need to construct a digital theology remains. Anthony Le Duc defines cyber/digital theology as "the systematic reflection on the transformative impact of the digital age on the various dimensions of one's faith life and his/her response to this ever-changing milieu."[87] There remains work to be done in this field, and to show why, this subsection surveys the state of the discussion.

In the 2012 book *Aquinas on the Web? Doing Theology in an Internet Age*, Jana M. Bennett proposes a much more robustly developed digital theology.[88] The book starts by exploring considered responses of theologians to Web 2.0 technology, whether to embrace it for online theological discussion or to reject it. Web 2.0 gives space for grassroots theologians or lay people to

---

85. Hassan, *The Information Society*, 18; Meadows, "Mission and Discipleship," 163–182.
86. Meadows, 173.
87. Duc, "Cyber/Digital Theology," 140.
88. Bennett, *Aquinas on the Web?*

participate in theological discussion.[89] While Web 2.0 does create a space for new or renewed theological discussions or those that have been ignored or forgotten, Bennett points out that online theological discussion has its constraints due to the nature of the digital medium. There remains the challenge of facilitating online theological arguments and forming a community of discernment for online theological discussions.[90]

Bennett moves on to discuss theological anthropology. She observes that humans have become cyborgs – "a different kind of creature on the web, a hybrid of human and technology" – as they use digital technology as an extension of their selves.[91] She argues that God is involved with human beings regardless of their being online or off-line, and in fact, "God is online." Therefore, becoming social cyborgs does not negate our encountering God.[92] The question to ask is how to be witnesses in the world in which Christian cyborgs find themselves. To answer this, Bennett discusses (1) how theological authority functions in a seemingly "democratic" medium, (2) the location of an online Christian community, and (3) the issue of Christian behavior online.[93]

While pointing out some drawbacks of the internet, such as addiction to online games, selfies, instant messaging, and pornography, which can alienate us from those around us and damage the wellness of our life, Bennett is even-handed in observing that vice happens off-line, too.[94] That said, it is clear that the internet does not really cater to certain virtues and practices.[95] The book proposes a solid digital theology, and in this it is a step beyond what we have seen to this point. But what it does not do is elaborate the further steps that the church needs to take in order to reach and disciple the youth who are already wholly immersed in digital media. Hence the driving question of this thesis in seeking an account of faithful youth discipleship for digital natives.

In *Networked Theology: Negotiating Faith in Digital Culture* (2016), Heidi A. Campbell and Stephen Garner proposed a networked theology, which is

---

89. Bennett, 10–29.
90. Bennett, 29–32.
91. Bennett, 71.
92. Bennett, 86.
93. Bennett, 87–163.
94. Bennett, 148–163.
95. Bennett, 173.

the convergence between digital technologies and theology.[96] The book stresses that digital media have changed "our relationship with information and others from static, controlled structures to dynamic, adaptive connections."[97] Digital communication technologies create new forms of social connection and information sharing, and they promote individual choice and freedom.[98] The network, which is reshaping our relationships with others and creating a network society, has important theological implications.[99] Technological innovations prompt Christians to experiment with new forms of worship and discipleship. Many churches see the internet as an essential tool for ministry.[100] Therefore, there is a need for an authentic theology of digital media that relates to our faith communities.

Campbell and Garner see themselves as doing contextual theology, "a theological endeavour seeking to articulate a practical theology rooted in the experience of the individual or community."[101] Bringing theology into conversation with the concept of the network enables us to discuss the impacts of digital media on Christian communities. Jesus gives us great examples of contextualizing the gospel in his parables of the kingdom of God, in which he described the kingdom as a small, growing mustard seed, the yeast in bread, a treasure hidden in a field, and so on. He used images that were familiar to the people of his time. In the same manner, the authors propose that it is possible to contextualize the parable of the kingdom of God in our time: "The kingdom of God is like a smartphone with endless battery life and unlimited data" or "The kingdom of God is like a wireless network connecting all kinds of people."[102] Seeing the kingdom of God as a network provides a guide for our interaction with God and others. The book also reflects on Jesus's teaching to love God and love our neighbors in the context of the networked world. The book explores the possibilities for encountering God and expressing his

---

96. Campbell and Garner, *Networked Theology*.
97. Campbell and Garner, 3.
98. Campbell and Garner, 9.
99. Campbell and Garner, 9.
100. Campbell and Garner, 1–2.
101. Campbell and Garner, 11.
102. Campbell and Garner, 13.

love to others both online and off-line.[103] The book also highlights both the pitfalls and the promise of digital media for Christian communities:

> The network can promote flattened rather than hierarchical structures, along with relationships that allow more dynamic interaction rather than being unresponsive and static. This creates sources of creativity and participation that promote connectedness within Christian community, with the "called out" people of God existing together in a system of interdependence and interaction. However, the network can also create tensions and anxiety when it seems to challenge or undermine aspects of the Christian life, particularly communal life and faith.[104]

With latest studies on digital technologies and a nuanced view of their impact on society and Christian community, the book offered a developed digital theology, which is helpful for Christians as they navigate their lives and live faithfully in the digital age – and also shape this culture for the sake of the gospel of Christ.

Going deeper with more theological ground than Thomas's *Digital Disciple*, Chris Shirley's article "Overcoming Digital Distance: The Challenge of Developing Relational Disciples in the Internet Age" (2017) proposes Jesus's model for discipleship (John 15:1–17) as the basis for disciple making in the digital age.[105] It is grounded within the context of human and divine relationships:

> In John 15:1–17, we find a three-point biblical description of the authentic disciple: to (a) live in Christ, (b) love one another, and (c) labor for the kingdom. These characteristics are built on a foundation of relationships with Jesus Christ, with the body of Christ, and with the world. Therefore, the implication is that disciple-making is a relational process, involving an ongoing and abiding relationship with the Lord, a face-to-face commitment to our brothers and sisters in Christ, and a passionate ministry

---

103. Campbell and Garner, 14.
104. Campbell and Garner, 14.
105. Shirley, "Overcoming Digital Distance," 376–90.

with those who need to hear the gospel and/or experience the support of the Christian community.[106]

Within the context of the "Network Society," churches must understand the pitfalls and promise of digital technology as they seek, in this context, to establish and enhance the essential spiritual relationships of abiding in Christ, fellowshipping with other disciples, and ministering to needs of others in the world and in the church.[107]

Hipps has described the paradox of technology: "Every medium when pushed to an extreme will reverse on itself, revealing unintended consequences."[108] The church's responsibility is to make wise choices about the digital tools God has given it to build spiritual relationships. In relation to this paradox, Shirley observes: "Social media highlights the importance of relationships, collaboration, and group life, but the personal, private, and distant nature of the online environment is counterproductive to the goal."[109] He calls the church to build authentic community which demands face-to-face interaction by making "intentional choices to walk away from the electronic community and spend more time building relationships inside and outside the church."[110] Shirley's model for discipleship is helpful for building spiritual relationships in the digital age, but it seems that he still holds a compartmentalized view of the online and off-line worlds and does not propose a solid theology of Christian community.

The question under dispute is whether spiritual formation can happen online. In their 2018 book *Ecologies of Faith in a Digital Age: Spiritual Growth Through Online Education*, Stephen D. Lowe and Mary E. Lowe provide a conceptual and theological ground for cultivating faith online using creation growth metaphors.[111] God's garden ecology, Jesus's parables such as the parable of the seeds, ecology of the body of Christ, and other ecological motifs in the Bible provide insights about connection, interconnection, and interaction for

---

106. Shirley, 377.
107. Shirley, 376.
108. Hipps, *Flickering Pixels*, 37.
109. Shirley, "Overcoming Digital Distance," 388.
110. Shirley, "Overcoming Digital Distance," 388.
111. Lowe and Lowe, *Ecologies of Faith*.

spiritual growth.[112] The study of ecosystems in nature has demonstrated the interconnectedness, which provides insights for how people grow.[113] Shifting from being informational to relational, digital ecologies provide connection, interconnection, and interaction, which can support humans' growth.[114] The authors observe, "The presence of digital ecologies is already shaping how people develop spiritually . . . Millennials are going online to find answers to their spiritual questions."[115] Lowe and Lowe argue that spiritual growth can happen at a distance through the work of the Holy Spirit: "The communion of the saints exists and grows both in spite of the dispersed nature of its existence in the world and through the effective ministry of the Holy Spirit."[116] The authors suggest that regardless of being online or off-line, "there must also be intentionality, reflection, engagement, and interaction between and among those gathered."[117] The book gives solid reasons for believing that spiritual formation can be achieved online if churches build digital ecologies that foster relationship and community.

The question remaining is how to build this digital ecology to foster spiritual formation. Stephen Garner (2019) explores several practices for online spiritual formation:[118]

- Digital storytelling: Mary Hess (2014), who developed digital storytelling as a key tool in spiritual formation, defines digital storytelling as "a community of practice that focuses on helping people to find their own voices, to hone stories from their own experience, and then to craft and share their stories using digital tools."[119]
- Digital photography: Intentional uses of digital photography support religious imaginations, connect individuals into

---

112. Lowe and Lowe, 11, 42–43, 50.
113. Lowe and Lowe, 172.
114. Lowe and Lowe, 114.
115. Lowe and Lowe, 115.
116. Lowe and Lowe, 74.
117. Lowe and Lowe, 85.
118. Garner, "Imaging Christ," 21–30.
119. Hess, "New Culture," 19.

communities, and form a part of spiritual practice contributing to discipleship.[120]
- "Reading" the Bible via apps and websites.[121]
- Didactic video games: Didactic or educational video games can perform evangelistic or apologetic functions or instruct the faithful.[122]

Garner reminds us that these practices should be done in the context of a worshipping community. Alongside the possibility of doing spiritual formation online, the internet also offers opportunity for online mission and evangelism. Therefore, this project will explore ways of discipling the youth and sharing the gospel with them online.

In this section, we have discussed Christian responses to social changes driven by the use of digital media. Christian responses range from pessimistic, to balanced, to optimistic – but all agree that there is a need for contextualization of the gospel in the digital age. Fore, Fortner, and Hipps sounded early calls to respond to the effects of digital media, while mid-stage developments on this topic have articulated a more nuanced view of digital culture, its effects on society, and the communication of the gospel. These mid-stage works did not, however, construct the developed digital theology needed to sustain their proposals. In parallel with the developments in the social-scientific study of digital media, Christians' response has developed over time with a solid digital theology beginning to emerge in the most recent literature. Bennett, Shirley, Lowe and Lowe, Campbell, and Garner propose a far more developed and doctrinally supple digital theology, neither fully embracing nor fully rejecting digital technologies.

My project will take, from these Christian responses, the call to develop a digital theology that takes into consideration both the positive and the negative influences of digital technologies as well as the need to find ways to communicate the gospel to youth whether they are online or off-line. This project will explore a space to reach out to youth who are lonely and lost in cyberspace – by drawing on the mainstream western theological tradition epitomized by Dietrich Bonhoeffer's work, which was concerned with the

---

120. Garner, "Imaging Christ," 24.
121. Garner, 24–25.
122. Garner, 26.

task of discipling youth as well as the task of reimagining Christian orthodox faith for the new era.

3. Theology of Youth Work

In this section, we will survey some recent literature on youth ministry and a theology of youth work, taking a special interest in their intersection with the sociological and theological discourses just surveyed. In the 2019 article "The Digital Way: Re-imagining Digital Discipleship in the Age of Social Media," Jodi G. Hunt presents ways that Catholic youth ministry can refashion the digital lives of youth and young adults.[123] She observes that youth ministry has "missed opportunities to fully develop youth and young adults into faithful and faith-filled digital disciples."[124] In order to help them become digital disciples, youth ministry and its practitioners must first acknowledge the significant role of digital technology in the lives of young people. Hunt suggests, "By offering meaningful youth nights, grounded in faith sharing, storytelling, and reflective praxis, youth and young adults can be guided back to reclaiming their own power and dignity in the digital world."[125] Youth ministry must also communicate the wisdom and beauty of God in digital language that the youth are familiar with. It is also significant for youth workers to accompany the youth as they navigate the digital world.[126] Hunt's call to form the youth into digital disciples is also applicable to youth ministry in Protestant churches. This section reviews books that are significant for formulating a theology of youth discipleship in the digital age.

a. God at the Mall

In the 1999 book *God at the Mall*, Pete Ward calls the church to do youth ministry that meets the needs of youth in their concrete context.[127] According to Ward, Christian youth work can be divided into two different traditions: *Inside-Out* and *Outside-In*. The Inside-Out tradition is characterized by work

---

123. Hunt, "Digital Way," 91–112.
124. Hunt, 92.
125. Hunt, 108–109.
126. Hunt, 109.
127. Ward, *God at the Mall*.

that starts with young people who have been brought up in the church, while the Outside-In tradition has concentrated on ministry among those who are outside the church.[128] The Inside-Out approach is favored by Christian youth workers because it is successful in socializing young people into the total life of the church.[129] The problem is that the social connections of young people are limited, for they tend to make friends with people who are socially very similar to themselves. If the youth group is formed around one type of young person, then the likelihood is that it will attract only similar young people. Therefore, youth workers need to find effective ways to reach out to the youth in the wider community.[130]

The Outside-In or *Incarnational* approach is more demanding since it requires youth workers to build trusting and non-judgmental relationships with young people outside the church and support them in their own struggles and crises. There is a huge gap to bridge before youth workers can share the gospel with them and build up or find an environment for spiritual nurturing.[131] Youth workers should be prepared to respect the existing values of the context of the youth that they are working with while contextualizing the gospel for them.[132] Ward concludes that both Inside-Out and Outside-In approaches in Christian youth work have value, can be used intertwined, and can supplement each other.[133]

Ward's theology of youth ministry is rooted in the characteristics and works of a missionary God who crosses boundaries to build relationship with humankind.[134] Youth ministry should reflect the purpose of God for his church, which is to build a community of people in communion with him and with one another. Relationship (communion) is at the center of being of the Trinitarian God, whom we know as Father, Son, and Holy Spirit – or Creator, Redeemer, and Sustainer. It is this God who calls us and inspires us

---

128. Ward, 8.
129. Ward, 16–17.
130. Ward, 16–17.
131. Ward, 20–21.
132. Ward, 23.
133. Ward, 27.
134. Ward, 33–34.

to reach out to young people.[135] Ward explains the practice of the mission of God in youth ministry:

> To be truly Christian, youthwork must carry within it the essential dynamic of the gospel story. We are called to proclaim this gospel in both our words and our deeds in ways that the young people can understand. The gospel story is rooted in God who is the same yesterday, today, and forever. This unchanging story, however, must be proclaimed afresh in each generation.[136]

As youth workers show care and concern for youth, they show the heart of God, who desires to have relationship with humankind. Youth workers need to not only care for youth but also proclaim the gospel to them. This proclamation of the gospel is fostered by godly living of youth workers as they serve as role models or mentors to youth.[137]

Ward proposes the shape of the gospel, which positions the work of contextualization of the gospel for youth in concrete contexts: the incarnation and the cross, redemption and repentance, transcendence and immanence, hope of the kingdom, and the work of the Holy Spirit. The incarnation of God as a human being requires us to accept youth where they are.[138] Redemption and repentance bridge the gap between youth and the gospel.[139] Youth ministry is inviting youth to encounter a transcendent and mysterious God – but a God who is also willing to reveal Himself to his children.[140] The task of youth workers is to proclaim the hope of the kingdom where sinners are set free.[141] These works cannot be carried out without the work of the Holy Spirit, who changes a person's life through both natural and supernatural encounters. There is a need for theological reflection upon the work of the Holy Spirit as youth workers choose which approach – or choose a combination of approaches – for youth ministry: focusing on the miraculous encounter with God in worship; focusing on the ministry of the word of God; or focusing on

---

135. Ward, 33–34.
136. Ward, 35.
137. Ward, 35.
138. Ward, 36.
139. Ward, 39.
140. Ward, 41–43.
141. Ward, 44.

youth work processes such as education, community work, empowerment, or counseling.[142]

Ward presents, in detail, a relational model of the incarnation approach (Outside-In). The stages of this relational model are contact, proclamation, nurture, and church. First, youth workers need to journey onto the territory of youth in order to establish contact and build relationships with them.[143] As relationships with the youth grow, the gospel is proclaimed naturally in ways that are relevant to youth in their specific context.[144] Then youth workers do Bible study with youth; teach them spiritual skills such as methods of prayer, discussion, and worship; and make them aware of the presence of local churches.[145] The last stage is helping youth to find a place in church.[146] This model can also bring benefits even to youth ministry that is located in a church context (Inside-Out).[147]

Ward highlights the need to understand the popular culture in which the youth immerse themselves. Youth workers act as a bridge between youth culture and church culture.[148] He points out the importance of cultural studies and also their need to be evaluated by the gospel:

> In the light of the gospel story, Christian youth workers will be looking for those aspects of popular culture that they can see being in tune with the gospel, while at the same time working for renewal and transformation of those aspects that are outside the sweep of God's inventions for society. Cultural studies therefore give us tools to understand the culture of groups of young people, but it is the gospel that gives us a perspective to see them in fresh light.[149]

---

142. Ward, 46–50.
143. Ward, 57.
144. Ward, 67.
145. Ward, 72–73.
146. Ward, 73–76.
147. Ward, 76–77.
148. Ward, 80–81.
149. Ward, 97.

The task of youth workers is providing a true contextualization of the gospel which requires "a rootedness in culture, a faithfulness to the Bible, and an openness to the tradition of the church."[150]

This book gives a valid call to contextualize the gospel for youth in their concrete context. In response to this call, this project will contextualize the theology of youth discipleship in the digital age.

b. Starting Right

Starting Right: Thinking Theologically About Youth Ministry is a handbook on youth ministry written by a number of authors from different backgrounds, with Kenda Creasy Dean, Chap Clark, and David Rahn as editors.[151] In the literature review in chapter 1, Kenda Dean sounds a call to think first of *"theological rocks"* for youth ministry.[152] She locates theology of youth ministry under practical theology. She uses the tasks of practical theology as a framework for doing youth ministry. This framework is used to organize chapters of the book written by different authors. The book is divided into four sections in accordance with the four tasks within practical theology reflections:[153]

1. Understand: What is going on?
2. Reflect: What we are doing?
3. Detect and evaluate: How well we are doing it by God's standard?
4. Project: How can we do it better?

The first section of this book explores the significance of practical theology reflection for youth ministry on understanding the context of youth ministry. This reflection contains considerations of theological resources such as Scripture, church teachings or doctrine, human reason, and sacred experience. Dean reminds the church of the call and the commitment to reach out to youth in their struggles and the need to understand their concrete situation.[154]

After describing the concrete situation of youth ministry, Section 2 moves on to reflections on current practice of youth ministry. Chap Clark discusses "The Myth of the Perfect Youth Ministry Model" to show that no model is

---

150. Ward, 112.
151. Dean, Clark, and Rahn, *Starting Right*.
152. Dean, Clark, and Rahn, 16.
153. Dean, Clark, and Rahn 20.
154. Dean, Clark, and Rahn, chap. 1.

perfect for youth ministry. To formulate a youth program in light of the mission of youth ministry, it is important to take into consideration the needs of youth – from general to specific to individual needs – and the available resources.[155] Then there is the discussion of doing youth ministry from various approaches, such as evangelism, Christian practices (for example, the sacraments, prayer, faith, baptism), student leadership, critical consciousness, community, and innovation. As Dean observes of these approaches, there may be a mix of various approaches. Moreover, there are some approaches that are not mentioned here. It is important to use our "theological rocks" to evaluate our current approach to and practices of youth ministry.[156]

Section 3, "Detecting Our Convictions and Evaluating Our Practices," calls churches to find the rationale for their practice of youth ministry in their concrete context. This section presents different theological frameworks for youth ministry proposed by various authors. Each framework has a different starting point such as repentance, grace, redemption, or hope. As Dean explains, the purpose of presenting various frameworks is to show how to use these frameworks or "theological rocks" to evaluate current practices of youth ministry, to check whether they are faithful to our calling.[157]

The fourth task is reconstructing youth ministry to more faithfully communicate God's intention rather than our own intentions. It discusses ways to walk more faithfully with youth, taking consideration of the community, the organizational, and the social contexts of our ministry. It presents ways to utilize networks, resources, and curricula, to organize programs, events, and counseling – and to assess our improvement and spiritual readiness for youth ministry calling.[158]

This book is a comprehensive and practical guide for doing youth ministry since it looks at youth ministry from various angles presented by different authors from various church traditions. What I take from this rather diverse material is the importance of having "theological rocks" for youth ministry as well as these authors' call to evaluate the practice of youth ministry in my own concrete context using the tasks of practical theology reflection. However,

---

155. Dean, Clark, and Rahn, chap. 6.
156. Dean, Clark, and Rahn, 108.
157. Dean, Clark, and Rahn, 227.
158. Dean, Clark, and Rahn, 283.

the book does not present an in-depth theology of youth discipleship for our day and age, which this project seeks to do.

c. Bonhoeffer as Youth Worker

In the book *Bonhoeffer as Youth Worker*, Andrew Root presents an inspiring historical account of Dietrich Bonhoeffer's journey with young people.[159] The main thread of the book is the claim that Bonhoeffer was the forefather of the "theological turn" to youth ministry that focuses on personal relationship with Christ.

Part 1 of the book is devoted fully to the history of Bonhoeffer from childhood to adulthood to death. Bonhoeffer started serving as a teacher in children's Sunday school then ministered to youth who had grown up in and then outgrown Sunday school. It is interesting how Bonhoeffer has different approaches with children (telling stories) than with youth ("heavy conversations" about thoughts and ideas).[160] This recognition is significant since the age groups are different. However, in many parts of this book, it is confusing and not helpful when Root puts together the terms "children" and "youth" or relates Bonhoeffer to children's ministry as if it is the same as youth ministry. However, Root did do a good job of showing how ministry to children and youth prompted Bonhoeffer "to see the church as the locale for experiencing the living Christ" and contributed to his theological works, especially his first book *Sanctorum Communio*.[161] I very much agree since Jesus said, "For the Kingdom of Heaven belongs to those who are like these children." (Mat 19:4). It was in ministry to young people that Bonhoeffer realized that "he must give his whole person," and he was ministered to by them.[162] This is very true of my experience as a youth worker, living, playing, and giving fully to youth, including letting them see my weaknesses, also, and being sharpened by them.

The book continues to present various significant youth ministry experiences of Bonhoeffer. The ten-year-old boy in tears in Barcelona contributed to the theological thinking of Bonhoeffer and his second book, *Act and*

---

159. Root, *Bonhoeffer as Youth Worker*.
160. Root, 57–58.
161. Root, 45; Bonhoeffer, *Sanctorum Communio*.
162. Root, *Bonhoeffer as Youth Worker*, 44, 60.

Being.¹⁶³ This also informed the task of youth worker in "helping them to wrestle with God's action in and through concrete lives."¹⁶⁴ The church is to give young people a place in the church community created by Jesus Christ.¹⁶⁵ Bonhoeffer's worship and serving experience at Abyssinian Baptist Church in Harlem also deepened his ministerial focus on youth ministry, pushing his conception of community to become even more concrete.¹⁶⁶ His class at Union Theological Seminary also "moved him into further reflection on youth work."¹⁶⁷ Bonhoeffer's ministry to young people from the summer of 1931 to mid-1933 was impressive: pastoral care with young adults at technical college, the teaching of confirmation classes, the running of a youth club, and secretary work for youth in the ecumenical movement. These are solid proof of Bonhoeffer's wide experience as a youth worker. In addition to all his successes, Bonhoeffer also encountered failure in ministry to young people: the sinking of his chaplaincy at a technical college where the students had little interest in knowing him, seeking his pastoral care, or attending the program events he offered.¹⁶⁸ Bonhoeffer shows why it is helpful for youth workers to learn from failure, too. During this period, Bonhoeffer also wrote *Creation and Fall*, though Root does not explore its relationship with youth.¹⁶⁹

The most impressive proof of Bonhoeffer's engagement with youth work is his eight theses on youth work. It reflects an in-depth and mature theological insight into youth ministry. Thesis 1 highlights the need of "Christian sobriety": the youth need to listen to the word of God, and the church needs to proclaim the word of God.¹⁷⁰ As Root observes, Bonhoeffer asserts that "youth ministry is first and foremost a theological task . . . a ministry that seeks the encounter of the divine with the human."¹⁷¹ This is very clear evi-

---

163. Bonhoeffer, *Act and Being*; the boy was in tears, asking Bonhoeffer whether he would see his dog again in heaven.
164. Root, *Bonhoeffer as Youth Worker*, 71.
165. Root, 78.
166. Bonhoeffer spent a significant amount of time in Harlem while he was a postdoctoral student in America at Union Theological Seminary during the 1930–31 school year.
167. Root, *Bonhoeffer as Youth Worker*, 86.
168. Root, 93. In October 1931, Bonhoeffer started his ordained appointment as chaplain to a technical college.
169. Bonhoeffer, *Creation and Fall*.
170. Root, *Bonhoeffer as Youth Worker*, 119.
171. Root, 120.

dence that Bonhoeffer made a "theological turn" away from idolizing youth spirit/culture/future roles and from focusing on just the technical things of doing youth ministry. This turn remains very helpful for youth ministry in this day and age. Theses 2 and 3 explain what the church community is and the place of youth in it, with theses 4 and 5 engaging the generational problem and the sober view of youth in the Bible. Theses 6 and 7 mention baptism – which removes the generational gap – and the right to protest in love. Thesis 8 presses the relative significance of "church association." Root comments that theses 1 to 6 move youth ministry to unity with the church whereas theses 7 and 8 need critique. However, I see that Bonhoeffer presents a very balanced view, especially during a time when the church was corrupted and the youth spirit was idolized.

Part 2 of *Bonhoeffer as Youth Worker* serves as an application of the books *Discipleship* and *Life Together* to youth ministry.[172] There is no doubt that the contents of these two books are appropriate for youth and youth workers because of their central theme: the call to follow Jesus Christ and to participate in Christ's community. However, it can be argued that these two books are applicable to all ages. Root did not indicate any sense in which they are especially relevant to youth ministry, although this could be argued from the character of youth in seeking truth, identity, experience, etc. Actually, Bonhoeffer did not mention youth in these two books except for the part about the rich young ruler. These things make part 2 very much like an appendix to the book. Overall, Root does well in exploring the history of Bonhoeffer in relation to, reflection on, and application to youth ministry. However, only the central portion of the book is directly related to Bonhoeffer as a youth worker, though Root claims that he deploys Bonhoeffer's "theological turn" in youth ministry throughout the book. Root might have directly focused on Bonhoeffer's works in youth ministry and his theological writing with themes directly related to youth – or prompted from youth work – such as the divinization of youth, parental authority, revolution of youth, and youth moral behavior, which can be found in other writings of Bonhoeffer such as *Ethics*.[173] Strong concluding statements might have been made toward the end of the book to prove that Bonhoeffer as a youth worker was the forefather

---

172. Bonhoeffer, *Discipleship*; Bonhoeffer, *Life Together*.
173. Bonhoeffer, *Ethics*, 139–140, 371.

of the theological turn in youth ministry. This thesis will launch from Root's claim that Bonhoeffer was a youth worker to explore Bonhoeffer's theology on discipleship, community, and youth more widely.

d. Networks for Faith Formation

In *Networks for Faith Formation*, Steven Emery-Wright and Ed Mackenzie highlight the significance of supporting networks for youths' spiritual formation.[174] The rationale for this is that God has created us for relationships. Furthermore, relationships are crucial for youth because they are in an important period of developing their identity, purposes, and faiths. As a result, youth need godly relationships for this process.[175] The book starts with a discussion of the theology of relationships drawn from the biblical portrayal of God as a God of relationship. This Trinitarian God is relational and wants to have relationship with humankind, who was created by him for relationship. Therefore, humankind is shaped through relationships. There is need for connection with the faith community.[176]

The book presents eight networks for faith formation with discussion from biblical studies, practical theology, and social studies.[177] The first one is personal practices such as prayer, Bible study, fasting, and journaling.[178] These practices are important, but they must be situated within a wider network of Christian community.[179] The church is a location where youth can encounter God through worship, God's word, sacrament, and catechesis, and exercise their spiritual gifts.[180] It is necessary for the church to help parents see their role in modeling faith to their children.[181] Friendship is very significant in shaping the identities of youth.[182] Therefore, the church needs to create contexts for youth to befriend other Christians with whom they can study

---

174. Emery-Wright and Mackenzie, *Networks for Faith Formation*.
175. Emery-Wright and Mackenzie, xvi.
176. Emery-Wright and Mackenzie, 2–3.
177. Emery-Wright and Mackenzie, xviii.
178. Emery-Wright and Mackenzie, 16.
179. Emery-Wright and Mackenzie, 22.
180. Emery-Wright and Mackenzie, 29–33.
181. Emery-Wright and Mackenzie, 43.
182. Emery-Wright and Mackenzie, 48.

the Bible, pray, worship together, have fun, and be mutually accountable.[183] Mentors can play a key role in building up youth in the image of Christ.[184] Small groups provide a good place for youth to be accountable to one another and encourage one another in their faith journeys.[185] Events and gatherings such as camps, festivals, and pilgrimages can provide a potential environment for encountering Christ.[186] Missions and service can be a location for youth to share their faith proactively and, in turn, can lead to spiritual growth.[187]

There are some limits to this book. The statement in this book that "the thicker the web of relationships, the more likely it is that faith in Christ will grow" is questionable.[188] The practices of silence, solitude, and prayer demonstrated by the Desert Fathers can challenge this statement. Christian relationships are just one of the loci for spiritual growth. The authors seem aware of this problem as they state:

> The importance of networks does not mean that an individual believer *cannot* come to faith without them, nor should it imply that all such networks are of equal value. God graciously draws people to himself through various means, and a person from an atheistic background who comes to faith in their late fifties is as valuable to God as the person born and nurtured within a Christian family.[189]

The problem with this book is that it does not define faith formation or give the exact location of those networks for faith formations. The first network, "Personal Faith," is not really a network. However, I take from this book the challenge to think about personal spiritual formation. As spiritual disciplines are very important for spiritual formation, this thesis will discuss them in Chapter 3.3. The other seven networks listed in the book – church, family, friends, mentors, small groups, events and gatherings, and mission and service – are the loci where youth can experience spiritual growth. Without

---

183. Emery-Wright and Mackenzie, 54.
184. Emery-Wright and Mackenzie, 68.
185. Emery-Wright and Mackenzie, 77–80.
186. Emery-Wright and Mackenzie, 91.
187. Emery-Wright and Mackenzie, 101.
188. Emery-Wright and Mackenzie, xvi.
189. Emery-Wright and Mackenzie, xv.

being grouped into a bigger group, These networks seem fragmented without being grouped into a bigger group: Christian community. Though the eighth network, mission and service, seems to move beyond Christian community, it is still located in the work of Christian community and of youth reaching out to the world. This book only focuses on Christian networks and neglects the networks from society at large such as teaching institutions, friendships beyond church, and vocational training, which can give input for the spiritual growth of youth. What I can take from this book is the call for the church and Christian communities to take up the responsibility of reaching out to and discipling youth.

e. Faith for Exiles

In the 2019 book *Faith for Exiles: 5 Ways for a New Generation to Follow Jesus in Digital Babylon*, David Kinnaman, Mark Matlock, and Aly Hawkins observe that the churches in North America are hemorrhaging their young people.[190] Today, 64 percent of all young adults from eighteen to twenty-nine years old who were once regular churchgoers have dropped out. This number has been increasing in the past ten years. The authors assert that today's society is especially hostile toward faith formation.[191] Young non-Christians are avoiding Christianity, and young Christians are abandoning church. In response, Kinnaman, Matlock, and Hawkins propose five spiritual practices for discipling youth in the digital age, whom they call the exiles in "digital Babylon."

As in Jesus's parable of the sower, in which a farmer scatters seeds on various kinds of ground, it is important to analyze the spiritual receptivity or resistance of the hearts of the youth with whom we are working today in order to provide suitable care for them.[192] In the digital age, we tend to navigate our lives and make sense of the world by turning to our digital devices. Growing up digitally, youth, especially, use smart devices as their counselors, entertainers, instructors, and even sex educators.[193] They do so because digital technologies and their contents look so powerful. The authors observe that

---

190. Kinnaman, Matlock, and Hawkins, *Faith for Exiles*.
191. Kinnaman, Matlock, and Hawkins, "Start Here."
192. Kinnaman, Matlock, and Hawkins, "Start Here."
193. Kinnaman, Matlock, and Hawkins, "Start Here."

this generation is the first generation of humans that cannot rely on the earned wisdom of older adults and traditions to help them navigate their lives in the changing world of a digital age. As a result, many young people turn to peers and digital algorithms.[194]

The authors call this age "digital Babylon." As we know, ancient Babylon was the pagan, multicultural crossroads that became the unwanted home of Judean exiles. Glorying in pride, power, prestige, and pleasure, this culture set itself against the purposes of God.[195] For those who grow up as Christians, whose understanding of the world is framed by the Bible, this may be understood as living through a shift from Jerusalem to "digital Babylon." The book describes our age as follows:

> Digital Babylon is not a physical place. It is the pagan-but-spiritual, hyperstimulated, multicultural, imperial crossroads that is the virtual home of every person with Wi-Fi, a data plan, or – for most of us – both . . . In digital Babylon, where information (and anything we could ever want or need) is instantly available at the godlike swipe of a finger, Almighty God has been squeezed to the margins. Those of us who long to keep him at the center of our lives constantly fight the centrifugal force of a world spinning us away from him . . . The Bible is one of many voices that interpret human experience; it is no longer viewed as the central authority over people and society.[196]

In this "digital Babylon," the idol is the demand to fit in and be up to speed at the pace of fiber optic. Screens promise more connectedness, but instead they cause loneliness, depression, and anxiety among young people. They are crippled by FOMO (the fear of missing out).[197]

Many young people live shallow lives, addicted to digital media, trying to fill the void in their hearts.[198] Statistically speaking, a typical young person spends nearly twenty times more hours per year consuming media than taking in spiritual content. For a typical Christian youth, the ratio is still more

---

194. Kinnaman, Matlock, and Hawkins, "Start Here."
195. Kinnaman, Matlock, and Hawkins, "Start Here."
196. Kinnaman, Matlock, and Hawkins, "Start Here."
197. Kinnaman, Matlock, and Hawkins, "Start Here."
198. Kinnaman, Matlock, and Hawkins, "Start Here."

than ten to one.[199] This poses a great challenge for the church in discipling youth, with the weight of information stacked against spiritual formation.[200] Since it is impossible to go back to Jerusalem, at least for now, the contemporary church needs to figure out how to shape the hearts and minds of youth spiritually here and now in the "digital Babylon."[201] This book takes this as the paradigmatic "exile" statement: "I want to find a way to follow Jesus that connects with the world I live in. God is more at work outside the church than inside, and I want to be a part of that. I want to be a Christian without separating myself from the world around me."[202] It suggests five helpful practices for making disciples in the "digital Babylon":

> Practice 1: To form a resilient identity, experience intimacy with Jesus. Practice 2: In a complex and anxious age, develop the muscles of cultural discernment. Practice 3: When isolation and mistrust are the norms, forge meaningful, intergenerational relationships. Practice 4: To ground and motivate an ambitious generation, train for vocational discipleship. Practice 5: Curb entitlement and self-centered tendencies by engaging in countercultural mission.[203]

These five practices are helpful for making disciples in the "digital Babylon."

This book has done an exciting job in describing this age as the "digital Babylon." It is obvious that digital technologies posed challenges for youth discipleship since youth are constantly consuming digital media on smart devices. However, the book has not described in depth these challenges and their root causes. Is it true that youth consume much more secular content and much less spiritual content than they did before the digital age? The book also takes the perspective of the church in North America, where Christians are used to being a majority, but now, in the digital age, young non-Christians are avoiding Christianity, and young Christians are abandoning church. However, coming from a secular Asian country, Vietnam, I think that the church there has always been in Babylon, not just now because of the digital age. Although

---

199. Kinnaman, Matlock, and Hawkins, "Start Here."
200. Kinnaman, Matlock, and Hawkins, "Start Here."
201. Kinnaman, Matlock, and Hawkins, "Start Here."
202. Kinnaman, Matlock, and Hawkins, "Start Here."
203. Kinnaman, Matlock, and Hawkins, "Start Here."

digital media may have negative impacts on youth, their benefits should not be neglected. Though this book does not provide a solid digital theology or a theology of youth discipleship, the five practices suggested in this book are nevertheless helpful for discipling youth of the "digital Babylon."

The literature on youth ministry and on theology of youth work is helpful for this work of communicating the gospel to youth in a digital culture. Ward calls for a contextualizing of the gospel for youth in their concrete context, while Dean suggests thinking of "theological rocks" of youth ministry. Root proposes that Bonhoeffer be accorded a pivotal role in forming a theology of discipleship, youth, and youth ministry. Emery-Wright and Mackenzie highlight the importance of Christian networks for spiritual growth in youth. Kinnaman, Matlock, and Hawkins suggest five spiritual practices for discipling youth in the "digital Babylon." What is still left to do is to weave these insights together to construct a theology for discipling youth in the digital age. That is the aim of this project. In summary, this literature review has surveyed studies of cultural changes in the digital age, Christian response to these changes, and contemporary theologies of youth work. The portrait developed of social changes in the digital age helpfully reveals the work needing to be done to communicate the gospel in ways that are relevant to the people of this age. How should the church of Christ respond to such dynamics and disciple the youth of this generation? Should the contemporary church use digital media in discipling youth? The literature considering Christian responses to the influence of digital media and theology of youth surfaces the call to develop a digital theology that takes into consideration both the positive and the negative influences of digital technologies as well as the need to find ways to communicate the gospel to youth where they are, whether on- or off-line. However, this literature still has not answered these questions. There remains a gap in the literature addressing digital theology for discipling youth. The next chapter will start to bridge this gap with a study of the impacts of digital media, especially on the youth of Gens Y and Z.

CHAPTER 2

The Impacts of Digital Media

Digital media have become an inseparable part of our lives, especially the lives of the youth of Gens Y and Z who find it difficult to put down their smartphones. The impact of digital media appears pervasive, yet it can be difficult to define exactly what is under discussion. This chapter describes how the use of digital media has become the way of life in society in general and has particularly obvious impacts on youth. The following sketch of recent developments in digital culture is intended to inform and instruct the church by providing some basic descriptions of the technologies and cultural trajectories with which churches will need to become familiar in order to walk with the youth generation in their contemporary faith journey. The task of this chapter is mostly descriptive, but the study of youth identity in the digital age and the practical implications for institutions to mentor youth will prepare the way for chapters to come that look directly at how the church may disciple the youth of this age.

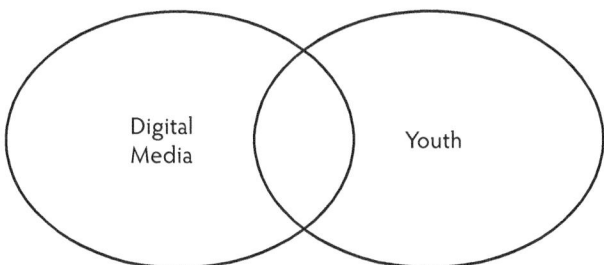

Figure 2.1. The convergence of digital media and youth

The literature review in chapter 1 surveyed cutting-edge insights from some social-scientific literature on the ways that culture is changing in the digital age. Scholars are divided in their views of the effects of digital media on society, some seeing it as more problematic and others, less problematic. Gaining a nuanced view of the cultural changes currently afoot will thus entail considering both the negative and the positive impacts of digital media. This chapter will build on the initial descriptions offered in chapter 1 to investigate more deeply the various impacts of digital media on society. It will focus on the topics of digital media and youth, and especially on the convergence between them (as illustrated in the figure above). It will proceed first by setting out a brief history of communication and the characteristics of the digital age. It will then look more closely at the impacts of digital media on youth, discussing the advantages and disadvantages that accrue due to its growing influence over the formation of the identities of youth. The final section of this chapter analyzes social studies on how institutions such as schools and families might most effectively mentor youth in this digital age.

1. The Impacts of Digital Media on Society
a. A Brief History of Communication

Before discussing how digital media affects society today, it is important to take a look at the history of communication. This allows us to see how communication shapes our brains and the way we process information, in turn shaping wider cultural patterns. In *Mythmakers: Gospel, Culture and the Media,* William F. Fore highlights how communicative media have affected cultural values throughout human history. "The media," he says, "do affect us, profoundly. In fact, the history of our communication technology is, in one sense, also a history of our cultures: oral, written, printed, and electronic."[1] Writing, for instance, changed the way people thought since people no longer needed to express themselves in the language that could be easily memorized. The shift from oral to written communication changed not only "what we think" but also "how we think" since it eliminated the need for communicators to present easily memorized speeches and develop highly accurate memories. Writing, in contrast, formally separates writer and reader,

---

1. Fore, *Mythmakers*, 29.

thus fostering more introspection and self-examination.[2] The development of printing affects societies greatly since widespread access to written documents promotes freedom of thought.[3]

With the invention of the telegraph in 1844, electronic communication moved humanity into a new era of communication in which discourse occurs apart from the physical means of transportation.[4] Robert S. Fortner's conclusion is that the digital age, with its distinctive characteristics

> is not merely the replacement of one system of transmission for radio and television, data and reportage, record-keeping and communication, by another. It is also the replacement of a multi-stranded, but continuous, line of culture (an analog culture) with one comprised of discrete bits (digitally-coded ones and zeros, if you will) in which the only relationship between any two bits is their proximity to each other – and that occurs nearly randomly.[5]

Digital technology presents a shift in culture as radical as the printing press did before. The next subsection discusses just how deeply digital communication technologies are embedded in our daily lives and how indelibly it shapes the lives of the people of our time.

b. Characteristics of the Digital Age

What makes digital communication profoundly different from any other form of communication is how its very medium of communication uproots the way culture was previously understood, shaping in turn how culture should now be defined. The first characteristic of the digital age is that information is delivered faster and more effectively than ever before. This enables people to make free choices among a much wider range of possibilities. Concurrently, digital technologies have severed the link between communication and information. Information can be treated as commodity and can be easily transferred, bought and sold, accessed and searched, and otherwise dealt with. People can get and process information as they wish with little permission

---

2. Fore, 29.
3. Fore, 32–34.
4. Fore, 34–35.
5. Fortner, "Gospel in a Digital Age," 3–4.

or granted authority.[6] The second characteristic of the digital culture is interactivity – the ability of a user to manipulate a technical system. This is made possible by interactive cable and the internet.[7] In contrast to television, which is passive, the internet is interactive. It allows the user to freely search and selectively engage information made up of discrete bits. Digital natives become used to being able to pinpoint what they want when they want it instead of having to sift through information displayed in its entirety as in older newspapers or TV programs.[8]

Another very important feature of the digital age is how networking technologies move us toward a network society.[9] Philip R. Meadows explains:

> From an everyday perspective, this trend can be seen in the transformation of "personal media" devices, such as mobile phones, toward greater integration with "social media" technologies, like Facebook. Computing devices become part of our lives as both individuals and communities. This is evident in the evolution of websites from rather static providers of information, to much more dynamic sites of collaboration, through the development of interactive "Web 2.0" technologies: from instant messaging to personal blogging, discussion forums, and various kinds of wiki-media applications. The transition toward a network society has the capacity to either replace or complement more traditional kinds of social relationship, though the trend is greater convergence between them.[10]

Technically speaking, the internet is nothing more than a vast web of connections. The "Network Society," Meadows suggests, is a convergence between cyberspace and physical life driven by a near complete connection to the internet via digital devices. Digital media becomes integrated with everyday life. For young people, this means immersion in a world in which cyberspace is inextricably interweaved with the flow of everyday life.[11]

---

6. Fortner, 10.
7. Fortner, 4.
8. Fortner, 11.
9. Meadows, "Mission and Discipleship," 165.
10. Meadows, 165–166.
11. Meadows, 165–166.

Digital technology enables telecommunication or "telepresence." Online chat and videotelephony services such as Facebook Messenger, WhatsApp, and Zoom make it possible for people to communicate with, or in some sense to be present with, someone else despite being separated by space. Social networking sites enable us to do this by chatting and sharing photos, videos, and status updates. Family members and friends can stay in touch easily despite being separated by long distances. Though this is not equivalent to the embodied presence of friendship that can be "smelled" and "touched," this can still allow for significant relational engagement.[12] Social networking sites such as Facebook, MySpace, and LinkedIn make it easier to form virtual communities of fan clubs for groups of like-minded people.[13] These communities can offer many things such as the sharing of knowledge, personal experience, and interest. Many of these groups may have some "off-line" meetings to strengthen relationships, for example, off-line fan club meetings out of Facebook or business meetings out of LinkedIn. However, it is also quite common for some people in these groups to never meet each other physically.

Thus, it is best to see the "Network Society" as a new form of sociality, concludes Meadows:

> Digital culture adds a virtual dimension to everyday life. On the one hand, digital technology can enhance and extend our embodied relationships in many ways, but it also has a compartmentalizing effect that divides our lives into different realms, and can even make virtual life an end in itself.[14]

Although Meadows proposes the possible convergence between cyberspace and physical life, his language of "compartmentalize" and "divide" shows that he has not moved fully beyond the popular views of separation between the virtual life and the physical life nor of separation between the virtual self and the "real" self. In short, digital technology presents a radical shift in culture, moving us toward a network society in which cyberspace and physical life converge. This raises questions about the impacts of digital media on youth.

---

12. Meadows, 169.
13. Meadows, 170.
14. Meadows, 170.

2. The Impacts of Digital Media on Youth

Digital media's greatest impact is on the youth of Gens Y and Z who were born into the digital age. The following section surveys ideas from some authors who write about the impacts of digital media on youth. Again, this information provides important descriptive background for the theological discussion to follow. It is easy for adults to point out the negative impacts of digital media on youth – attention deficit disorder, poor communication, game addiction, violence, the lack of work ethic, and so on.[15] Those negative impacts cannot be the whole picture. As discussed earlier in the literature review, Don Tapscott argues that the youth of this age are not dumber, nor do they have shorter attention spans. Rather, they are brighter and exhibit new ways of thinking, interacting, working, and socializing. He strongly defends youth as relating to technology in a different way than their parents' generation.[16] He names eight positive characteristics of the Net Generation:

> They prize freedom and freedom of choice. They want to customize things, make them their own. They are natural collaborators, who enjoy a conversation, not a lecture. They'll scrutinize you and your organization. They insist on integrity. They want to have fun, even at work and at school. Speed is normal. Innovation is part of life.[17]

These characteristics seem positive, but they need to be analyzed further to discern whether they are really all positive and enriching to the youth of this generation. Given the focus and scope of this project, there are two main impacts of digital media on youth that I will now examine in more depth in order to highlight some central dynamics that need to be understood in order to mentor the youth of this generation well. We will examine first whether they are "smarter" than their parents' generation and second whether they are "better at collaboration."

---

15. Tapscott, *Growing Up Digital*, 3–5.
16. Tapscott, 2.
17. Tapscott, 6.

a. Dumber or Smarter?

In the book *The Dumbest Generation*, discussed in the literature review, Mark Bauerlein asserts that young people today are dumber than previous generations.[18] He states the following:

> This is the paradox of the Dumbest Generation. For the young American, life has never been so yielding, goods so plentiful, schooling so accessible, diversion so easy, and liberties so copious. The material gains are clear, and each year the traits of worldliness and autonomy seem to trickle down into ever-younger age groups. But it's a shallow advent. As the survey research shows, knowledge and skills haven't kept pace, and the intellectual habits that complement them are slipping.[19]

His claim is that this generation should be more intellectual because they enjoy more opportunity to access knowledge than previous generations. However, they are not acquiring more knowledge. Bauerlein is correct that life now is more convenient than ever before, but he does not acknowledge any of the new challenges that young people today have to face in the digital age. Each generation has different challenges. Growing up in the "Peep culture," Hal Niedzviecki observes, young people are bombarded with all the social media that deeply influence their lives, trying to make them become "Peep persons."[20] Shoshana Zuboff observes the greatest challenge that the young people of this generation face is "Addiction by Design" of social media that make it impossible for them to escape.[21]

Bauerlein asserts that though young people today seem adept with technology and good at multitasking, they have less knowledge and skills, especially in academic matters, as compared to previous generations.[22] He seems to focus on some traditional knowledge and skills that he thinks are important, but the new age presents a new set of intellectual skills that previous ages do not have. From this perspective, Tapscott argues that the youth of Gens Y and Z are smarter than their parents' generation:

---

18. Bauerlein, *Dumbest Generation*, 7.
19. Bauerlein, 32.
20. Niedzviecki, *Peep Diaries*, 29–30.
21. Zuboff, *Age of Surveillance Capitalism*, 449–450.
22. Bauerlein, *Dumbest Generation*, 35.

> As the first global generation ever, the Net Geners are smarter, quicker, and more tolerant of diversity than their predecessors. They care strongly about justice and the problems faced by their society and are typically engaged in some kind of civic activity at school, at work, or in their community.[23]

Tapscott believes that the youth of Gens Y and Z are smarter because digital media has changed the way their brains are wired. Growing up digitally, youth are immersed every day in a deluge of information from a multitude of sources. This forces them to learn to balance the digital and physical worlds.[24] This also presents an intellectual challenge when youth have to make sense of different kinds of information that may be contradictory or confusing.[25] They find it difficult to reconcile posts on social media with conflicting views. As a result, Gens Y and Z have learned to be skeptical when online.[26]

Some people may argue that youth are not good at reading books. Bauerlein asserts that they do not read very well.[27] However, reading online requires different skills.[28] The youth of Gens Y and Z do not always start at the beginning. They do not operate in a sequential way. Using tools like keywords in Google, hypertext, and "clicking, cutting, and pasting," today's young people can search for and organize information containing links to other information.[29] This forces them to develop critical thinking and investigation skills, among others. They must become critics of the information they receive or see on social media.[30] Also, youth are prepared for multitasking.[31] They can turn on the computer or smartphone to simultaneously interact with several different windows or applications by, for example, talking on the phone, listening to music, doing homework, and reading a magazine or

---

23. Tapscott, *Growing Up Digital*, 6.
24. Tapscott, 10.
25. Tapscott, 113.
26. Tapscott, 81.
27. Bauerlein, *Dumbest Generation*, 35.
28. Tapscott, *Growing Up Digital*, 112.
29. Tapscott, 105.
30. Tapscott, 21.
31. Tapscott, 9.

watching television.[32] All these particular skills have significant impact on their brain development.[33]

Some studies suggest that Gens Y and Z's brains process, operate, and function differently than those of the older generations.[34] Scientists say that the second critical period of brain development occurs roughly during the adolescent and teenage years.[35] They also explain that the continual and intense use of a particular brain region can lead it to respond like a muscle, increasing its size and presumably its efficiency.[36] Therefore, the constant use of digital technology during the adolescent and teenage years leaves significant impacts on their brains. Neurological research shows that the way we receive information – by reading a book, watching a movie, or listening to someone on the telephone – has a big impact on the brain, and that impact is even more important than the actual content of the message. For example, a brain scan done by Erica Michael and Marcel Just shows that the brain constructs the message differently for reading than it does for listening. According to them, listening to an audiobook leaves a different set of memories than reading does.[37] Researchers show that the Net Generation remembers less from the traditional newscast – which narrates from beginning to the end – than they do from interactive versions that give them a chance to click to hear the news or learn more details.[38] Growing up digital has also forced the youth of the Net Generation to learn how to read images such as pictures, graphs, and icons. They may be more visual than their parents are. A study of Net Gen college students showed that they learned much better from visual images than from text-based ones.[39]

Tapscott's capstone evidence that the Net Generation is the smartest generation rests on comparing IQ scores. The statistics show that raw IQ scores have been climbing by three points a decade since World War II and have

---

32. Tapscott, 20.
33. Tapscott, 30.
34. Tapscott, 101.
35. Tapscott, 30.
36. Tapscott, 99.
37. Tapscott, 104.
38. Tapscott, 104.
39. Tapscott, 106.

been increasing across racial, income, and regional boundaries.[40] The evidence suggests that the top students are reading more and performing well in school. The reasons for those who are falling behind have little to do with the internet and more to do with a failing educational system, family problems, poverty, and other social causes. Tapscott therefore suggests that these poorer students would be better served if the educational system changed to embrace the way they learn, think, and process information.[41]

Tapscott concludes:

> This generation is not dumber. Far from it. Many of the Net Geners are using technology to become smarter than their parents ever could be. I believe they know when they have to focus. They think and process information in a different way than most boomers do, but that doesn't stop them from coming up with brilliant insights, or new models of doing business and winning an election.[42]

We can see the truth of Tapscott's claim by looking at the many successful startup companies of this generation. These startups are mostly run by young people with innovative ideas on using digital technologies to reach the market. A typical example of this is Facebook, founded by Mark Zuckerberg and his fellow Harvard college students. The Net Generation is driving the democratization of content creation as young people generate and exchange online blogs, photos, music, movie reviews, and commentaries on everything from products to politics. This new paradigm in communication will have a revolutionary impact on everything it touches – from music and movies to political life, business, and education – shifting the power from authorities to ordinary individuals.[43]

In contrast to the augment of Bauerlein that young people today are dumber, Tapscott is reasonable in arguing that they are not less intellectual than the previous generations if the typical achievements of this digital age mentioned above are taken into account. However, he may well have overstated his case by claiming that youth are smarter. His proof of the growing IQ

---

40. Tapscott, 30.
41. Tapscott, 118.
42. Tapscott, 115.
43. Tapscott, 40, 62.

score is important, but there are other indications, such as the EQ score, that should be examined. Youth can be better online communicators compared to the older generations, but face-to-face contacts can be another story. It is important to take note that he does not give evidence or say that the IQ scores of the Net Generation are improved because of digital technology. Raw IQ scores have been climbing since World War II.[44] Therefore, the evidence of IQ scores here has little significance in the discussion of the impacts of digital media on youth.

Furthermore, from the evidence of youths' new skills and the study of brain development presented by Tapscott, it seems that their intelligence has not grown but rather changed as they relate to the culture of their age. Each generation has different challenges and opportunities. Ancient people were smart in their own ways when they built pyramids, palaces, and monuments without modern technologies. It is still difficult for modern people to build the same structures with all the modern tools available. Ancient people made many discoveries that were beneficial to their lives and have been beneficial to the lives of generations coming after them. Measuring intelligence across time and space is not straight forward. *Phronesis*, lived wisdom rather than just IQ or the volume of knowledge or skill sets, needs also to be measured. Being smart means having good stewardship of all one's gifts, using all the resources available to meet the challenge of contemporary lives, and doing good for humanity. Jay N. Giedd gives the fair observation that serves as a perfect closing for the argument:

> Remarkable advances in technologies that enable the distribution and use of information encoded as digital sequences of 1s or 0s have dramatically changed our way of life. Adolescents, old enough to master the technologies and young enough to welcome their novelty, are at the forefront of this "digital revolution." Underlying the adolescent's eager embrace of these sweeping changes is a neurobiology forged by the fires of evolution to be extremely adept at adaptation.[45]

---

44. Tapscott, 30.
45. Giedd, "Digital Revolution," 101.

In short, it is fair to say that the current generation of youth, being the first to grow up surrounded by digital media, not only is greatly adept at utilizing modern technology for their convenience and entertainment but is ardently doing so. It is, however, reductive to claim they are smarter or dumber than previous generations.

b. More Self-Absorbed or Better at Collaboration?

People sometimes observe that today's youth might be smart in their use of digital technology but that their social skills are lacking. Niedzviecki observes that the "Peep culture," enabled by digital technology, leads to narcissism and self-absorption.[46] Tapscott's retort to this challenge is to emphasize the ways in which the youth of this generation are very good at collaboration. They are transforming the internet from a place where people mainly find information to a place where people share information, collaborate on projects of mutual interest, and create new ways to solve some of their most pressing problems.[47] Wikipedia, the global encyclopedia written and edited by tens of thousands of contributors worldwide, is a classic example of this new web of collaboration.[48] They do not just take what they are given either. They are the active initiators, collaborators, organizers, readers, writers, authenticators, and even strategists. They do not just observe; they participate. They inquire, discuss, argue, play, shop, critique, investigate, ridicule, fantasize, seek, and inform.[49]

People can argue that young people are not socializing since they only like to be in the virtual world. However, they do not shy away from socializing. Rather, they find more efficient ways to do it. For example, they prefer email to talking because email is faster than talking. This is why Net Geners often prefer to communicate with people at work via electronic means rather than meeting them unless it is a first-time meeting or an important negotiation.[50] They are better at collaborating online than adults and have no problem incorporating the fruits of that collaboration smoothly into the physical world. For them, there is no boundary between the virtual and physical worlds.

---

46. Niedzviecki, *Peep Diaries*, 111.
47. Tapscott, *Growing Up Digital*, 40.
48. Tapscott, 53.
49. Tapscott, 21.
50. Tapscott, 94.

People may argue that youth are absorbed totally by virtual reality when going online, especially while playing games. My research has not been able to locate a single case where virtual life takes over physical life as an end in itself. Yes, there are cases of teenagers playing online games to their death due to lack of sleep and nutrition. Those are rare and extreme cases, however, and it can be argued that those teenagers were competing with someone over the internet. It was the community that they were seeking, not the game itself. Virtual life cannot completely take over physical life. The convergence between cyberspace and physical life creates "hybrid identities" in the youth of the Net Generation. This term means that virtual reality in social media blends with the real in youths' everyday lives. The reason that youth yearn for online communities is that they want to find a place to negotiate their hybrid identities.[51]

We can see this from the way youth play video games. Video games attract youth because they can play with others. According to Tapscott, video games help youth to tap into the collective form of intelligence that is heightened through collaboration with other people and with machines.[52] Today, youth can easily collaborate and make friends in an increasingly digital society. This has prompted Lina Eklunda and Sara Roman to conduct a study on the potential effects of digital gaming on youths' friendships.[53] They conclude that "shared identities related to digital gaming influence individuals' off-line, everyday social relationships as, in the analyses of changes over time to youth's school networks, digital gaming seems to motivate friendship formation."[54] Youth development theory (discussed in the next section) shows that friendships are significant to youths' well-beings and identity formations. Peer relationships do not necessarily replace family ties, but adolescents spend most of their time with friends. They tend to befriend others who have similar cultural tastes and social identities to them.[55] Eklunda and Roman suggest that youth prefer other gamers who are their friends in school. As gamers who are in the same school, they want to get to know each other in school

---

51. Faix, "Hybrid Identity," 70.
52. Tapscott, *Growing Up Digital*, 114.
53. Eklunda and Roman, "Do Adolescent Gamers?," 284–289.
54. Eklunda and Roman, 284.
55. Eklunda and Roman, 284.

and build up friendships which, in turn, affects their identity formation.[56] Thus, it can be said that digital gaming can motivate friendship formation.[57]

In short, the Net Generation is neither smarter nor dumber than previous generations since each generation has its own set of challenges and opportunities. Youth are better at collaborating online than adults and have no problem incorporating online friendships smoothly into the physical world. It is understandable that their adeptness at using technology is born out of accessibility and familiarity. With this research in mind, we now turn to discuss youth identity in the digital age.

3. Youth Identity in the Digital Age

As discussed in the literature review, Niedzviecki observes that the "Peep industry," enabled by digital technology, leads to narcissism and self-absorption.[58] Zuboff points out that Gens Y and Z are the first generations growing in and being trapped in the "digital hive with no exit" created by surveillance capital.[59] This gives them no necessary space to cultivate a healthy identity.[60] This section discusses youth identity formation in the digital age by first laying out the theories of identity then exploring the influence of digital media.[61]

a. Theories of Identity

David Buckingham defines identity thus:

> The fundamental paradox of identity is inherent in the term itself. From the Latin root idem, meaning "the same," the term nevertheless implies both similarity and difference. On the one hand, identity is something unique to each of us that we assume is more or less consistent (and hence the same) over time . . . It is what distinguishes us from other people. Yet on the other hand, identity also implies a relationship with a broader collective or

---

56. Eklunda and Roman, 287.
57. Eklunda and Roman, 288.
58. Niedzviecki, *Peep Diaries*, 111.
59. Zuboff, *Age of Surveillance Capitalism*, 21.
60. Zuboff, 455.
61. This section previously appeared in: Vo, "Youth Identity in the Digital Age," 58-82.

social group of some kind. When we talk about national identity, cultural identity, or gender identity, for example, we imply that our identity is partly a matter of what we share with other people. Here, identity is about identification with others whom we assume are similar to us (if not exactly the same), at least in some significant ways.[62]

Buckingham's definition of identity is helpful as it covers both the similarity and the difference that this term conveys. The tensions that surround debates about identity are derived from the "unique" aspect of the self and from the "similarity" aspect of multiple identifications with others on the bases of "social, cultural, and biological characteristics as well as shared values, personal histories, and interests."[63] Human beings are the product of both their unique, personal biographies and the social circumstances surrounding them. Biographical identity is interwoven with social identity. As human beings living in society, we are not entirely free to choose our own identities. The rise of globalization, social mobility, insecurity in personal relationships, and digital media, which influence community life, may cause fragmentation and uncertainty in one's understanding of his or her identity, especially for youth who are already going through identity crises.[64] From the definition of identity, Buckingham observes that there are two main approaches to identity, which are directly related to youth identities: the psychological approach and the sociological approach.[65]

1) Identity Formation: The Psychology of Adolescence

Buckingham did not mention Sigmund Freud, but Freud's psychosexual theory (1905) is a well-known theory of development. Believing that life is built around tension and pleasure due to the buildup of libido (sexual energy), Freud describes human identity formation in relation to the accumulation and discharge of sexual energy as we mature biologically. He proposes that identity develops in a series of five predetermined psychosexual stages: oral,

---

62. Buckingham, "Introducing Identity," 1.
63. Buckingham, 1.
64. Buckingham, 1.
65. Buckingham, 2.

anal, phallic, latency, and genital.⁶⁶ Adolescence, referred to as the genital stage, is seen as playing a critical role since, at this stage, teens begin to forge their own sense of identity. They begin to explore romantic relationships and develop a sense of balance between all areas of life. Those who successfully complete this stage will have developed a warm, caring, and well-adjusted identity.⁶⁷

In Buckingham's view, it was G. Stanley Hall's classic account of adolescence in his book *Adolescence*, published in the early years of the last century, that founded the psychological approach to defining youth identity.⁶⁸ Hall described adolescence as a period of "storm and stress" that possibly leads to rebellious actions and risky behaviors. This is also a period of intense orientations toward their friends.⁶⁹ In Buckingham's story of the rise of the psychological account, it was Erik Erikson who then described adolescence as a phase of identity crisis. In this phase, adolescents go through "role confusion," which they need to resolve. This a critical period of identity formation when adolescents overcome confusion and become more aware of their uniqueness, strengths, weaknesses, and who they want to become in the future. The outcome of this period, if they resolve it successfully, is a settled role in life and a coherent sense of personal identity. The alternative outcome is "maladaptation." Though identity is developed by the individual, it is a process that happens in the context of a society where personal identity is recognized and confirmed. One notable characteristic of this period is that adolescents desire to spend much more time socializing with their peers.⁷⁰

Influenced by Freud's ideas, Erikson also believes that personality develops in a series of predetermined stages, but unlike Freud's more individualist theory of psychosexual stages, Erikson's theory describes the impact of social experience across the whole lifespan.⁷¹ Erikson observes that changes in modern society and technology prolong the transition from adolescence to adulthood. This slowdown can become frozen and therefore a final or "initial

---

66. McLeod, "Freud's Psychosexual Stages." Freud used the term "sexual" in a very general way to mean all pleasurable actions and thoughts.
67. Cherry, "Comparing Erikson's vs Freud's Theories."
68. Hall, *Adolescence*.
69. Buckingham, "Introducing Identity," 2; Hall, *Adolescence*, Hall, *Youth*.
70. Buckingham, "Introducing Identity," 2–3; Erikson, *Identity*.
71. Cherry, "Comparing Erikson's vs Freud's Theories."

identity formation" rather than a transitory period within adolescents' faddish attempts to establish their subculture.[72] In this period, they are actually looking for a role model in whom they can put their trust, yet at the same time they often express cynical mistrust in fear of a foolish commitment. They are willing to trust their peers and elders who fit their imaginations, aspirations, and self-images, but they object violently to those whom they think pedantically limit their self-image.[73] Disturbed by their inability to settle on an "occupational identity," young people tend to temporarily identify themselves with superstars and heroes. At the same time, they show intolerance to those who are "different" than them.[74] Those who are not sure of their identity can withdraw from interpersonal intimacy or throw themselves into "promiscuous" intimacy with real self-abandon.[75] One positive and stable thing about adolescents is that they are gifted at acquiring new technological trends and able to identify themselves with new roles in society brought by the latest technology.[76] However, they should be careful with the negative effects of the glorification of youth that mass media might provoke.[77]

Buckingham's critical resistance to Hall and Erikson's developmental theories is that he finds them too normative in the ways they assume adolescence as a distinctive stage with a beginning and an end. These theories see adolescence as a state of "becoming" rather than "being."[78] Buckingham thinks that human development is more appropriately seen as a matter of gradual progression. However, these development theories are still useful in our discussion of youth and their involvement with digital media as they help us understand the characteristics of youth and their strengths and struggles. Buckingham agrees with Erikson's notion of adolescence as a "psychosocial moratorium," a period of "time out" when the youth try different potential identities including engaging in risky behavior.[79] In short, the psychological approach to identity proposes that adolescents have distinct characters

---

72. Erikson, *Identity*, 128.
73. Erikson, 128–129.
74. Erikson, 132.
75. Erikson, 135.
76. Erikson, 130.
77. Erikson, 232.
78. Buckingham, "Introducing Identity," 3.
79. Buckingham, 3; Erikson, *Identity*, 143.

marked by personal identity conflict and intense orientations toward peers as proposed by Hall and Erikson. This is a critical period of identity formation for adolescents as they become more aware of themselves, think of their roles in society in the future, and try different potential identities including engaging in risky behavior.

2) Youth Culture and the Sociology of Youth

Sociological theories take a different approach to defining adolescence than do psychological accounts. A traditional, functionalist account of socialization presumes that "the young person is a passive recipient of adult influences."[80] A typical view held by proponents of this approach is that youth who are marginalized are "at risk" and in need of various forms of treatment provided by social workers, teachers, counselors, or psychiatrists. This theory positions the problem to highlight social factors such as poverty rather than the psychological problems of "raging hormones." As compared to the psychological account of youth, this theory does not focus on personal identity conflict but focuses on the social problems youth face. This approach holds that the characteristics of youth depend on social context, such as social class, gender, and ethnicity. This also leads youth to establish relevant subcultures, which can be subordinate or subversive. This approach also focuses attention on the social dimension of youth identities with relevant focus on their interactions with digital media. Digital media can provide youth with opportunities for constructing or expressing their own identities and for resisting adult authority. Youth can use digital media to express their subcultural allegiances or claim "spaces" that escape adult control. They can also use media production to address relevant social issues.[81]

Even though psychological and sociological accounts of youth take different approaches, Buckingham observes that "both are essentially concerned with the ways in which young people are gradually prepared, or prepare themselves, to take up their allotted roles in adult life."[82] Both the psychological account and the traditional, functionalist account of socialization are equally normative in seeing the young person as a "becoming" rather than a

---

80. Buckingham, "Introducing Identity," 4.
81. Buckingham, 4.
82. Buckingham, 4.

"being" in their own right.[83] Both the approaches discussed so far are directly concerned with youth identities and are helpful in understanding youths' identities with respect to "inner self" and social influence.

There are, however, other approaches that emphasize the "performativity" of social identity. Some sociologists view that identity as "a fluid, contingent matter – it is something we accomplish practically through our ongoing interactions and negotiations with other people." Therefore, it is more of identification rather than identity.[84] Rob Cover builds his theory of digital identity on Judith Butler's theory of identity as "performative":[85]

> Butler's theory of performativity is based on the idea that identity and subjectivity is an ongoing process of becoming, rather than an ontological state of being, whereby becoming is a sequence of acts, that retroactively constitutes identity . . . The self or "I" is made up of a matrix of pregiven identity categories, experiences, and labels repetition, lend to the illusion of an inner identity core.[86]

According to Butler's theory as Cover deploys it, neither off-line nor online behaviors and actions emerge from a core inner identity but are only a set of performances that retroactively give an illusion of a core, essential self.[87] While never complete or without flaw, identities are performed "in accord" with cultural demands for coherent senses of self, which are necessary for social participation and belonging.[88] In a society of digital surveillance, we police each other's identity performances for coherence.[89]

In the digital age, social networking extends the performance of identity from "real life" to virtual space. Drawing on Butler's theory of identity performativity, Cover suggests that the online performance of subjectivity is expressed in two typical ways: (1) managing one's social network profile and

---

83. Buckingham, 4.
84. Buckingham, 6.
85. Cover, *Digital Identities*, xiii.
86. Cover, 3.
87. Cover, 12.
88. Cover, xiv, 12.
89. Cover, 13.

(2) maintaining online friendship lists and engaging with those "friends."[90] He argues that profile management is an act of identity performance. An initial profile creation frequently involves submitting gender, age, sexual preference, nationality, and relationship status. According to Cover, creating and modifying the user profile are required for social participation and can be viewed as a set of acts that are repeated over time to produce an illusion of an inner self.[91]

Friendship lists management provide a somewhat different framework for the performance of identity as Cover proposes:

> Although not wholly disconnected from profile management, the act of friending and relating to others through social networking on Facebook is a separate set of performances of identity expression. This second "field" of online performance focuses on the social or relational, producing conformity through interactive identification with others: friends, acquaintances, strangers, persons known only online, coworkers, employees, students and teachers, parents, and family – all typically presented under the problematically simple label of "friends."[92]

This online relationality is expressed through the creation and maintenance of friends lists and through engaging with those friends such as by updating, commenting, responding, and tagging. According to Cover, these acts are identity performances conveyed through the frameworks of relationality and belonging. Within the narrative of coherent identity performance seeking, this act is carried out not only for social participation but also for "friendship" with those in the friend lists who often unwittingly surveil.[93] Even though Facebook and other social networking sites provide a convenient tool for identity performance, Cover points out that the acts of online identity performativity, such as managing profiles and friending, can rend the coherence of an identity narrative and create "extra work" for identity self-management.[94] Online friends can surveil and easily point out any breach in identity coherence. Archives of wall posts and status updates may contain

---

90. Cover, 3.
91. Cover, 16.
92. Cover, 16.
93. Cover, 16.
94. Cover, 4.

information that is in contrast with other parts of the social networking site. Unwanted photo posting and tagging by others can also breach the coherence of identity performance.[95]

While Cover's study is upfront with the study of digital media and identity, his view of identity as performativity is problematic in that his view of the self is so fluid that it might reasonably be said that he denies there being any "inner" identity at all. In his view, people respond to the environment online and off-line as chameleons changing color in accord with the surrounding environment. However, chameleons do have identity at least in biological sense. The questions to ask are whether people have one coherent inner identity and how it might be understood to relate to the social environment. Up to this point, this project takes Buckingham's review on the development theory and social theory as a guide and views that there is an "inner identity", but Cover's observations highlight the shaping effects of the cultural and social environment. Youth participation in cyberspace can clearly influence the formation of their "inner" identity. This project will discuss a theology of self-identity in chapter 4. For now, we continue the discussion of the social influence of digital media on the identity formations of youth.

b. The Influence of Digital Media on Identity Formation of the Youth of Gens Y and Z

Social networking sites such as Facebook have great impact on the self-confidence and self-concept of youth. In his 2009 book *The Church of Facebook*, discussed in the literature review in Chapter 1, Jesse Rice observes that Facebook influences our personal identities profoundly. He adopts Sherry Turkle's term of the "tethered self" when describing the new phenomena brought by Facebook and mobile technology such as iPhones and BlackBerrys – and the changes they bring to the way we think about ourselves. We are tethered to nonstop online communication and activities; people can always be reached online.[96] There are tens of millions of us who check Facebook anywhere and anytime, several times a day or several times an hour, whether at work, at

---

95. Cover, 22.
96. Rice, *Church of Facebook*, 140.

home, at church, or while we are meeting friends. This ability to be always online changes the way we define ourselves.[97]

With nonstop connectivity to ensure that they are within reach of someone, youth have no time or space to cultivate healthy self-concepts, and their self-confidences are linked to their connectivity with others.[98] Kids' early adoptions of cell phones can prevent them from resolving difficult tasks on their own since they can always stay in touch with parents and get help from them.[99] In the same way, youth start using Facebook as soon they are thirteen years old, and they are exposed to a vast network of people from whom they can receive guidance, encouragement, and camaraderie. As a result, they depend on the advice and opinions of others and lose their ability to navigate life on their own.[100] The author observes that adults are also influenced by this phenomenon as we are faced with many online voices that distract us from forming feelings, thoughts, and actions of our own. We are tempted to follow public opinion to be "liked" rather than be ourselves. As a result, we lose our authentic self that requires us to stand on our own feet – to make our own judgments and decisions which may sometimes go against public opinion. Constant connections for public affirmation and approval hinder the formation of an authentic self.[101]

Being constantly online prevents us from being fully present in the moment, leading to a blurry picture of our "selves." We are easily distracted by colorful, moving objects offered by smartphones, and we constantly feel that we are missing out on something online. As a result, we cannot stay focused on our conversations with family members, friends, and colleagues. We could be unclear about where we stand in relationship to the people and objects around us at the present moment.[102] Rice observes:

> It's almost as though we're living an out-of-body existence . . . Our self-concept becomes "enshrouded" in temporal distractions that can cloud our direction and even make the ground

---

97. Rice, 141.
98. Rice, 142–143.
99. Rice, 143.
100. Rice, 144.
101. Rice, 145–146.
102. Rice, 146–147.

beneath us an untrustworthy place to stand. . . . Our lives unfold, moment by moment, and the only way we can truly experience them is *in the moment*. Being always-on can thwart awareness of the present moment, keeping our attention ever focused on the new rather than the now.[103]

The constant checking of Facebook posts, emails, etc., keeps us "disembodied" and unable to live and relate properly to those around us.[104] Rice seems to have a compartmentalized view of virtual and physical life. He does not elaborate on the disembodiment of the self and does not propose a theology of "self." The question to ask is whether there is actually a disembodiment of the self. This project will discuss this question in "Theology of Self-Identity," chapter 4. However, Rice's discussion on the influence of social network and digital connections on identity formation is valid and can bring us to more up-to-date discussion on this topic.

In the digital age, youth identity is greatly influenced as their lives are immersed in the "hive" or the instrumentarianism society as Zuboff puts it in her 2019 book, *The Age of Surveillance Capitalism*.[105] In this society, youth behaviors are modified to conform to social norms created by peer pressure and computer algorithm. Social media such as Facebook create social pressure and tuning on the youth. Zuboff explains:

> Facebook has learned to bite hard on the psychological needs of young people, creating new challenges for the developmental processes that build individual identity and personal autonomy . . . Business and tech analysts cite "network effects" as a structural source of Facebook's dominance in social media, but those effects initially derived from the demand characteristics of adolescents and emerging adults, reflecting the peer orientation of their age and stage.[106]

In fact, Facebook founders and original designers were themselves adolescents and emerging adults. Therefore, they designed the system to fit the

---

103. Rice, 147–149 (emphasis original).
104. Rice, 149.
105. Zuboff, *Age of Surveillance Capitalism*, 445.
106. Zuboff, 446.

psychological needs of adolescent users and college students by reducing the social world to a community of "friends" who are not necessary friends and "likes" that provide a questionable sense of confirmation of one's value, fueling the anxieties of the youth.[107] Facebook's design intentionally triggers the psychological needs of young people, making it difficult for them to unplug from Facebook and the consequences of attachment to this social network. Like Facebook, other social media such as Instagram, Snapchat, and TikTok deploy all the same psychological mechanisms.

The developmental accounts of G. Stanley Hall and Erik Erikson, as discussed previously, observe that adolescence is a period of intense orientations toward their peers. Facebook takes advantage of the psychological vulnerabilities of youth during this period by hooking them up with online friends. The youth also depend on smart, connected devices for all daily activities such as logistics, communication, information, and social networking. This makes unplugging almost impossible for youth. Their sudden disconnection from the network can result in craving, depression, anxiety, loneliness, and acute disorientation.[108] According to Zuboff, these feelings of disorientation and loneliness show the youths' psychological dependency on their "online" peers. Studies show that Generation Z – the generation of those who were born after 1996 and have no memory of life before the rise of digital media – rely on many social media platforms, which they use simultaneously for psychological sustenance. The majority use a smartphone and are online "on a near-constant basis." This dependency affects their identities and how they view themselves and their happiness.[109] By their own assessment, they have been negatively affected by their habit of comparing themselves and their lives with others.[110]

Zuboff describes the effects of social media on youth:

> The magnetic pull that social media exerts on young people drives them toward more automatic and less voluntary behavior. For too many, that behavior shades into the territory of genuine compulsion. Social media is designed to engage and

---

107. Zuboff, 447.
108. Zuboff, 446.
109. Zuboff, 447.
110. Zuboff, 448.

hold people of all ages, but it is principally molded to the psychological structure of adolescence and emerging adulthood, when one is naturally oriented toward the "others," especially toward the rewards of group recognition, acceptance, belonging and inclusion. For many, this close tailoring, combine with the practical dependencies of social participation, turn social media into a toxic milieu. Not only does this milieu extract a heavy psychological toll, but it also threatens the course of human development for today's young and the generations that follow.[111]

Zuboff observes that this technology was invented not by Facebook but by the gaming industry with its "Addiction by Design" principles of engrossing, immersive, and immediate. It leads to a loss of self-awareness, automatic behavior, and a complete absorption.[112] Facebook imitates this by sending users "a little dopamine hit every once in a while" and "variable reinforcement" by "likes" and comments.[113] "In short," observes Zuboff, "young people crave the hive, and Facebook gives it to them, but this time it's owned and operated by surveillance capital."[114]

As discussed above in relation to Erikson's observations about the prolonging of the period between adolescence and adulthood, today psychologists call this period "emerging adulthood," denoting the years between eighteen and the late twenties as a new phase of life. The main challenge of this phase is "the differentiation of 'self' from the 'others.'"[115] However, life in the digital "hive" poses an essential challenge to this process. Young people wait anxiously for the approval of their existence through likes or comments from their online friends.[116] They fail to keep a healthy balance between "the inner and the outer, self and relationship," as Zuboff observes. "Not surprisingly, these include an inability to tolerate solitude, the feeling of being merged with others, an unstable sense of self, and even an excessive need to control others as a way of keeping the mirror close. Loss of the mirror is the felt

---

111. Zuboff, 449.
112. Zuboff, 449–450.
113. Zuboff, 451.
114. Zuboff, 460.
115. Zuboff, 452.
116. Zuboff, 454.

equivalent of extinction."[117] Social media hinder youth from cultivating their inner resources or "self."

Many studies on the relationship between social media use and mental health show that the typical psychological process that most defines the Facebook experience is "social comparison."[118] It is normal that we compare ourselves with others as we go through life. However, in the past, people lived in communities with people who were not very much different from them. Today Facebook accelerates social comparison since people are now comparing themselves with others who live in different parts of the world. This triggers negative thoughts as people think others are happier than them.[119] Zuboff observes the unprecedented effect of social media on youth:

> Social media marks a new era in the intensity, density, and pervasiveness of social comparison processes, especially for the youngest among us, who are "almost constantly online" at a time of life when one's own identity, voice, and moral agency are a work in progress. In fact, the psychological tsunami of social comparison triggered by the social media experience is considered unprecedented."[120]

Zuboff explains that because social media drives young people from real-life encounters, they sense the need to share something of their life to establish social connection and communality. However, this sharing of personal life on social media is often crafted with marvelous biographical information, photos, and updates designed to attract likes and comments. This is called profile "inflation" which negatively affects youths' feelings of self-worth as they compare themselves with others on social media. This in turn leads to more profile inflation and more negative self-evaluation, especially in the context of the larger social networks where youth connect to many distant friends.[121]

---

117. Zuboff, 455.
118. Zuboff, 461.
119. Zuboff, 462.
120. Zuboff, 462.
121. Zuboff, 462.

This social comparison also surfaces in the phenomena of FOMO ("fear of missing out").[122] It is a form of social anxiety defined as the negative feeling that your friends have or are doing something better than you. FOMO has been identified with compulsive Facebook use. As young people obsessively check their Facebook feeds hoping to find relief in the form of social reassurance, they became more dissatisfied with life. As a result, they are stuck in a loop of unending searching.[123] The imperative to compare also includes body surveillance as young people compare their physical appearances with those of others who seem to have better looks on Facebook than them. As young people compare themselves with others on social networks, they present themselves as data objects for inspection. Their sense of self-worth depends on physical appearance and what others perceive.[124] This phenomenon has also been discussed in *The Peep Diaries*, which is discussed in the literature review, with all the psychological dangers that accompany such constant comparison – people "desire to be watched and to watch others being watched."[125]

The advice from researchers is that social media users should cut down their use of social media and focus on "real-world relationship" since Facebook use does not promote well-being.[126] However, this is difficult to do since surveillance capitalism is always at work to ensure that youth cannot escape from the digital "hive" where there is no place for them to cultivate a healthy personal space.[127] Therefore, the need to teach young people to cultivate inner resources and practice solitude is much more urgent than ever.

While Zuboff does well in presenting all the negative aspects of "life in the hive" and the disruption of youth identity formation caused by digital media and surveillance capitalism, there are positive aspects that should not be neglected. Katie Davis did a study on the joint effects of interpersonal relationships and digital media use on adolescents' senses of identity.[128] She administered questionnaires to a sample of 2079 students (57% female)

---

122. Zuboff, 462.
123. Zuboff, 643.
124. Zuboff, 464.
125. Niedzviecki, *Peep Diaries*, 111.
126. Zuboff, *Age of Surveillance Capitalism*, 465.
127. Zuboff, 471, 477–479.
128. Davis, "Young People's Digital Lives," 2281–2293.

between the ages of 11 and 19 years (M = 15.4 years) attending one of seven secondary schools in Bermuda. She found:

> Friends also played a mediating role in relation to aspects of adolescents' digital media use. Specifically, the negative association detected between online identity expression/exploration and self-concept clarity was mediated partially by low friendship quality. Going online to communicate with one's friends appeared to play a more positive role in adolescents' sense of identity. The results showed that online peer communication affected self-concept clarity indirectly through its positive impact on friendship quality.[129]

According to Davis, online peer communication has a positive impact on youths' friendship quality, positively affecting the clarity of their self-conceptions.

In terms of youths' digital media use, the result of this study showed a positive correlation between online peer communication and friendship quality. Despite some problematic dynamics, such as cyberbullying and addiction, the existing evidence suggests that online peer interactions are mostly positive for most adolescents.[130] Furthermore, according to this study, if the youth have good friends in real life, they tend to go online to connect with their existing friends. Buckingham agrees, observing: "There is little evidence that most young people are using the Internet to develop global connections; in most cases, it appears to be used primarily as a means of reinforcing local networks among peers."[131] As youth spend time online to communicate with their friends with whom they have good relationships in real life, their friendships can grow, and in turn, this helps them to have a better self-image. Online communication can positively influence youths' friendships, which in turn affect their sense of identity correlatively. The result of this research is reasonable. As we have discussed in developmental theories earlier, Erik Erikson describes adolescence as a phase of identity crisis. A primary developmental task of adolescence is forming a coherent, meaningful, and socially

---

129. Davis, 2281.
130. Davis, 2290.
131. Buckingham, "Introducing Identity," 14.

validated personal identity. In this process, friendship plays a crucial role as youth spend much more time socializing with their peers.[132]

Friends play a validating role in adolescent identity formation since youth identify themselves with their peer groups and express themselves with their close friends. In the digital age, digital media and social network sites create a new context in which for youth to explore friendship and personal identity.[133] Good friendship, both online and off-line, can therefore have clear positive effects. Davis observes:

> This online peer communication does not appear to be displacing adolescents' offline friendships but rather augmenting them, with positive residual effects on their self-concept clarity. These findings illustrate just how integrated online and offline lives have become in recent years as smartphones, broadband internet access, and social media platforms have permeated Western societies.[134]

Katie Davis's findings here agree with some ideas presented in the book *The App Generation*, discussed in the literature review. Howard Gardner and Katie Davis point out that a benefit of digital media is that it can support senses of belonging and self-disclosure, which are important in forming intimate bonds during adolescence.[135] Sandra Weber and Claudia Mitchell add that youth not only consume but also produce digital media productions in order to express themselves and craft a clear identity.[136] Their audience may be themselves and their circle of friends, yet through the visual structure and content of their websites or Facebook walls, youth are negotiating their identities within general pop culture and their circles of friends who give them feedback on their posts. This can strengthen a sense of belonging and promote self-disclosure and reflexivity.[137]

Coming back to Gardner and Davis's point, good apps can promote a strong sense of identity and deepen friendship. Furthermore, it can help

---

132. Buckingham, 2–3; Davis, "Young People's Digital Lives," 2281.
133. Davis, 2281.
134. Gardner and Davis, *App Generation*, 2290.
135. Gardner and Davis, 108.
136. Weber and Mitchell, "Imaging, Keyboarding," 7.
137. Weber and Mitchell, 41.

youth who face ostracism in their off-line contexts by allowing them to forge a sense of belonging in a sympathetic community online.[138] However, Gardner and Davis present not only the positive aspects of digital media but also the negative ones. Apps with their own design can enable certain actions while restricting others.[139] Some apps can enable youth to form a stronger identity, while other apps lead them to become "someone else's avatar," as Gardner and Davis observe:

> With respect to identity formation: Apps can short-circuit identity formation, pushing you into being someone else's avatar (that of your parents, your friends, or one formulated by some app producer) – or, by foregrounding various options, they can allow you to approach identity formation more deliberately, holistically, thoughtfully. You may end up with a stronger and more powerful identity, or you may succumb to a pre-packaged identity or to endless role diffusion.[140]

Overall, apps give "packaged identities" formulated by some app producer. Gardner and Davis agree with Zuboff that digital media and apps minimize focus on an inner life and personal reflection needed for youth to cultivate their inner identities.[141] While digital media can open up new opportunities for youth to express themselves online, it can take away their time and opportunity to explore "off-line" life.[142] Youth can spend so much time looking at posts from other people on social media since they are afraid of missing out and they want to be connected with the world where community lives are declining as Niedzviecki observes in *The Peep Diaries*.[143] This may result in an "impoverished sense of self" and make community lives worse.[144]

In summary, studies have shown that digital media has a significant influence on youths' socio-emotional development since it gives them opportunities for self-exploration, improving self-esteem, practicing self-presentation

---

138. Gardner and Davis, *App Generation*, 108.
139. Gardner and Davis, 24.
140. Gardner and Davis, 32–33.
141. Gardner and Davis, 61.
142. Gardner and Davis, 91.
143. Niedzviecki, *Peep Diaries*, 8.
144. Gardner and Davis, *App Generation*, 91.

and self-disclosure, obtaining support, lessening rejection in the off-line world, gaining autonomy, and exploring identity. It also offers opportunities for creating and exchanging ideas, connecting with peers, and furthering global education. Social networking sites satisfy the need of youth for belonging and popularity. It also helps youth who are lacking socio-emotional skills to interact more with other people. For example, they can share their emotional experiences and receive support from online support groups. Youth can present and experiment with possible identities online and receive feedback, which might help them to solidify their identity. Along with positive influence, digital media can present negative impacts such as aggressive behaviors caused by playing violent video games, racist behavior, sexual harassment, and cyberbullying.[145] It can also lead to a lack of self-control and to the collapse of traditional communities defined by a physical place and face-to-face contacts. Excessive use of the internet replaces socialization with friends and schoolwork.[146]

Developmental theories show the significance of the adolescent period in forming an inner identity now being strongly affected by the "Network Society" as suggested by social theories. Social media can enhance the peer-to-peer communication that is crucial for youth identity formation, but there are risks involved. The design of digital media and apps can enslave youth in the "hive" and take away the solitude and resources needed for them to cultivate their inner identity. In later chapters, this project will continue to discuss how to help youth cultivate solitude and an inner identity from a theological perspective. For now, we will continue the discussion by asking what social science can tell us about how to mentor youth who are embedded in the current social media environment.

4. Mentoring Youth

Scholars have proposed that digital media greatly affects the development of personality, identity, and sexuality. As digital media acts as the central medium for entertainment, learning, communicating, shopping, expressing, self-discovering, and building online communities, the sense of self and the

---

145. Savina et al., "Digital Media and Youth," 84–85.
146. Savina et al., 85–86.

values of youth are thus reinvented accordingly.[147] Though digital media has many positive impacts on youth, the negative effects are likewise multiple. These include, but are not limited to, addictions of many kinds, pornography, unhealthy relationships with the physical world or the community, and a lack of respect for authority and discipline. As we walk with youth, it is imperative to recognize and acknowledge both the positive contributions digital media has to offer as well as the negative repercussions it can inflict upon them. The reality is that youth are using digital media to cultivate culture and create meaning for their lives. Our role is thus to teach them to engage the popular culture with both responsibility and discernment.[148] As adults, we need to acknowledge these cultural changes by altering the way we approach them and how we organize our schools, families, and churches.[149]

a. Education

On the surface, we can observe that digital media do not necessarily alter traditional education's approach and methods but can complement them. Apps can encourage pursuit of traditional education's goals by digital means such as mastering concepts; learning arithmetical operations; and identifying geographical locations, historical figures, or key processes – biological, chemical, or physical.[150] At a deeper level, Tapscott suggests that youth who are immersing themselves in digital technology are forcing a modification in pedagogical methods from a teacher-focused approach based on instruction to a student-focused model based on collaboration.[151] Many Net Geners learn more by collaborating, both with their teacher and with each other. Furthermore, by using the internet, they have access to most of the world's knowledge. This freedom and ease of access is transforming education as it allows learning to now take place where and when they want it.[152] Youth are

---

147. Khoon, "Youth and the Internet," 89–97; Bailey, "Welcome to the Blogosphere," 173–188; Buckingham, *Youth, Identity, and Digital Media*; Emery-Wright, *Understanding Teenage Sexuality*.

148. Emery-Wright and Mackenzie, *Networks for Faith Formation*, 121.

149. Tapscott, *Growing Up Digital*, 11.

150. Gardner and Davis, *App Generation*, 179–180.

151. Tapscott, *Growing up Digital*, 11.

152. Tapscott, 77.

proven to be more responsive to this surfacing method, which is focused on customization and collaboration.[153]

Though appearing somewhat overly optimistic about youths' abilities to learn in this new age, there are many points worth considering from Tapscott's suggestions regarding the approach to education in this digital age.[154] In summary, these points include:

1. Focus on the change in pedagogy, not on the technology. Learning 2.0 is about dramatically changing the relationship between a teacher and students in the learning process. Once that is accomplished, then use technology to create a student-focused, customized, and collaborative learning environment.
2. Cut back on lecturing.
3. Empower students to collaborate.
4. Focus on lifelong learning, not on teaching to the test.
5. Use technology to get to know each student.
6. Design educational programs according to the eight norms: choice, customization, transparency, integrity, collaboration, fun, speed, and innovation.
7. Reinvent yourself as a teacher, professor, or educator.

As educators consider ways to reform teaching approaches to respond to the impact of digital technology, Buckingham suggests that it is helpful to look at both the positive and the negative impacts of digital technology. On one hand, advocates of technology say that digital technology promotes student-centered learning, new styles of thinking, motivation, and achievement. On the other hand, critics point out that the use of computers in schools undermines students' creativity by emphasizing mechanical rote learning and promotes instant gratification rather than developing the patience needed for the hard work of education.[155] In the process of reforming education, it is important that educators not go to the extreme of romanticizing youth in their technological expertise, critical intelligence, and social responsibility since there are substantial social studies refuting this view.[156]

---

153. Tapscott, 91.
154. Tapscott, 91.
155. Buckingham, "Introducing Identity," 16.
156. Buckingham, 14.

Elena Savina's survey on the negative impacts of digital media on education and how to tackle them is worth considering. Schools should carefully consider introducing tablets – carefully since their entertaining features could distract, especially young students or those with deficits in executive functioning. Tablets might be better for individual work than for collaborative learning. Schools need to develop effective practices and policies regarding digital media use that balance student autonomy, privacy, safety, legal rights, and restrictions. It is important to support both students and teachers in their active engagement in collaborative media production. At the same time, schools need to promote face-to-face interactions among students in order to develop their prosocial skills and a sense of community.[157]

While digital media offers massive opportunities for learning, creativity, and discovery with easily accessible, readily available, and rich information, it can easily delude its learner. The non-linear form that information appears in on the internet and the visual form of its presentation can easily seduce one's attention and prompt shallow exploratory behavior rather than deep and systematic search. The result can be superficial networks of associations rather than a well-structured knowledge base. Therefore, using the internet as an informational source without digital literacy skills may result in a fragmented knowledge network and compromised deep comprehension processes. Moreover, people tend to remember where to find information online rather than the information itself. Schools need to foster media literacy, which involves critical thinking necessary to evaluate the reliability of online sources, selecting relevant information and integrating information obtained from different sources. This also involves self monitoring and executive attention skills in order to combat the many distractions on the internet. The fact is that the youth of today's generation are not being well equipped with media literacy skills, and many children and adolescents are not proficient at using the internet as an educational source.[158]

One point that educators also need to consider is the learning process outside of the classroom. Today, digital media offers youth a whole range of informal learning processes with highly democratic relationships between "teachers" and "learners." Buckingham observes:

---

157. Savina et al., "Digital Media and Youth," 87.
158. Savina et al., 84.

Young people learn to use these media largely through trial and error. Exploration, experimentation, play, and collaboration with others – both in face-to-face and virtual forms – are essential elements of the process. Playing certain types of computer games, for example, can involve an extensive series of cognitive activities: remembering, hypothesis testing, predicting, and strategic planning.[159]

Gaming, online networks, and amateur production pose challenges to traditional education.[160] In terms of media production, learning in this informal context involves interacting with friends whose responses fuel and shape youth media production.[161] Since digital media plays a significant role in redefining education both within and outside the classroom, there is a need to equip educators and students with media literacy. This involves "not only ways of understanding, interpreting, and critiquing media, but also the means for creative and social expression, online search and navigation, and a host of new technical skills," Buckingham suggests.[162] This can bridge the gap in media engagement between learning inside and outside the classroom.[163]

Kirsten Drotner also addresses the learning issue in the digital age: how can schools build forms of creativity and learning that youth are experiencing in their everyday uses of digital media? Social media and online gaming usually occur in the context of youthful communities and peer learning and sharing. There is a gap between traditional teaching methods and youths' digital involvement and learning beyond the school. Children may find that teaching materials in schools cannot meet their expectations in terms of multimodal presentation, selection, and interaction. This poses the challenge to traditional schooling approach in developing multimodal literacies at school. Textbooks, combined with oral presentations, are still the main teaching materials in most schools in the world, despite the fact that children grow up surrounded with and educated by digital media and also create their own productions. Digital media offers children and young people the experience

---

159. Buckingham, "Introducing Identity," 16–17.
160. Buckingham, *Youth, Identity, and Digital Media*, viii.
161. Weber and Mitchell, "Imaging, Keyboarding," 42.
162. Buckingham, *Youth, Identity, and Digital Media*, viii.
163. Buckingham, viii.

of flexible and collaborative learning.¹⁶⁴ Drotner does not propose taking any of the extremes of abandoning traditional school's approach or upholding a strict "formal" learning.¹⁶⁵

Rather, Drotner proposes the balanced approach that schools should continue to scaffold pupils' learning processes without forfeiting their opportunities to think and work creatively with their digital media's involvement.¹⁶⁶ She offers some observations about how this might be undertaken, practically.

> Different societies offer different answers to these questions, which are partly dependent upon their educational traditions. For example, Singapore is currently reforming its school system to allow for more differentiated and creative work processes, while in Northern Europe and the United States, the pendulum is swinging in the opposite direction: here policy makers put increasing emphasis on national tests and on evidence-based learning along well-defined lines, in order to counter what are perceived as the unduly permissive tendencies of the past. Whatever the educational policies favored, it seems clear that in their leisure time many children and young people are already busily rehearsing for a future in which the handling of mediatized complexities is key.¹⁶⁷

Drotner concluded that formalized schooling is vital for the formation of digital literacy because in school, pupils' individual resources are harnessed for joint processes of learning that push the boundaries of these resources in ways that leisure time and internet communities of practice cannot do. She adds, "in training pupils to handle the complexities of a heavily mediatized world, and the forms of identity work that it entails, educators will need to draw on children's out-of-school experiences, which increasingly involve complex negotiations between self and others."¹⁶⁸ Overall, Drotner argues that schools have a new role to play in providing media literacy that will equip youth in their media's involvement and both online and off-line learning.

---

164. Drotner, "Leisure Is Hard Work," 175–178.
165. Drotner, 179–180.
166. Drotner, 181.
167. Drotner, 181.
168. Drotner, 181.

Monica Pini, Sandar I. Musanti, and Teresa C. Pargman also agree that schools should provide critical literacy to students.[169]

> The school is the place where this critical media literacy has to be developed. Even though children are acquiring and creating some new forms of digital literacy, their ability to explore and learn to operate computers or other devices by themselves is not enough to achieve digital critical literacy. Children need to learn how to: search for information, critically read the information available to them, interpret different perspectives, be able to develop criteria to select, interpret information and know how to participate in and renew a debate.[170]

They propose that schools should take a dialogic approach in teaching that acknowledges youth identity and cultural consumption practices. This requires teachers to build a teaching approach that considers students' motivations, attitudes, and capabilities and that invites them to participate in a meaningful learning dialogue. Teachers should consider encouraging students' curiosity for using digital devices and software for learning purposes and promoting innovation and adaptation to new situations. Furthermore, it is necessary to acknowledge students' digital media skills in communication and social expression.[171] Last, teachers should consider students' backgrounds and interests. Teaching strategies should pay attention to youths' interests, promote reflection and awareness of the use of digital technology, and increase technological abilities.[172]

While Drotner and Pini discuss pedagogical strategies being developed by schools, Shelley Goldman, Meghan McDermott, and Angela Booker discuss the potentials and the challenges of "informal" learning in out-of-school contexts. They propose that learning is participatory.[173] People can have access to digital technology, which provides important new possibilities for self-expression and communication. This does not mean, however, that digital technology, in itself, makes the difference in learning. It requires interaction

---

169. Pini, Musanti, and Pargman, "Youth Digital Cultural Consumption," 58–79.
170. Pini, Musanti, and Pargman, 76.
171. Pini, Musanti, and Pargman, 76.
172. Pini, Musanti, and Pargman, 77.
173. Goldman and Booker, "Mixing the Digital," 186.

and participation. Learning happens when people are engaged in activities with each other. These authors give a call to think of "social technologies" – the other forms of social interaction – and the teaching approach that surrounds the technologies:

> These "social technologies" embody particular social relationships, expectations of producing media together, and ways of working that engage young people in dialogue, and support and challenge them to recognize their own capacity for inquiry and action. Learning doesn't necessarily happen instantly, but develops over time as youth have the structured opportunity to reflect on and critique what they have done, with the goal of improving the next time around. "Social technologies" give digital media purpose as a means for youth to craft new identities as learners, and potentially as social leaders.[174]

Digital technology serves as a communicative vehicle and platform for dialogue, discourse, connection, and self-expression. A mix of social, cultural, and digital technologies brought youth to new levels of participation, which enable them to learn.[175]

In short, digital media change the way that youth learn in school and beyond. Therefore, schools and educators need to walk with youth by equipping them with critical media literacy. Schools and educators should take a dialogic approach in teaching that acknowledges youth identity and cultural consumption practices and brings out the best in them. More interaction and collaboration in learning should also be provided. Teachers should utilize digital platforms to bridge the gap between teacher and student, to know each student, to befriend them, and to accompany them in their studies and in their lives beyond the classroom.

b. Family

Besides educators, parents also need to walk with youth in this digital age. Katie Davis's study finds that besides friends, mothers also play an important role in adolescents' lives. The experience of positive relationships with their

---

174. Goldman and Booker, 193–194.
175. Goldman and Booker, 203.

mothers had a positive impact on adolescents' levels of self-concept clarity, partly as a result of the mediating role of high friendship quality. Davis concludes that though digital natives may appear, on the surface, to be quite different from their parents, they still require supportive, face-to-face relationships in order to thrive.[176]

Obviously, parents play a key role in youths' media consumption as they purchase, model, and have authority to monitor digital media use. Savina also gives helpful guidelines for parents in the digital age as they negotiate these issues. Parents have to think of strategies to promote healthy media use for their children in order to minimize its possible negative effects. It is recommended that parents limit children's entertainment screen time to one to two hours per day and that they not expose children younger than two to screen media for any amount of time. It is helpful for parents to control children's media use before bedtime to avoid negative effects on sleep. They also need to set a good example for their children in using digital media in a healthy way. Furthermore, parents and children might watch some programs together so that they can share ideas with one another. Parents can encourage children to spend time interacting with people face to face by increasing quality family time and imposing rules about not using digital media during mealtime or family time.[177]

Savina's suggestions are ideal but difficult to apply to monitoring adolescents' screen time. In the digital age, the dynamic has already changed between parents and children, especially adolescents, since the latter are now experts on the internet, an enigma so important that it challenges the authority previously solely held by the parents. Instead of trying to reverse the situation, Net Gen parents should work together with their children in creating an environment that invites more interaction and openness. Net Geners are quick to recognize that the best way to achieve power and control is *through* people, not *over* people. Open families are those that continue to learn, adjust, and evolve.[178] Once again, Tapscott suggests some helpful guidelines for parenting youth:[179]

---

176. Davis, "Young People's Digital Lives," 2281.
177. Savina et al., "Digital Media and Youth," 86.
178. Tapscott, *Growing Up Digital*, 240.
179. Tapscott, 241.

1. Create an open family based on multi-directional communication, mutual trust, and respect for a fluid notion of authority.
2. Prioritize spending quality time with one another.
3. Spend time playing with each of the children.

In short, social studies on this subject suggest that parents should educate children in their digital practices and spend quality time with them.

Thus far, we have discussed the impacts of digital media on society and especially on youth who grow up surrounded by digital media. Digital media significantly impacts youth identity formation. The "Network Society" has strongly affected the process of forming an inner identity, a significant task of the adolescent period. The design of digital media and apps can enslave youth in the "hive" and take away the solitude and resources needed for them to cultivate their inner identity. The overall implication that emerges from these social studies, taken together, is that we need to teach youth to engage with digital media with responsibility and discernment. In order to walk with them and bring out the best in them, it is necessary for institutions such as school and family to invent better ways to accommodate them. In this rapidly evolving context, how should the church of Christ disciple the youth of this generation, whose personal identities are profoundly influenced by digital culture? How should the church, Sunday school teachers, youth workers, and Christian parents mentor the youth of the digital age in their journeys of faith? To answer these questions, the next chapter will develop an appropriate theology of discipleship or spiritual formation. This will pave the way for the theologies needed for youth discipleship in chapter 4 and the contextualizing of youth discipleship for the digital age in chapter 5.

CHAPTER 3

Theology of Spiritual Formation

Chapters 1 and 2 explored the social context for discipling youth in the digital age. This chapter will discuss the theology of discipleship or spiritual formation. It first offers a brief history of the term "spiritual formation" in order to set the stage for a more detailed engagement with the theologies of spiritual formation found in John Calvin, Dietrich Bonhoeffer, Henri Nouwen, and other modern Western writers. The last section will focus on gaining a better theological purchase on the significance of solitude by examining the practice of solitude in the Christian tradition, beginning with the Desert Fathers. The central argument of this chapter is that spiritual formation is encountering Christ in the context of community and daily life. It starts with solitude, in which the believer opens their life to God in preparation to listen for his voice in every moment of life.

1. The History of the Term "Spiritual Formation"

Before discussing the theology of spiritual formation, it is helpful to look back on the history of the term "spiritual formation" to clarify the relationship between spiritual formation and discipleship. Willard summarizes the history of spiritual formation:

> Now, spiritual formation talk has emerged within evangelical circles because of a pervasive felt need – felt on the part of many people within the laity as well as within the clergy – for "something more" than the group and individual activities that have been recognized and encouraged in conservative religious circles

in recent decades . . . So discipleship was marginalized to something that was a special function. In my circles, it always had to do with soul-winning . . . The subsequent rise of talk about spiritual formation occurred because of the felt (though often unarticulated) need to find something deeper: something that actually lead to the transformation of life, that actually moved people in the direction of "the good tree," that looked into the tangled depths of the heart and said, "There must be a way of doing something about that."[1]

According to Willard's observation, spiritual formation emerges to care for spiritual life or inner life, while discipleship seems to focus on soul winning or the outworking of faith. Recent decades have seen a rediscovery of the Christian tradition in the evangelical church of the importance of caring for the spiritual lives of its members and meeting the gaps that previous "discipleship" programs in the church have overlooked.[2]

Other authors explain the relationship between spiritual formation and discipleship in various ways. Doug Paul defines discipleship as "the intentional relational process of one Christian investing into the life of another Christian, through the power of the Holy Spirit, so that the person being discipled becomes more like Jesus."[3] He adds that discipleship is an intentional process aiming to bring about Christian spiritual formation: "Discipleship, however, is a kind of Spiritual Formation. And in many ways, it's the gateway for the outworking of the intentional spiritual formation we are looking for in the rest of our life."[4] Paul sees that discipleship is more than just soul winning or the outworking of faith. It also cares for spiritual life and brings about spiritual transformation. Moving from the mystical view of spiritual formation implied by Doug Paul, James C. Wilhoit locates spiritual formation in the concrete location:

> Spiritual formation is *the* task of the church. It represents neither an interesting, optional pursuit by the church nor an insignificant

---

1. Dallas Willard, "Spiritual Formation."
2. Dallas Willard.
3. Paul, "Why the difference."
4. Paul. I have left Paul's capitalization of the term "spiritual formation" as it is in his original text.

category in the job description of the body of Christ. Spiritual formation is at the heart of its whole purpose for existence. The church was formed to form. Our charge, given by Jesus himself, to make disciples, baptize them, and teach new disciples to obey his commands (Matt 28:19–20). The witness, worship, teaching, and compassion that the church is to practice all require that Christians be spiritually formed.[5]

Wilhoit views that spiritual formation is the task of the church, which involves making disciples and nurturing them in their spiritual life.

Diane J. Chandler defines spiritual formation as "an interactive process by which God the Father fashions believers into the image of his Son, Jesus, through the empowerment of the Holy Spirit by fostering development in seven primary life dimensions."[6] In Chandler's view, spiritual formation is holistic, from soul winning to faith nurturing. Kenneth Boa shows the relationship between spiritual formation and discipleship when he describes spirituality as a gem with many facets. He looks at spirituality in twelve different facets, such as relational spirituality, disciplined spirituality, devotional spirituality, nurturing spirituality, warfare spirituality, and corporate spirituality.[7] He places discipleship under nurturing spirituality:

> Nurturing spirituality involves a lifestyle of discipleship and evangelism, and these two processes reinforce each other. Discipleship is concerned with the post-conversion half of the spectrum of spirituality.[8]

> A whole spectrum of spiritual formation ranges from unwillingness even to consider the claims of Christ to the spiritual maturity of a reproducing disciple.[9]

Boa views that discipleship is concerned with the post-conversion period, while spiritual formation covers the whole range from pre-conversion to

---

5. Wilhoit, *Spiritual Formation*, 15–16, emphasis original.

6. Chandler, *Spiritual Formation*, 19.

7. Boa, *Conformed to His Image*, 20–23. Kenneth Boa is the president of Reflections Ministries and the president of Trinity House Publishers.

8. Boa, 367.

9. Boa, 369.

post-conversion. However, the term discipleship covers evangelism to the same extent that the term spiritual formation does. Making disciples involves sharing the gospels with nonbelievers, converting them, and nurturing their faith as the Great Commission says: "Therefore go and make disciples of all nations, baptizing them in the name of the Father and of the Son and of the Holy Spirit, and teaching them to obey everything I have commanded you. And surely I am with you always, to the very end of the age" (Matt 28:19–20).

What all these theologians share is an agreement that discipleship is focused on soul winning or the outworking of faith, while spiritual formation is directed toward the spiritual care of believers. However, in-depth studies of the terms and their usage show that if done holistically, both discipleship and spiritual formation aim at the same goals. They both refer to the whole process of conversion and sanctification. Therefore, I suggest that the terms spiritual formation and discipleship can be used interchangeably. A brief study of the history of the term "spiritual formation" surfaces the need to explore the theology of spiritual formation to safeguard the practice of discipleship or spiritual formation in our modern day, especially within the evangelical tradition that seeks the deepening of faith.

2. Theology of Spiritual Formation

This section discusses the theology of spiritual formation by engaging deeply the ideas of two Reformed theologians, John Calvin and Dietrich Bonhoeffer, as well as an influential writer on spirituality, Henri Nouwen. At the same time, it continues the dialogue with modern authors on these themes by discussing nine common emphases in the definitions of spiritual formation they propose. (See the Appendix for more details of the survey. Calvin's contribution is that his work suggests a mature theology of spiritual formation. Bonhoeffer, too, has a theological account of spiritual formation, which is intentionally linked with a theology of discipleship, community, and youth and which shall be discussed in more detail in chapter 4. With a strong emphasis on Christ and the word of God, he is also a master of reimagining orthodox Christian faith for the new era. Nouwen's contribution relates to his engagement with the theme of spiritual practice, especially the tradition of practicing solitude that goes back as far as the Desert Fathers. Since solitude is an important locus for spiritual formation, I will discuss its significance at the end of the discussion on the theology of spiritual formation, after engaging with Calvin, Bonhoeffer, and Nouwen.[10]

a. John Calvin

The focus of this subsection will be exploring Calvin's theology of spiritual formation as it parallels the common themes of spiritual formation suggested by modern writers. My treatment follows the reading of Julie Canlis, whose discovery of Calvin's theology of spiritual formation is groundbreaking. In contrast to much modern writing on spiritual formation, which is often sparsely supported by doctrinal scaffolding, Calvin's *Institutes* provides a much more robust grounding for spiritual practice by locating it in a Trinitarian context. As Canlis observes,

> Demonstrated even by the way he organizes the Institutes, Calvin declares: all must begin with the Trinity. Before we even enter into the words on the first page, the Trinity gives shape to Calvin's understanding of where we have come from and where we are going. The Institutes shimmers with this unstated presence of a trinitarian, personal God who is above, before, ahead of, behind, and all around us – loving us, calling us, breathing life into our beings. The Institutes follows the steady pursuit of (Book I) God the Father, who creates us for love and fellowship, and who incarnates the Word as (Book II) Jesus the true Son, who has come to redeem us from sin and show us what this fellowship is really like. The Spirit (Book III) continues this wooing, building the life of Jesus the Son into our broken lives so that we can truly be God's children who, as the church (Book IV), live a familial life responding to this Triune God of grace.[11]

According to Calvin, spiritual formation is fundamentally to live as God's children. It is a work of grace accomplished by the Trinitarian God: God the Father creates us, Jesus redeems us, and the Holy Spirit builds the life of Jesus in us.

---

10. The sub-subheadings 1) to 9) run through the subheadings a, b, and c. Sub-subheadings 1) to 4) are ideas present in Calvin, 5) and 6) come via Bonhoeffer, and 7) to 9), via Nouwen.

11. Canlis, "Calvin's Institutes," 17.

Spiritual formation is encountering Christ or being conformed to Christ. Canlis observes that Calvin's contribution is to supply a strong theological basis for conformity-to-Christ language:

> Calvin's theology, for all its clarity and polemic usefulness, loses its centre when it is pulled away from sonship – both the Sonship of Jesus and, consequently, our own adoptive sonship. If we are going to read Calvin's theology as it was intended, for spiritual formation, then it must begin here, with Calvin's grasp of the transformative impact of sonship.[12]

"In 'union with Christ,'" Calvin says, as elucidated by Canlis,

> Jesus' Father becomes our Father, we become children, and we enter the family dynamic. We move from being orphans to suddenly sitting around a table, eating the family food, being included in the Father's legacy, and getting in on everything in this family economy.[13]

In my view, Canlis's interpretation of Calvin is accurate, especially when it is clearly situated within a Calvinistic doctrine of predestination and as she develops it in the form of an account of spiritual formation. Calvin's concept of predestination – often referred to as Calvinism's "central doctrine" - is presented in chapters 21–24 of the third book of the *Institutes of the Christian Religion*. Calvin's doctrine is summarized in the title of chapter 21, "On the Eternal Election by Which God Predestines Some to Salvation, Others to Destruction."[14] Calvin's account flows from the concept of God's glory and providence found in Scripture, and it is linked closely to Christ, who is taken as the pattern of all election and who is the author and assurer of salvation. Election is preeminently a demonstration of God's gracious will in Christ, shown forth in his calling, justification, and sanctification of the elect. In God's special calling of an individual, God gives proof that this person has been chosen in Christ before the foundation of the world. When an individual is called, they receive the Spirit of adoption who unites them

---

12. Canlis, 16.
13. Canlis, 20.
14. Parker, *Calvin*, 113.

with Christ (III.24.1).[15] The soteriological ground of predestination is the intention of God that men be conformed to the image of Christ and partake of his merits.[16] The election, which is willed by God, does not excuse but rather empowers believers to live a godly life, holiness being the sole goal of election (III.23.12).[17] Given this grounding of spiritual formation in the doctrine of election, we can now confirm that Canlis has offered an astute interpretation of Calvin in saying that for Calvin, spiritual formation is most basically the activity of living as God's children. It is a work of grace done by the Trinitarian God. We now inquire whether there is any part for us to play in spiritual formation.

1) Intentionality

Among many modern authors who write or have written about spiritual formation, Michael Burer and James C. Wilhoit are the only two authors who mentioned explicitly the *intentional* aspect of spiritual formation.[18] I will first introduce their ideas and then critically probe them. This will discuss whether humans can intentionally participate in God's transformation in the lives of believers in view of Calvin's theology presented above.

Burer defines spiritual formation as "the intentional transformation of the inner person to the character of Christ."[19] He explains what he means by intentional as follows. "It is intentional in two ways: It is part of God's will for the individual believer, and the individual believer makes a conscious choice about it."[20] However, there is a need to explore how these "two ways" coexist. Burer anchors this view in Romans 12:1–2.

> Therefore, I urge you, brothers and sisters, in view of God's mercy, to offer your bodies as a living sacrifice, holy and pleasing to God – this is your true and proper worship. Do not conform to the pattern of this world, but be transformed by the renewing

---

15. Parker, 119.
16. Muller, *Christ and the Decree*, 37.
17. Battles, *Analysis of the Institutes*, 268.
18. Michael Burer is Associate Professor of New Testament Studies at Dallas Theological Seminary. James C. Wilhoit is the Scripture Press Professor of Christian Formation and Ministry at Wheaton College.
19. Burer, "Towards a Biblical Definition."
20. Burer, "Towards a Biblical Definition."

of your mind. Then you will be able to test and approve what God's will is – his good, pleasing and perfect will.

Burer expounds this text: "Paul is focusing on the believer's participation in the process of sanctification, as it were, and the 'will of God' is meant to be the overarching standard by which the believer functions."[21] However, there is a need to elaborate the meaning of "participation" with God in the process of sanctification and the "will of God."

Burer concludes of spiritual formation:

> I wish to offer a revised definition of spiritual formation in light of the fresh light thrown on it by Romans 12:1–2: "An act of worship in response to God's mercy and grace which involves the intentional transformation of the character to be like Christ and the intentional transformation of the actions to conform to God's will."[22]

In his definition, though, Burer always places "intentional" right next to "transformation". The word "intentional" can be misleading as it tends to trigger ideas about our sole, deliberate effort or tasks in the process of transformation. A better question to ask is in what sense is spiritual formation an act of worship? As believers respond to God's mercy and grace in worship, God brings transformation into their lives. Burer mentions "intentional" when describing believers' participation in the process of sanctification. However, if we take Calvin's Trinitarian theology of sanctification seriously, it can only be initiated by grace alone, not by human effort. There is no place for humans to initiate a process of transformation. What we can do is respond to God's grace. Transformation can only come from God through Christ alone as Canlis observes Calvin's theology on spiritual formation: "And this, not incidentally, is the only place where Calvin believed the transformation of our hearts and lives could occur – in an ongoing encounter with Jesus the Christ."[23]

While Burer mentions spiritual formation as an intentional, personal task, Wilhoit calls it an "intentional communal process." After discussing three sets of images of spiritual life – nurture (agriculture, gardening, human growth,

---

21. Burer, "Towards a Biblical Definition."
22. Burer, "Towards a Biblical Definition."
23. Canlis, "Calvin's Institutes," 16.

intimacy), the journey (race, battle, struggle), and death and resurrection (dying with Christ, being born again) – Wilhoit suggests that "Christian spiritual formation refers to the intentional communal process of growing in our relationship with God and becoming conformed to Christ through the power of the Holy Spirit."[24] However, spiritual formation is not about our personal tasks or the tasks of the church. God's will is that we enter our relationship with him through Christ. Here, again, Calvin's theology can shed some light, as Canlis observes.

> It is the hard task of laying tasks aside in order to contemplate and receive the words, "This is my beloved Son, in whom I am well pleased" we hear (Matt 3: 17). Only when we hear that word can our tasks have any meaning at all. Spiritual formation is all about entering this Father-Son relationship, about living out the truth of our adoption, it is formation as relation.[25]

It becomes more obvious why Canlis's observation can be affirmed if we recall Calvin's placement of spiritual formation with his robust account of justification and sanctification. When believers are called, they receive the Spirit of adoption who unites them with Christ:[26]

> Though the Lord, by electing his people, adopted them as his sons, we, however, see that they do not come into possession of this great good until they are called; but when called, the enjoyment of their election is in some measure communicated to them. For which reason the Spirit which they receive is termed by Paul both the "Spirit of adoption," and the "seal" and "earnest" of the future inheritance; because by his testimony he confirms and seals the certainty of future adoption on their hearts. (III.24.1)[27]

---

24. Wilhoit, *Spiritual Formation*, 23.
25. Canlis, "Calvin's Institutes," 24.
26. Parker, *Calvin*, 119.
27. John Calvin, *Institutes*. All quotations from Calvin's Institutes in this chapter are taken from this source unless otherwise indicated.

God's will is that believers enter into relationship with him through Christ, being conformed to his image and partaking of his merits:[28]

> But Paul reminds us that the end for which we are elected is "that we should be holy, and without blame before him," (Eph 1:4). If the end of election is holiness of life, it ought to arouse and stimulate us strenuously to aspire to it, instead of serving as a pretext for sloth. (III.23.12)

Spiritual formation is not about tasks but about encountering Christ. Spiritual formation can be pursued through spiritual practices, Henri Nouwen states:

> By their solitude, silence, and unceasing prayer the Desert Fathers show us the way. These disciplines will teach us to stand firm, to speak words of salvation, and to approach the new millennium with hope, courage, and confidence. When we have been remodelled into living witnesses of Christ through solitude, silence and prayer, we will no longer have to worry about whether we are saying the right thing or making the right gesture, because then Christ will make his presence known even when we are not aware of it.[29]

Nouwen's exploration of the spirituality of the Desert Fathers will be discussed in detail later in the subsection *Henri Nouwen* and the section *The Practice of Solitude*.

In short, Burer mentions the "intentional" aspect of spiritual formation with regards to participation in God's transformation in the lives of believers, while Wilhoit mentions it as the task of the church. However, from Calvin's theology, the "intentional" aspect is a dangerous view since spiritual formation can only come from God alone, not human effort. Spiritual formation should be located under the overarching grace of God.

2) Grace

In Calvin's theology of spiritual formation presented earlier, spiritual formation is not intentional human work, but it is the work of grace accomplished

---

28. Muller, *Christ and the Decree*, 37.
29. Nouwen, *Way of the Heart*, 94.

by the Trinitarian God. From eternity, the triune God has freely determined Christ to be the author and assurer of election.[30] To illustrate this point, Calvin turns to a series of sayings recorded in the fourth gospel, found in John 6:37 – "All that the Father gives me will come to me" – as well as John 6:39, 45; 17:6, 12. This cluster of verses explicitly asserts that the elect belonged to God the Father, who gave them to the incarnate Son (III.22.7).[31] Christ is predestined to be the head of the elect, and they are predestined to be his members. And he is the source of grace that flows through them and the assurance of their salvation. We know of our election as it is manifested and confirmed in Christ. Our election is not to be inferred from works, but rather the assurance of our election ultimately rests on Christ, who is the "mirror" of election.[32] Calvin explains:

> Christ proclaims aloud that all whom the Father is pleased to save he has delivered into his protection (John 6:37–39, 17:6, 12). Therefore, if we would know whether God cares for our salvation, let us ask whether he has committed us to Christ, whom he has appointed to be the only Savior of all his people. Then, if we doubt whether we are received into the protection of Christ, he obviates the doubt when he spontaneously offers himself as our Shepherd, and declares that we are of the number of his sheep if we hear his voice (John 10:3, 16). Let us, therefore, embrace Christ, who is kindly offered to us, and comes forth to meet us: he will number us among his flock, and keep us within his fold. (III.24.6)

Election is preeminently a demonstration of God's gracious will in Christ shown forth in calling, justification, and sanctification.[33] Calvin concludes his case by citing Romans 8:29–30: "'Whom he did predestinate, them he also called; and whom he called, them he also justified,' that he may one day glorify." (III.24.1)

This segment will explore the aspect of grace in spiritual formation. Not many authors explicitly mention grace in their definitions of spiritual

---

30. Muller, *Christ and the Decree*, 37.
31. Parker, *Calvin*, 117.
32. Muller, *Christ and the Decree*, 36.
33. Muller, 25.

formation. Jeffrey P. Greenman, Kenneth Boa, and Nathan Foster are exceptions to this general tendency. In Greenman's definition, "spiritual formation is our continuing response to the reality of God's grace shaping us into the likeness of Jesus Christ, through the work of the Holy Spirit, in the community of faith, for the sake of the world."[34] He elaborates this definition of grace as "the unmerited gift of God's love and mercy toward sinners, shown supremely in Christ's life, death and resurrection."[35] As grace is shown in God's act of dealing with human sin through the cross of Christ, spiritual formation "involves grace-based disciplines of confession, forgiveness and reconciliation."[36] According to Greenman, believers receive spiritual transformation as they respond to God's grace. This response involves the disciplines of confession, forgiveness, and reconciliation, which are based solely on God's grace, not human merit. His definition of spiritual formation reflects the biblical logic of divine grace preceding human work; "we love because he first loved us." (1 John 4:19) Christians are to respond in faith, trust, and obedience to Christ and let him transform their lives.[37]

Greenman, however, overstates when he asserts that "divine action takes priority over human action. God's gift precedes and makes possible the human task of discipleship, witness and service."[38] He does acknowledge the human contribution of intentional action: "Spiritual formation necessarily involves intentional action and commitment, yet we recognize that divine grace is not opposed to human effort, but rather opposed to earning divine favor."[39] According to Greenman, divine action overpowers everything, and we make no contribution to spiritual formation. It is utterly a work of God's grace. According to Calvin, spiritual formation means learning to live as God's children. This happens through the work of grace done by the Trinitarian God: God the Father creates us, Jesus redeems us, and the Holy Spirit builds the life of Jesus in us.[40] It is important to take note that Christians are not

---

34. Greenman and Kalantzis, *Life in the Spirit*, 24.
35. Greenman and Kalantzis, 24.
36. Greenman and Kalantzis, 24–25.
37. Greenman and Kalantzis, 25.
38. Greenman and Kalantzis, 25.
39. Greenman and Kalantzis, 25.
40. Canlis, "Calvin's Institutes," 17.

passive in faith but must practice grace-based disciplines, especially solitude, to be discussed in the last section of this chapter.

Sharing a similar view of grace and of becoming like Jesus, Kenneth Boa defines spiritual formation as "the grace-driven developmental process in which the soul grows in conformity to the image of Christ."[41] He describes spiritual formation as a journey or a pilgrimage to become "conformed to the image of His Son." (Rom 8:29) "The spiritual life is an all-encompassing, lifelong response to God's gracious initiatives in the lives of those whose trust is centered in the person and work of Jesus Christ."[42] Spiritual formation is a Christ-centered journey in the Spirit beginning with the gifts of forgiveness and life in Christ and progressing through faith and obedience.[43] The most relevant claim made here for his thesis is Boa's conclusion that the task of the Christian life is a balancing "between radical dependence on God and personal discipline as an expression of obedience and application."[44]

We need to not only trust God but also obey him. These are the grounds out of which Bonhoeffer's warning against cheap grace spring in *Discipleship*. Our responses to God's grace are repentance, the discipline of community, the confession of sin, discipleship, and bearing Jesus's cross.[45] In this regard, Nathan Foster suggests that spiritual practices are a response to God's grace:

> As we submit our will to spiritual practices, God's grace brings forth character transformation. This seems to be the dominant means God uses to bring about change in our lives. Christian spiritual formation is the process of becoming people formed into the likeness of Christ's character.[46]

Grace is freely given to us, but it is not "cheap," as it requires us to respond in faith and obedience. This is where grace-based spiritual disciplines and

---

41. Boa, *Conformed to His Image*, 515.
42. Boa, 19–20.
43. Boa, 19–20.
44. Boa, 21.
45. Bonhoeffer, *Discipleship*, 44.
46. Foster, *Making of an Ordinary Saint*, 16. Nathan Foster is the son of Richard Foster. He is an associate professor of social work and theology at Spring Arbor University, where he holds the Andrews Chair in Spiritual Formation.

practices can come in as Henri Nouwen helps us explore these disciplines from the Desert Fathers.[47]

Calvin gives us the theological foundation for these spiritual practices that focus on encountering Christ only, as Canlis observes:

> A big task of being spiritually formed is to begin to recognize this possibility for Christ-encounter all around us. Spiritual formation in the Institutes does not revolve around set spiritual practices. Nor does it begin with an understanding of grace and the gifts that God longs to give us. These gifts have a face – Jesus. This world we have entered is a Christ-saturated world. All "spirituality" we have is encounter with Christ.[48]

While the modern authors on spiritual formation – Jeffrey P. Greenman, Kenneth Boa, and Nathan Foster – remind us of the significance of God's grace, which is the overarching and foundational condition for spiritual formation, Calvin gives a deeper theological foundation in locating spiritual formation in the Trinitarian context of the work of grace that enables us to become God's children. Since grace is not "cheap" as Bonhoeffer suggests, we need to respond to God's grace in faith and obedience. This is where the spiritual disciplines dated back to the Dessert Fathers can be located, as Henri Nouwen suggests. However, Calvin reminds us that spiritual disciplines are not first a set of practices, but they concern encountering Christ.

3) Inspiration or Empowerment from the Holy Spirit

As already noted, according to Calvin, spiritual formation is fundamentally living as God's children. It is a work of grace accomplished by the Trinitarian God: God the Father creates us, Jesus redeems us, and the Holy Spirit builds the life of Jesus in us. The works of the Spirit in the lives of believers begin with the calling and the illumination of the mind. Calvin distinguishes two kinds of calling: the universal call when the gospel is preached, and the special call when the Spirit illuminates the mind:

> There are two species of calling: for there is a universal call, by which God, through the external preaching of the word, invites

---

47. Nouwen, *Way of the Heart*, 92.
48. Canlis, "Calvin's Institutes," 19.

> all men alike, even those for whom he designs the call to be a savor of death, and the ground of a severer condemnation. Besides this there is a special call which, for the most part, God bestows on believers only, when by the internal illumination of the Spirit he causes the word preached to take deep root in their hearts. Sometimes, however, he communicates it also to those whom he enlightens only for a time, and whom afterwards, in just punishment for their ingratitude, he abandons and smites with greater blindness. (III.24.8)

By the preaching of the gospel, all are called to repentance and faith, whereas the special call or the Spirit of repentance and faith is not given to all. Therefore, "not all have been endowed with eyes and ears so as to understand." (III.22.10) Calvin maintains that the same sermon is preached to 100 people, but only 20 will embrace it with faith when the Spirit illuminates their minds while others will reject it.[49] Calvin explains the reasons:[50]

> It is also incontrovertible, that to those whom God is not pleased to illumine, he delivers his doctrine wrapt up in enigmas, so that they may not profit by it, but be given over to greater blindness. (III.24.13)

> The covenant of life is not preached equally to all, and among those to whom it is preached, does not always meet with the same reception. This diversity displays the unsearchable depth of the divine judgment, and is without doubt subordinate to God's purpose of eternal election. But if it is plainly owing to the mere pleasure of God that salvation is spontaneously offered to some, while others have no access to it. (III.21.1)

When believers are called, they are united with Christ by the Spirit.[51]

This segment explores the work of the Holy Spirit in spiritual transformation. Most of the authors, namely Wilhoit, Boa, and Greenman, mention the role of the Holy Spirit in spiritual formation. Wilhoit explains the main reason for relying on the Holy Spirit in spiritual formation: "Since it is a spiritual

---

49. Parker, *Calvin*, 117–120.
50. Parker, 117–120.
51. Parker, 119.

process, it is also important that we rely on the power of the Holy Spirit rather than relying on our power and skill."[52] Wilhoit is right but does not himself elaborate the work of the Spirit. Describing spiritual formation as a journey or a pilgrimage to become "conformed to the image of his Son" (Rom 8:29), Kenneth Boa shares the same view that we need to rely on the power of the Holy Spirit rather than our skill, knowledge, programs, and written materials.[53] Boa says that we need to constantly depend on the presence of the Holy Spirit, but he also does not explain how to do so. Nor does he elaborate on the work of the Spirit. Greenman explains that believers receive spiritual transformation as they respond to God's grace and that it is the work of the Spirit to give believers spiritual transformation (2 Pet 1:4).[54] Like Wilhoit and Boa, Greenman also does not elaborate on the work of the Holy Spirit.

Again, Calvin's setting the work of the Holy Spirit in the Trinitarian context helps to clarify what these modern authors do not explain: that "we really are loved, because of the one, saving will of the triune God – the Father effecting, the Son ordering, and the Spirit empowering (I.13.18). God's Fatherhood is made available to us in Christ, the Son."[55] Canlis points out that, for Calvin, the work of the Holy Spirit is to concretize the Fatherhood of God in specific contexts. Jesus is the concreteness of God, and this concreteness is brought alive in the believer's union with Christ through the Spirit. She adds, "Without the Spirit, God is no more than a kindly, fatherly figure. With and by the Spirit, we are engrafted into the Son, who shares his Father with us."[56] The central work of the Holy Spirit is to engraft the believer into the life of Christ. The Holy Spirit's work is to inform us about our identity in Christ rather than our own tasks or effort in spiritual formation.[57] Spiritual transformation is the natural result of life in the Spirit. Nouwen aptly describes the marks of a life in the Spirit: being free from false attachments and living with peace and joy even when surrounded by conflict and sadness.[58]

---

52. Wilhoit, *Spiritual Formation*, 17.
53. Boa, *Conformed to His Image*, 19–20, 371.
54. Greenman and Kalantzis, *Life in the Spirit*, 26.
55. Canlis, "Calvin's Institutes," 21.
56. Canlis, 22.
57. Canlis, 23.
58. Nouwen, *Spiritual Formation*, xxix.

It is the work of the Holy Spirit to engraft believers into the life of Christ so that we can live life in its fullness. The question is how to respond to the work of the Holy Spirit in our lives. As discussed above, many authors mention the roles of the Spirit in spiritual formation, but not many authors elaborate on how to respond to the Holy Spirit. Here, we need to come back to Richard Foster's spiritual disciplines of meditation, prayer, fasting, solitude, and submission in order to respond to the Spirit.[59] Nouwen also reminds us of the continuous response to the Holy Spirit: "Therefore, we need to begin with a careful look at the way we think, speak, feel, and act from hour to hour, day to day, week to week, and year to year, in order to become more fully aware of our hunger for the Spirit."[60] We can also learn from the practice of the presence of God from Brother Lawrence. The story of his conversion and commitment to his Christian faith at eighteen years old highlights the essential point. Seeing a tree stripped of its leaves then later sprouting new leaves, flowers, and fruit, he received a high view of the providence and power of God.[61] This vision fostered a sensitivity to the presence of God in everyday life. The love of God became for him the end of all his actions, to the extent that he was even pleased when he could take up a straw from the ground for the love of God.[62] It is the work of the Holy Spirit to reveal God in our daily lives. The thing we need to do is to cultivate the habit of listening to him in every moment of life.

To recap, Wilhoit, Boa, and Greenman, mention the role of the Holy Spirit in spiritual formation. Calvin goes deeper into the work of the Holy Spirit on engrafting us into Christ. The Holy Spirit tells us about our identity in Christ. Richard Foster, Nouwen, and Brother Lawrence elaborate how the spiritual disciplines can be understood as a preparation for responding to the work of the Holy Spirit in the daily life of the believer.

4) *Process of Transformation*

As Calvin describes it, spiritual formation is encountering Christ or being conformed to Christ. This is not a onetime action but an ongoing journey

---

59. Foster, *Celebration of Discipline*, 17–77, 120–156.
60. Nouwen, *Spiritual Formation*, xxii.
61. Brother Lawrence, *Practice of the Presence*, 3.
62. Brother Lawrence, 4.

of transformation that will be further discussed in this segment. Almost all modern authors speak about spiritual formation as a process of transformation. The consensus view of this term is that it emphasizes that sanctification is not a onetime event but an ongoing or lifetime process. Paul Pettit presents the consensus view.

> When we use the term *formation,* we mean the on-going process of the believer's actions and habits being continually transformed (morphed) into the image of Jesus Christ. Make no mistake: maturing as a Christian is a process. It is not a second step, a higher plane, a sacred blessing, or a lightning bolt moment when God invades and brings the Christian to perfected place. A lifelong transformation is set into motion when one places his or her faith in Jesus and seeks to follow him (discipleship, apprenticeship).[63]

Spiritual formation leads to life change. Pettit further specifies that some of these changes can be seen immediately, while other transformations take longer.[64] Drawing from biblical images, Wilhoit describes the spiritual life as nurture and journey that are a lifetime process.[65] Boa also describes spiritual formation as a journey or a pilgrimage that is carried out by the Holy Spirit not by us.[66] Richard Foster reminds us to stay away from the temptation of the "fast food" culture as we do spiritual formation. As spiritual formation is a process of transformation, we should commit ourselves to the long-term relationship with God and cultivate patience as we disciple young people.[67]

Once again, however, none of these authors clearly set out a view of why spiritual formation is not a onetime process but an ongoing one. Here, Calvin's approach is again substantive in explaining why spiritual formation must flow from the ongoing encounter with Christ. Formation is the mode the long-term relationship with Christ takes for Calvin as Canlis explains.

---

63. Pettit, *Foundations of Spiritual Formation*, 21.
64. Pettit, 19.
65. Wilhoit, *Spiritual Formation*, 19.
66. Boa, *Conformed to His Image*, 19–20.
67. Foster, "Ten Counsels."

And this, not incidentally, is the only place where Calvin believed the transformation of our hearts and lives could occur – in an ongoing encounter with Jesus the Christ. An encounter with Jesus was not something one could label and date (as Calvin himself refused to label and date his own conversion), then to be put on display in one's spiritual archives. From Calvin's perspective, it was a new way of living and being, and its shape was sonship. "Adoption . . . is not the cause merely of a partial salvation, but bestows salvation entire."[68]

Spiritual formation, for Calvin, means union with Christ and being conformed to his image.[69]

Calvin gives a strong theological foundation for the notion of being spiritually formed by suffering as children of God. Transformation happens in the same way that we were justified: participation in Christ and in his sufferings.[70] As Jesus mentions in John 16:33, "in this world you will have trouble." Suffering is characteristic of the circumstance we are living in. Participation in Christ and being conformed to Christ do not exclude suffering. As Canlis observes, "Calvin specifically links adoption and cross-bearing, in order that adoption doesn't usher us into a feel-good realm or into unreality itself. Salvation comes through a cross-shaped life."[71] God predestined us to be conformed to the image of Christ (Rom 8:29), but he did not predestine suffering, since it is part of the fallen world. The transformational character of suffering is predestined for us since we participate in Christ, who suffered and conquered the world. God appointed suffering to make us conformed to Christ. He creatively used the suffering of this broken and fallen world to work out the good of it for the sake of believers. Canlis observes from Calvin, "Suffering is, in Christ, subject to the recapitulating love of the Father who, through the Spirit, draws near to his children – first to comfort, and one day finally to heal. In between that first and final embrace, our transformation occurs."[72] In union in Christ, who still bears the marks of suffering,

---

68. Canlis, "Calvin's Institutes," 16.
69. Canlis, 20.
70. Canlis, 25.
71. Canlis, 25–26.
72. Canlis, 26.

humiliation, death, and resurrection in his body, we are driven away from a "self-contained person" into the family of God, which together witnesses to the "true human identity" that is restored in us by Christ.[73]

Being conformed to Christ is not a clear-cut thing as Canlis observes from Calvin's theology:

> Calvin is anything but vague. We are not to imitate Jesus. We are not to consent intellectually to Jesus. We are not to receive the gifts of Jesus, as if they could in some way be "imputed" to us apart from him. We are to "grow into one body" with him. We are to undergo, what Calvin terms a few chapters later, "that joining together of Head and members, that indwelling of Christ in our hearts – in short, that mystical union" (Calvin, Institutes, III.11.10).[74]

Canlis calls Calvin's theology filial: "Calvin, like other Reformers, revelled in the Christological, but I believe his theology is better known as filial. In nearly every possible way, and at every critical theological juncture, Calvin paints the Christian life in familial terms, as children with their loving Father."[75] As the children of God, we need to pass the understanding of the gospel into "daily living, and so transform us." (III.6.4)[76] Spiritual formation is union with Christ in his death and resurrection. This means surrendering totally to the lordship of Christ and conforming to his image.

Almost all authors, including Pettit, Wilhoit, Boa, and Foster, mention spiritual formation as a process of transformation yet do not explain the in-depth reasons behind this assertion. Calvin helpfully explains that spiritual formation is an ongoing process of transformation because it is a necessarily continuing encounter with Christ – and particularly in his suffering. In this subsection, we have seen that Calvin conceives a robust theology of spiritual formation as a way of living as God's children. It is by a work of grace accomplished by the Trinitarian God: God the Father creates us, Jesus redeems us, and the Holy Spirit builds the life of Jesus in us. Spiritual formation means encountering Christ or being conformed to Christ. It is the work of actively

---

73. Canlis, 26.
74. Canlis, 20.
75. Canlis, 20.
76. Canlis, 17.

participating in the mystical union that is created between Christ and the believer by the Holy Spirit. This definition of spiritual formation lays a solid foundation for the theology of spiritual formation discussed in this chapter and the theology of youth discipleship in the digital age discussed in chapter 4. Calvin has clarified and developed the theological definition of spiritual formation. It remains necessary to explore the loci of it.

b. Dietrich Bonhoeffer

Calvin mentions the Bible – the Law (Old Testament) and the Gospels (New Testament) – in book II (chapters 7–10) of his *Institutes* and the church in book IV. He adds that people can only understand the mysteries of God revealed in Scripture through the Spirit's illumination:

> If we confess that what we ask of God is lacking to us, and He by the very thing promised intimates our want, no man can hesitate to acknowledge that he is able to understand the mysteries of God, only in so far as illuminated by his grace. He who ascribes to himself more understanding than this, is the blinder for not acknowledging his blindness. (II.2.21)

> Hence without the illumination of the Spirit the word has no effect; and hence also it is obvious that faith is something higher than human understanding. (III.2.33)

The Holy Spirit illumines the minds and hearts of believers as they read the Scriptures. Calvin believes that it is significant that believers read the Scriptures for themselves, as Wesley Kort observes:

> For Calvin, nothing is more crucial, more basic, or more determinative for the Christian life than the reading of Scripture. Everything else depends upon and follows from it, and if anything has standing in and for the Christian life, it derives from or is analogous to the reading of Scripture. It is the occasion when or the site where the basic, transforming event in a person's life occurs. The church is a company of readers, and preaching borrows its status of Word of God from Scripture.[77]

---

77. Kort, *Take, Read*, 35.

In contrast with Calvin, Bonhoeffer, it seems, develops the biblical foundations of Christian formation even more explicitly. He presents being engaged with the word of God and Christian community as the central loci for spiritual formation.[78] This subsection will show that the Bible is the foundation for the spiritual formation, which takes place in the context of the faith community.

5) *Accordance to Biblical Standards*

We have investigated the theme of grace and the intentional aspect of spiritual formation, which involves the believer's response to God's grace. The logical next step is to ask what practical guidelines might best help Christians respond to the grace of God. For Bonhoeffer, the Bible played a central role in Christian discipleship, observes Lisa E. Dahill. The primary loci orienting Bonhoeffer's account of spiritual formation "are the Word, the Christian community (specifically the experience of friendship), and public life in the world."[79] This was certainly true in Bonhoeffer's own practice of spiritual formation, Dahill suggests.

> For Bonhoeffer, Scripture was the central means of grace. His conversion took place through learning to read the Gospels, and particularly the Sermon on the Mount, in a new way – that is, as personally implicating. It was here that he came to experience Jesus himself as a living presence and his Lord and that he learned to pray for the first time.[80]

In his youth work, Bonhoeffer similarly emphasized the importance of preaching and teaching the word of God to young people.[81] In his *Eight Theses on Youth Work,* Bonhoeffer emphasizes that the church needs to focus on preaching the word of God to youth, regardless of the day and age.[82] For Bonhoeffer, the Bible is the central means of grace providing the standard for the practice of Christian spiritual formation. But given the vast scope of

---

78. Dahill, *Reading from the Underside*, 101.
79. Dahill, 101.
80. Dahill, 101.
81. Root, *Bonhoeffer as Youth Worker*.
82. Bonhoeffer, *Berlin: 1932–1933*, Volume 12, *Dietrich Bonhoeffer Works*, edited by Larry L. Rasmussen and translated by Isabel Best and David Higgins (Minneapolis, MN: Fortress Press, 2009), 515–516.

the Bible's teaching, there is a need to recognize and understand the central message of the Bible.

Wilhoit highlights that the gospel of Jesus Christ is the foundation for spiritual formation and that we should teach the gospel not only to nonbelievers but also to believers, who should be constantly reminded of their iniquities and come back to God to receive forgiveness and refreshment of their spiritual lives.[83] He helpfully emphasizes that true spiritual formation will always carry out a twofold task in relation to the gospel: first, it will promote a deep understanding, greater trust, and spiritual cleansing and healing, and second, it will confront false gospels and idols, including the consumer-oriented culture, which has affected the church.[84] Last but not least, Wilhoit secures the whole process of spiritual formation with the backdrop of the God who forms us in love.[85] Wilhoit is helpful in reminding us to teach and preach the gospel to both believers and nonbelievers, but Jesus seems to play a small role in all of this. At this juncture, Dallas Willard sheds some light: "When we talk about spiritual formation, we are talking about framing a progression of life in which people come to actually do all things that Jesus taught."[86] Spiritual formation is living a life in accordance with Jesus's teaching in the Bible.

The Bible plays an important role in spiritual formation. However, how should we approach it? What source of practice do we need to exercise in relation to the Bible? Henri Nouwen proposes an updated version of the traditional monastic discipline of *lectio divina*:

> The term *lectio divina* comes from the Benedictine tradition and refers primarily to the sacred or devotional reading of the Bible. My growing suspicion is that our competitive, productive, skeptical, and sophisticated society inhibits our reading and being read by the Word of God. *Lectio divina* means to read the Bible with reverence and openness to what the Spirit is saying to us in the present moment. When we approach the Word of God as a word spoken to me, God's presence and will

---

83. Wilhoit, *Spiritual Formation*, 26–33.
84. Wilhoit, 31–33.
85. Wilhoit, 35.
86. Willard, "Spiritual Formation."

can be made known. The regular practice of *lectio divina* presents occasions when my story and God's story meet, and in that moment something surprising can happen. To read the Bible in this way means therefore to read "on my knees" – reverently, attentively, and with the deep faith that God has a word for me in my unique situation.[87]

Long before Nouwen, Calvin, too, was influenced by the monastic practice of *lectio divina*.[88] As Kort observes, "Calvin could not have accomplished what he did with his doctrine of reading Scpriture if it were not for the tradition of *lectio divina*. By his doctrine of Scripture, he took this practice out of its monastic setting and inserted it into the life of every Christian."[89] For Calvin, reading the Scriptures is never an indivitualistic pursuit nor is it understood as an act of private piety, as Kort notes:

> A Christain life based on reading is inescapably solitary, but Calvin's solitary reader is not comprehesible using understandings of privacy or the individual current in our own culture. Calvin would have nothing to do with the priviledged place we give to privacy or with either our ontology or ethic of the individual . . . For example, in his commentary on 2 Pet. 1:20, which speaks against private interpretation, Calvin takes "private" to mean not solitary but privately concocted and self-serving. The saving knowledge of God made available by the Holy Spitrit in the process of reading is anything but "private" in our sense of individualistic. Calvin did not advocate private religion or the primacy of personal religious experience. The Holy Spirit that imparts saving knowledge to the heart of the solitary reader is the Holy Spirit that at the same time unites that reader with other Christians so constituted. Reading is solitary, a process, like dying, of divestment, but the saving knowledge of God is shared and is not a priviledged possion of separate individuals.[90]

---

87. Nouwen, *Spiritual Formation*, xxiii.
88. Kort, *Take, Read*, 23.
89. Kort, 23.
90. Kort, 35.

Personal devotion to the Scripture is important and necessary, but we should not neglect the corporate aspect of spiritual formation, as Nouwen suggests:

> I read the Word alone. I enter into silence and solitude. I may talk with a specialist to help me walk the way of the heart. But these are not enough. Spiritual formation is not an exercise of private devotion but one of corporate spirituality. We do not have personal experiences of God, but together we are formed as the people of God. Spiritual formation requires not only the *inward journey* to the heart, but also the *outward journey* from the heart to community and ministry. Christian spirituality is essentially communal . . . In community we learn true humility. Without community, we become individualistic and egocentric.[91]

Nouwen mentions corporate spirituality, but it seems not to have a place for the corporate practice of group *lectio divina*, such as preaching, small group Bible study, Sunday school, or one-to-one Bible reading, which is significant to build up one another in Christian living. Since group *lectio divina* is very important in youth ministry, I will discuss it in the section "Contextualizing the Theology of Spiritual Formation in Youth Ministry in Vietnam" of chapter 5.

Bonhoeffer, in contrast, draws explicit attention to the importance of preaching and teaching the word of God to young people. He considers the Bible as one of the loci of spiritual formation as does Nouwen. The above discussion suggests how the Bible can be understood as the central means of grace along with the gospel of Jesus Christ as the foundation for spiritual formation. Spiritual formation is living a life in accordance with Jesus's teaching in the Bible. The Bible not only sets standards for spiritual formation but brings spiritual transformation through the Holy Spirit as believers study Jesus's teaching and apply it to their daily lives. This is not only in personal devotion but also in the corporate life of the church. This brings us to the next point about the relationship between spiritual formation and the faith community.

---

91. Nouwen, *Spiritual Formation*, xxvi.

6) Grounding In the Context of the Faith Community

Calvin also states that Christians can be spiritually formed by the church, as Canlis observes:

> Book IV of the Institutes articulates what it is to be a family, with God as our Father and "the Church as our Mother." Just as union with Christ is anchored in Christ's humanity, so Calvin anchors our spiritual growth in concrete, human things. Far from being an add-on to the spiritual life, the church is the nurturer, the maternal environment where we are brought into fellowship and, therefore, into maturity (IV.1.1).[92]

While the Desert Fathers emphasize the importance of solitude in spiritual formation in the context of ascetic life, Bonhoeffer talks about spiritual formation in the context of community. In *Act and Being* and *Life Together*, Bonhoeffer draws heavily on the idea that Christians can encounter Christ in the church community.

Authors such as Wilhoit, Greenman, Paul Pettit, and Henri Nouwen mention faith community in their definitions of spiritual formation. Among them, Paul Pettit is the main spiritual formation author who speaks about community in spiritual formation. He defines spiritual formation:

> First, spiritual formation is the holistic work of God in a believer's life whereby systematic change renders the individual continually closer to the image and actions of Jesus Christ. And second, the change or transformation that occurs in the believer's life happens best in the context of authentic, Christian community and is oriented as service toward God and others."[93]

He sees spiritual formation as mutual influence: "Christians are to be *in process* and undergoing renovation so that the individual believer is able to influence and interact with *others* in a more Christlike manner. Christians are *in process* for *influence*."[94] He explains that spiritual formation takes place in the context of community because the individual believer is one small part of a greater whole. A believer is in union with Christ and is a part of his body,

---

92. Canlis, "Calvin's Institutes," 24.
93. Pettit, *Foundations of Spiritual Formation*, 19.
94. Pettit, 19. emphasis original.

which includes other members.[95] He emphasizes that spiritual growth cannot take place outside of community. Each member has a unique contribution to the body of Christ. Therefore, serving God and others is an imperative and a natural outcome of a life devoted to Christ.[96]

Greenman shares the same ideas that spiritual formation cannot take place if the believer lives in isolation:

> The wisdom of the church over two millennia is that this sort of transformation of heart, mind and spirit is not something that can be pursued satisfactorily by individuals in isolation. Spiritual formation involves personal spiritual disciplines, such as prayer, confession, fasting and biblical meditation as well as corporate participation in the congregation's shared life of worship, fellowship and teaching.[97]

According to Greenman, spiritual formation involves both personal and corporate spiritual disciplines. He states that Christ's body is the communal context for spiritual formation.[98] Richard Foster also suggests the corporate disciplines: confession, worship, guidance, and celebration.[99] All these spiritual disciplines should be tested and applied in the faith community. Kenneth Boa also does not neglect the notion of community in his approach to spiritual formation: "We come to faith as individuals, but we grow in community. A meaningful context of encouragement, accountability, and worship is essential to spiritual maturity since it involves the others-centered use of spiritual gifts for mutual edification."[100] Wilhoit also describes spiritual formation as an "intentional communal process."[101] This agreement about the importance of the communal aspect of spiritual formation is significant, and it highlights that spiritual formation should not be an individualistic process but should be experienced by the whole church family in order to witness to the need for sanctification of the whole of society.

---

95. Pettit, 272.
96. Pettit, 274.
97. Greenman, *Life in the Spirit*, 26.
98. Greenman, 26–27.
99. Foster, *Celebration of Discipline*, 177–251.
100. Boa, *Conformed to His Image*, 23.
101. Wilhoit, *Spiritual Formation*, 17.

In the context of the faith community, it is important to take note of the role of the sacraments in spiritual formation. Greenman sees the Eucharist as a prominent "means of grace" reinforcing Christian faith:

> The ecclesial practice of prayer and the Lord's Supper (or Eucharist) have a special prominence among the "means of grace" that God has appointed to strengthen our faith. For this reason, my proposed definition asserts that spiritual formation takes place "in the community of faith." Christians belong to one another as members of Christ's body, which becomes the communal context for mutual encouragement, mentoring and accountability in the journey toward Christlikeness.[102]

Wilhoit also emphasizes the formative power of the ministry of God's word and the sacraments because they are forums in which Christians learn to open themselves to God. In them the truth about their lives is proclaimed, including the salvific work that Christ has done on their behalves. The sacrament of communion is thus a central ecclesial practice in which the trust of the believer in the proclamation of forgiveness is invited ever anew.[103] Eric Stoddart points out:

> In the Eucharist we receive the body and blood that relativises all constructions of risk. In Him, we are freed for freedom – but for the freedom to choose to suffer for others, freed to resist injustice and freed into a contingent world in which safety is not promised, but instead into an unsafe peace.
>
> The Eucharist is not where we go to escape from the world, its technologies and its systems of surveillance. It is the moment in which we are offered a particular promise that He is present so that we might come to ourselves. We are dismissed to love and serve the Lord – to be surprised by those other sacramental moments when, within our technologised world, we encounter God's Spirit in the little explosions of liberation that reintegrate what we have rent asunder.[104]

---

102. Greenman, *Life in the Spirit*, 26–27.
103. Wilhoit, *Spiritual Formation*, 99.
104. Stoddart, *Theological Perspectives*, Kindle Locations 3909–3914.

In Stoddart's view, this sacrament makes the church visible and accountable to the world, which is fragmented by digital surveillance technology.

In *Act and Being*, written in 1929–30, Bonhoeffer likewise highlights the importance of the notion that people can experience the revelation of God in the church community through the ministry of God's word and the sacraments.[105] Regardless of youth culture in the digital age, youth remain part of the church community in which they have direct access to the experience of Christ through the preaching of God's word, the sacraments, and acts of love. In pulling together these theological threads of a theology of spiritual formation, Bonhoeffer offers the church a foundation for its working toward Christian community in relation to spiritual formation. He experienced the Christian community, specifically the experience of friendship, as the indispensable locus of spiritual formation.[106]

Christ is the one who establishes the true community that is the church, Bonhoeffer states in thesis 3 of his *Eight Theses on Youth Work*. The church-community is Christ's presence as the true Lord and Brother. Being in the church-community means being in Christ; being in Christ means being in the church-community.[107] Bonhoeffer asserts that the true church community is defined and established by Christ. It includes people saved by Christ. Bonhoeffer elaborates this idea in *Life Together*:

> Christianity means community through Jesus Christ and in Jesus Christ. No Christian community is more or less than this. Whether it be a brief, single encounter or the daily fellowship of years, Christian community is only this. We belong to one another only through and in Jesus Christ.[108]

The faith community is an important locus for spiritual formation. This leads to the question of which practices of corporate spirituality cohere with this account of ecclesial formation. As quoted above, according to Bonhoeffer, believers can experience spiritual transformation through corporate spirituality – preaching, the sacraments, and loving one another.[109]

---

105. Bonhoeffer, *Act and Being*, 115.
106. Dahill, *Reading from the Underside*, 101.
107. Bonhoeffer, *Berlin*, 516.
108. Bonhoeffer, *Life Together*, 11.
109. Bonhoeffer, *Act and Being*, 115.

In claiming that the faith community is an important locus for spiritual formation, Bonhoeffer points forward to theological thinkers to come who also emphasize that Christians can experience the revelation of God in the church community. Wilhoit, Greenman, Paul Pettit, and Henri Nouwen highlight the importance of the faith community in their definitions of spiritual formation. Bonhoeffer goes deeper, stating that the faith community established by Christ is an indispensable locus for spiritual formation. Calvin also locates spiritual formation in the context of the faith community, but he more strongly emphasizes its ontological basis as the believer's union with Christ. This subsection has shown how Bonhoeffer perceives the Bible to be the central means of grace, with the gospel of Jesus Christ being the foundation for the spiritual formation taking place in the context of the faith community.

c. Henri Nouwen

Calvin offers a solid theology of spiritual formation as encounter with Christ, and Bonhoeffer can be seen as developing his account of the Christian community as the locus of spiritual formation. However, neither Calvin nor Bonhoeffer explain how this encounter with Christ happens in the daily life of the believer. This question is answered by Henri Nouwen, who suggests that spiritual formation is encountering Christ through spiritual practices, which center on a practice of solitude that dates back to the Desert Fathers.[110] Solitude is a way that God shapes believers into Christ's image:

> Solitude shows us the way to let our behaviour be shaped not by the compulsions of the world but by our new mind, the mind of Christ. Silence prevents us from being suffocated by our wordy world and teaches us to speak the Word of God. Finally, unceasing prayer gives solitude and silence their real meaning. In unceasing prayer, we descend with the mind into the heart. Thus we enter through our heart into the heart of God, who embraces all of history with his eternally creative and recreative love.[111]

When we are remodeled into Christ's image, we will be his witnesses to the world. Loving our neighbors is the outcome of solitude, silence, and prayer.

---

110. Nouwen, *Way of the Heart*, 27, 31–32.
111. Nouwen, 92.

Nouwen's understanding of solitude presumes that solitude cannot effectively be apart from others in being ineradicably communal. During the last ten years of his life, Nouwen served as a pastor of Daybreak, the L'Arche community where he worked with individuals with intellectual and developmental disabilities.[112] During this time, he accompanied Adam Arnett, a core member at L'Arche Daybreak with profound developmental disabilities.[113] As he describes Adam in his book *Adam: God's Beloved*,

> Adam was my friend, my teacher, and my guide: an unusual friend, because he couldn't express affection and love in the way most people do; an unusual teacher, because he couldn't think reflectively or articulate ideas or concepts; an unusual guide, because he couldn't give me any concrete direction or advice.[114]

Nouwen also closely watched the friendship between Adam and Father Bruno, who spent some time in solitude at L'Arche Daybreak after finishing his eighteen-year term as abbot of the Camaldolese monastery in Big Sur, California:

> As I saw them together I thought, "What better companion could Adam have than this quiet, peaceful monk! Isn't Adam's life similar to his? Peace is speaking to peace. Solitude is greeting solitude. Silence is dwelling with silence. What a grace!"[115]

Father Bruno reflected, "As I spend long hours with Adam, I find myself drawn into an ever deeper solitude. In Adam's heart, I have touched a fullness of divine love."[116] For Nouwen, solitude is not an escape from others but a different modality of being with others in community.

7) Interest in the Sake of Others and the World

Spiritual formation should not be an individualistic process, but it should be experienced by the whole church and family – and then reach out to the whole society. Authors such as Greenman and Pettit mention that spiritual

---

112. Jonas, *Essential Henri Nouwen*, xxxiv.
113. Nouwen, *Adam*, 7–8.
114. Nouwen, 7–8.
115. Nouwen, 33.
116. Nouwen, 33.

formation is not only for the sake of individual Christian's lives but also for the sake of others in the community and the world. Greenman mentions the aspects of evangelism, mission, and social work, which are the outcomes of spiritual formation. Spiritual transformation involves not only loving God but also loving our neighbors as ourselves (Luke 10:27). This includes our participation in Christ's mission to the world, reflecting Christ as "the salt of the earth" and "the light of the world" (Matt 5:13–14). He observes that outward-focused spiritual disciplines such as hospitality and "works of mercy" always accompany inward-focused disciplines: "Spiritual formation at its best involves a reciprocal dynamic between gathering and scattering, contemplation and action, silence and speech, being and doing, receiving and giving."[117] Richard Foster describes the importance of the outward discipline of service: "As the cross is the sign of submission, so the towel is the sign of service."[118] Serving others flows from a heart that prays, "Lord Jesus, as it would please you, bring me someone today whom I can serve."[119] He reminds us to listen to the prompting of the Holy Spirit in order to know whether to say "yes" or "no" to calls of service.[120]

While Bonhoeffer also considers public life in the world as the third locus for spiritual formation,[121] Nouwen states that the works of evangelism, mission, and social work, which are the outcome of spiritual formation, not only bring benefit to the world but also, in turn, enrich Christians' personal lives and the life of the faith community:

> Christian spirituality not only flows from community but creates community. It nurtures the life of the Spirit in us, within us, and among us. The Spirit of God dwells in the center of our heart and is the center of our life together . . . It is therefore not surprising that prayer and community are always found together because the same Spirit who prays in us is the Spirit who binds

---

117. Greenman, *Life in the Spirit*, 27.
118. Foster, *Celebration of Discipline*, 157.
119. Foster, 171.
120. Foster, 173.
121. Dahill, *Reading from the Underside*, 101.

us together into the body as we are called to love each other and work for a renewed world.[122]

Prayer and community are joined since Christians need the empowerment of the Spirit in serving the community. Nouwen asserts that we are called by the Spirit to reach out to the needy. "To serve means to minister, to love and care for others, and to recognize in them the heart of God. A true disciple of Jesus will always go to where people are feeling weak, broken, sick, in pain, poor, lonely, forgotten, anxious, and lost."[123]

He explains the spiritual practices of the Desert Fathers, from whom we can learn about the relationship between inner spiritual practices – such as solitude, silence, and prayer – and the outward practice:

> The purification and transformation that take place in solitude manifest themselves in compassion.[124]
>
> If you ask the Desert Fathers why solitude gives birth to compassion, they would say, "Because it makes us die to our neighbour."[125]
>
> But let us not be too literal about silence. After all, silence of the heart is much more important than silence of the mouth ... Silence is primarily a quality of the heart that leads to ever-growing charity ... Charity, not silence, is the purpose of the spiritual life and ministry. About this all the Desert Fathers are unanimous.[126]

Modern authors on spiritual formation affirm that spiritual formation is not only for the sake of the individual Christian's life but also for the sake of others in the community and the world. Nouwen grounds this claim in the calling of the Spirit to reach out to the needy that the Desert Fathers demonstrated to be the outcome of solitude, silence, and prayer.

---

122. Nouwen, *Spiritual Formation*, xxvii.
123. Nouwen, xxviii.
124. Nouwen, *Way of the Heart*, 34.
125. Nouwen, 34.
126. Nouwen, 64.

8) *Inner Person*

As presented at the outset of this chapter, there has been a rediscovery of the Christian tradition in the evangelical church of the need to care for the spiritual lives of its members, which many church "discipleship programs" have not done well. This involves caring for the inner person of Christians. Most of the authors in this survey, such as Michael Burer, Kenneth Boa, Dallas Willard, Diane J. Chandler, Henri Nouwen, and Richard Foster, mention the inner person in their definition of spiritual formation. Burer explains why he mentions the inner person: "It involves the inner person in that it concerns itself with character, thoughts, intentions, and attitudes more than actions, habits, or behaviors; it has the character of Christ as its goal and standard of measure."[127]

Henri Nouwen uses the language of the heart to name this "inner person": "Spiritual formation requires taking an inward journey to the heart. Although this journey takes place in community and leads to service, the first task is to look within, reflect on our daily life, and seek God and God's activity right there."[128] He uses the language of the heart to name the inner person for biblical reasons.

> The word *heart* is used here in its full biblical meaning of that place where body, soul, and spirit come together as one . . . Our heart determines our personality, and the place where God dwells, but also the place to which the Evil One directs fierce attacks, causing us to doubt, fear, despair, resent, over-consume, and so on. Thus to live the spiritual life and to let God's presence fill us takes constant prayer, and to move from illusions and isolation back to the place in the heart where God continues to form us in the likeness of Christ takes time and attention.[129]

Calvin mentions the work of the gospel in the inner lives of believers. The gospel possesses the whole soul and stay at the inmost affection of the

---

127. Burer, "Towards a Biblical Definition."
128. Nouwen, *Spiritual Formation*, xix.
129. Nouwen, xvii.

heart (III.6.4).[130] The power of the gospel not only penetrates the heart but also transforms it.[131] Calvin explains the nature and value of prayer from the heart:

> As faith springs from the Gospel, so by faith our hearts are framed to call upon the name of God (Rom. 10:14). And this is the very thing which he had expressed some time before – viz. that the Spirit of adoption, which seals the testimony of the Gospel on our hearts, gives us courage to make our requests known unto God, calls forth groanings which cannot be uttered, and enables us to cry, Abba, Father (Rom. 8:26). (III.20.1)

Caring for the inner life is significant in spiritual formation. However, how should believers open their hearts to receive the work of the gospel of Christ? Henri Nouwen suggests five practices to cultivate the heart for God: *reflection* on the living documents of our own hearts and time, *lectio divina*, *silence*, *community*, and *service*.[132] He also highlights the importance of the practice of silence:

> Without silence, the Word of God cannot bear fruit. One of the most depressing aspects of contemporary life is the almost complete absence of silence. I wonder if the Word of God can really be received in the center of our hearts if our constant chatter and noise and electronic interactions keep blocking the way of the heart . . . The mystics all agree that silence is the royal road to spiritual formation. I have never met anyone seriously interested in the spiritual life who did not have a growing desire for silence.[133]

Learning from the spirituality of the desert, Nouwen captures the practice of silence well in his book *The Way of the Heart*. This practice prevents the world from shaping us in its image and cultivates life in the Spirit.[134] Calvin

---

130. Canlis, "Calvin's Institutes," 16.
131. Canlis, 16.
132. Nouwen, *Spiritual Formation*, xxi–xxii.
133. Nouwen, xxv.
134. Nouwen, 15.

affirms that silence flows from our confidence in our status as children of God, which "consists in quieting frightened consciences before God." (III.19.9)[135]

In the digital age, which can form a "dangerous network of domination and manipulation" and bring about many noises and distractions, the practice of silence is so important to us as "the Desert Fathers praise silence as the safest way to God."[136] "First, silence makes us pilgrims. Secondly, silence guards the fire within. Thirdly, silence teaches us to speak . . . Silence is the home of the word. Silence gives strength and fruitfulness to the word."[137] The Desert Fathers remind us to keep the true silence in which an encounter with our loving Father could take place.[138] Solitude leads to silence before God, which is an important step in spiritual formation, but it cannot be complete without prayer.[139]

Nathan Foster shares his experience as he practiced solitude in the midst of ordinary life: "Solitude allowed me to face myself and my emptiness. I learned that boredom can be a wonderful gift and that silence is God's primary language."[140] Silence may be especially important in our contemporary life with its immersion in digital media. Silence can mean submission to God and preparing our heart for God. It can be a medium by which Christ speaks to us, but it is not God's primary language, since God can use other mediums to speak to us through the church, his word, the sacraments, or acts of love.[141] To recap, many authors mention the cultivation of the inner person in their definitions of spiritual formation, but few mention how to cultivate it. Henri Nouwen suggests fives practices to cultivate the inner life for God, and Richard Foster introduces the inward disciplines: meditation, prayer, fasting, and study, and the outward disciplines: simplicity, solitude, submission, and service – which can also, in turn, enrich the inner life.[142] Nathan Foster applies the spiritual disciplines in daily, modern, ordinary life. These ideas are valid and helpful if understood as empowered by the Holy Spirit to

---

135. Canlis, "Calvin's Institutes," 23.
136. Nouwen, *Way of the Heart*, 21, 43.
137. Nouwen, 48–49.
138. Nouwen, 60.
139. Nouwen, 69.
140. Foster, *Making of an Ordinary Saint*, 190.
141. Bonhoeffer, *Act and Being*, 115.
142. Foster, *Celebration of Discipline*, 17–97.

creatively apply these proposals to the particular context of our lives and the lives of the youth who we are ministering to.

9) Conformity to the Image or Character of Christ

Though having different models or views of spiritual formation, all modern authors in this survey mention that spiritual formation is conforming to the image or character of Christ. However, what is the true meaning of being conformed to the image or character of Christ? This segment argues that being conformed to the image or character of Christ means encountering Christ in daily life. This requires solidtude, which means opening ourselves before God in the context of the faith community or in personal daily life.

Among contemporary authors on spiritual formation, Diane J. Chandler proposes a comprehensive definition of being conformed to the image or character of Christ, which is based on the concept of *imago Dei*. Therefore, I will discuss her view in detail in order to elaborate what might be meant by the injunction to be conformed to the image of Christ. Moving beyond the nonphysical and mystical aspects of spiritual formation, Diane J. Chandler mentions the whole-person theology in the definition of being conformed to the image or character of Christ:

> The word spiritual relates to more than simply the nonphysical and mystical components of life . . . Christian spiritual formation is defined as an interactive process by which God the Father fashions believers into the image of his Son, Jesus through the empowerment of the Holy Spirit by fostering development in seven primary life dimensions (spirit, emotions, relationships, intellect, vocation, physical health and resource stewardship).[143]

It is helpful that Chandler emphasizes that spiritual formation is not mystical but is an interactive process. Her approach is very practical, especially for young people, in engaging a person's spirit, emotions, relationships, intellect, vocation, physical health, and resource stewardship.

However, though she claims that her approach is multidimensional and holistic,[144] it begins to seem fragmented as she breaks human lives into seven

---

143. Chandler, *Spiritual Formation*, 18–19.
144. Chandler, 19.

dimensions. Even though she mentions relationship, her model also shows a lack of emphasis on the notion of community in spiritual formation. Another limit of her model is its tacit assumption that spiritual formation is an individualistic process between me and God. Spiritual formation is not just a process in which I receive something from God then I give it to other people. It is about the nurture I receive from the Holy Spirit through participation in Christian community and then, in turn, contribute to the church. Chandler's definition answers the "what," but the "how" to do spiritual formation is not very clear or helpful. In her model, God's love and grace, and *imago Dei* are at the core. This is unified and systematic, but then the "interactive process" is quite blurred. Nor does Chandler clearly specify the role of human action in this process.

In her model, Chandler places the *imago Dei* at the core, next to God's love. Chandler defines spiritual formation as "the process of being restored into the image of God!"[145] She discusses four perspectives on the *imago Dei*: humankind's capacity to think and reason, humankind's capacity for relationship, humankind's dominion over the earth, and humankind's divine goal and destiny.[146] Chandler concludes that she does not hold a single view on this but argues for a multidimensional approach. In practice, her approach seems vague and problematic since her presentation of the theological account of *imago Dei* presents the views of only one particular perspective to the neglect of others. In the section *Theology of Self-Identity* in chapter 4, I will suggest that the term "image of God" cannot be defined by probing deeply into human nature but must be defined by human relationship with God made possible through Christ. It is through this relationship that people reflect Christ's obedience to God and love for his neighbors. It seems over-simplistic as Chandler puts *imago Dei* at the core as the only theological foundation for spiritual formation. Spiritual formation is not just about going back to the "Garden" – God's initial design – but it is about moving toward heaven. Spiritual formation is not just restoration but growing in perfection in Christ, who is the perfect *imago Dei*. Even though she mentions that Christ is the perfect *imago Dei* and that we are moving from *imago Dei* to *imago Christi* and then *gloria Dei*, putting *imago Dei* at the core as the only foundation is

---

145. Chandler, 17.
146. Chandler, 32–38.

quite forced and over-simplified,¹⁴⁷ though Chandler could have explained that *imago Dei* means encountering Christ and being transformed into his image (2 Cor 3:18).

While Chandler defines being conformed to the image of Christ as an interactive process of being restored to *imago Dei*, other authors mention being "conformed to Christ" from different angles. Wilhoit describes the process of being conformed to the image of Christ as taking Christ's easy yoke:

> We must teach the commands of Christ as "a package deal." These are not mere laws to follow; Jesus invites us to take on his easy yoke (Matt. 11:20–30). These commands are two-sided and contain both the command and the means of change. Spiritual disciplines are Jesus-endorsed spiritual practices (e.g., solitude, fasting, and meditation) that foster positive spiritual change and enable us to become the kind of people who genuinely desire to carry out these commands. When we understand the two-sided nature of Jesus's commands, we no longer view them as heavy burdens but see them as an invitation to a more sensible way of living.[148]

However, as we have seen in Calvin's theology, spiritual formation is not just about taking the yoke of Christ but is about taking the identity of Christ.

Kenneth Boa describes spiritual formation as a journey or a pilgrimage to become "conformed to the image of his Son (Roman 8:29)."[149] He proposes the idea of Exchanged Life Spirituality, which means grasping our true identity in Christ. Our old life has been exchanged for the life of Christ in his crucifixion and resurrection (Rom 6; Gal 2:20). This moves from works and legalism to grace and liberty because it centers on the work of Christ.[150] This is a threefold process described in Romans 6: "*knowing* one's identity in Christ (6:3–10), progresses to *reckoning* or considering these truths to be so (6:11), and climaxes with *yielding* or presenting oneself to God (6:12–14)."[151] However, it is important to take note that it is not about head knowledge

---
147. Chandler, 64.
148. Wilhoit, *Spiritual Formation*, 39.
149. Boa, *Conformed to His Image*, 19–20.
150. Boa 101–123.
151. Boa, 114.

but is about heart knowledge. It is not work but grace, "because you are not under law, but under grace." (Rom 6:14) From another angle, Greenman defines self-sacrifice as the expression of being conformed to Christ. Being "conformed to Christ" involves embracing a life of self-sacrifice and humble service for the sake of others demonstrated by Jesus in his earthly ministry (Mark 10:42–45; John 12:12–17; Phil 2:1–11).[152] Nathan Foster defines being "conformed to Christ" as practicing what Jesus did, not by our own effort, but by his power.[153] He also shares his journey of becoming like Jesus through practicing spiritual disciplines such as the disciplines of study, meditation, and simplicity.[154]

Though all the above authors mention being "conformed to Christ" at a certain level, it seems not very clear or holistic. It is also still not in depth and not deeply rooted in theology and tradition. Here, Nouwen helps us in returning to the Desert Fathers. He recounts the story of St. Anthony (born around 251), the "father of monks," which is helpful for us to understand the true meaning of being "conformed to Christ":

> When he [St. Anthony] was about eighteen years old he heard in church the Gospel words, "Go and sell what you own and give the money to the poor . . . then come and follow me" (Matthew 19:21). Anthony realized that these words were meant for him personally. After a period of living as a poor labourer at the edge of his village, he withdrew into the desert, where for twenty years he lived in complete solitude. During these years Anthony experienced a terrible trial. The shell of his superficial securities was cracked and the abyss of iniquity was opened to him. But he came out of this trial victoriously – not because of his own willpower or ascetic exploits, but because of his unconditional surrender to the Lordship of Jesus Christ. When he emerged from his solitude, people recognized in him the qualities of an authentic "healthy" man, whole in body, mind, and soul. They flocked to him for healing, comfort, and direction.[155]

---

152. Greenman, *Life in the Spirit*, 26.
153. Foster, *Making of an Ordinary Saint*, 16.
154. Foster, 111, 190.
155. Nouwen, *Way of the Heart*, 19–20.

The story of St. Anthony shows that "we must be made aware of the call to let our false, compulsive self to be transformed into the new self of Jesus Christ."[156] Being conformed to Christ is "unconditional surrender to the Lordship of Jesus Christ."[157] To recap, from the discussion of Calvin and Bonhoeffer's theology and Nouwen's exploration of the Desert Fathers' spirituality, we can reach the conclusion that spiritual formation is encountering Christ in the context of community and daily life. This is the work of the Holy Spirit to engraft us into the mystical union with Christ. This process requires solitude in which we can open our lives to God and listen to his voice. This brings us to the next section discussing the practice of solitude.

3. The Practice of Solitude

Solitude is an important locus for spiritual formation. Nouwen explains the outcome of the practice of solitude that goes back as far as the Desert Fathers: "In solitude I get rid of my scaffolding: no friends to talk with, no telephone calls to make, no meetings to attend, no music to entertain, no books to distract, just me – naked, vulnerable, weak, sinful, deprived, broken – nothing."[158] Solitude is very necessary for youth, who are constantly captivated by social media, which hinder them from cultivating a healthy self-identity. Nouwen adds:

> Solitude is thus the place of purification and transformation, the place of the great struggle and the great encounter. Solitude is not simply a means to an end. Solitude is its own. It is the place where Christ remodels us in his own image and frees us from the victimizing compulsions of the world.[159]

In solitude, we open ourselves for Christ, who conforms us into his image and frees us from all the captivations and addictions of the digital culture.

The story of St. Anthony discussed in the previous section shows not only what being conformed to Christ is but how to do it. This starts with the spiritual practice of solitude: "Without solitude we remain victims of our society

---

156. Nouwen, 20.
157. Nouwen, 20.
158. Nouwen, 27.
159. Nouwen, 31–32.

and continue to be entangled in the illusions of the false self."[160] St. Anthony is very helpful in reminding us of the practice of solitude, especially in the midst of our busy lives surrounded by all the modern technologies. However, the question to ask is how to practice solitude. Do we need to withdraw to the desert? Does solitude fit into the context of spiritual formation in the faith community? Based on the practice of solitude from the Desert Fathers, Nouwen elaborates the meaning of solitude: "Solitude is not a private therapeutic place. Rather, it is the place of conversion, the place where the old self dies and the new self is born, the place where the emergence of the new man and the new woman occurs."[161] Therefore, solitude does not depend on physical location. Solitude means encountering Christ wherever we are. It means surrendering to the lordship of Christ. It can happen in the context of the faith community or in our personal daily lives. It is interesting to see how the story of St. Anthony influences people's lives.

The story Augustine also demonstrates that solitude does not depend on physical location. Augustine converted to Christianity after listening to the story of Ponticianus's and his friends' first reading of the life of St. Anthony. This story inspired Augustine to listen to the voice of God telling him to put away his old life of sin and live a life of holiness, which led to his conversion: "Not in rioting and drunkenness, not in chambering and impurities, not in contention and envy, but put ye on the Lord Jesus Christ and make not provision for the flesh in its concupiscences." (Rom 13:13–14) Even though Augustine was inspired by the ascetic life of St. Anthony, Augustine's conversion did not happen in the context of ascetic life. His friends told him their story of reading St. Anthony's life, then he was prompted by a childlike voice telling him to "take up and read," then he opened the Bible and read Romans 13:13–14.[162] After his conversion, Augustine did not go to the desert like St. Anthony, but he lived a life of holiness and served the church. From the story of Augustine, we see that his conversion and his spiritual formation take place in the contexts of both community and personal daily life. For Augustine, his spiritual formation starts with solitude, which means listening to God's voice and surrendering to God as we can observe from his *Confessions*.

---

160. Nouwen, 25.
161. Nouwen, 27.
162. Augustine, *Confessions*, 411–415.

As discussed above, spiritual formation means encountering Christ. From the story of the Desert Fathers and Augustine, this starts with solitude, which means listening to God's voice and obeying. The Desert Fathers practice solitude in the context of ascetic life, while Bonhoeffer talks about spiritual formation in the context of the community. He asserts that a Christian can encounter Christ in the church community. Solitude means opening ourselves before God and listening to God's voice. This can happen either in the context of the faith community or in personal daily life. In today's society, where youth are surrounded by digital media, we need to teach them what it means to practice solitude in the faith community and personal daily life either online or off-line.

In conclusion to this chapter, this discussion was presented in themes on spiritual formation raised by modern authors. Therefore, it is also helpful to have a summary of what the modern authors say about spiritual formation. Some authors in the survey mention the aspects of intentionality, grace, and accordance to biblical standards in their definitions of spiritual formation. A few more authors mention the aspect of the faith community and that spiritual formation is for the sake of others and the world. Most authors mention the inner person, the Holy Spirit, and the process of transformation, and all authors in the survey mention that spiritual formation is conforming to Christ's image. Even though presented in separated segments, all these themes related to spiritual formation are somehow overlapped and closely linked to one another. Most of the definitions of spiritual formation describe the "what," "who," "why," and "where" of spiritual formation but give little answer to "how" to do spiritual formation. Richard Foster and Henri Nouwen stand as exceptions in suggesting the spiritual disciplines – as well as Nathan Foster, who seeks to apply these spiritual disciplines in modern ordinary daily life. Though these modern writings seem weak in theology, the study of Calvin, Bonhoeffer, and Nouwen on spiritual formation has suggested a more solid theological backup for these modern practices of spiritual formation.

Calvin conceives a strong theology of spiritual formation as encounter with Christ and conformity to Christ. Bonhoeffer reminds us of the significant role of the Bible as the central means of grace in spiritual formation. According to Bonhoeffer, the gospel of Jesus Christ is the foundation for the spiritual formation that takes place in the context of the faith community. Nouwen helps us understand that spiritual formation is not about tasks but is about encountering Christ through spiritual practices, among which the practice of solidude is given priority. From the discussion with Calvin and Bonhoeffer's theologies and Nouwen's exploration of the Desert Fathers' spirituality, we can reach the conclusion that spiritual formation is encountering Christ in the context of community and personal daily life. This is the work done by the Holy Spirit, who engrafts us into the mystical union with Christ. This process starts with solitude, which means opening our lives to God and listening to his voice. In the next chapters, I will continue to explore what this means among the youth of Gens Y and Z.

CHAPTER 4

The Theologies Needed for Youth Discipleship Given by Dietrich Bonhoeffer

This chapter analyzes the impacts of digital media on discipleship and begins to construct a theology of discipleship for youth in the Christian community that takes this analysis into account. The majority of this chapter will discuss the theologies of Dietrich Bonhoeffer on self-identity, discipleship, community, and youth, which are significant in constructing a theology of discipling youth. Today's youth are surrounded by digital media, which has become embedded in their everyday lives, and compared to which traditional sermons are dull and arid. The aggressive speed of digital media makes the pace and content of the teachings seemingly outdated. As a result, they find the teachings in church irrelevant to their lives. The arrival of the digital age has profound implications for culture, self-identity, and the gospel. To respond well demands that Christians and theologians listen to and understand the world's viewpoints, beliefs, and needs in order to faithfully contextualize the message, present the Scripture in the language of youth, and finally, bridge the generational gaps caused by the digital culture. The starting point of this chapter is the traditional Christian affirmation that the content of the Christian gospel remains unchanged as do the life-changing experiences both here on earth and in the life thereafter that it describes. By implication, discipleship, as the process of leading people into this Christian gospel, entails a following of Jesus in both the physical as well as the virtual world.

The church is entrusted with the task of nurturing the growth of faith in youth. If it evades this task, youth can slip into nominal or stagnant faith regardless of the numbers of Bible studies, cell group meetings, fellowships, and retreats provided. A disconnection between God and the daily lives of youth thus becomes a barrier as they find themselves unable to integrate the doctrine that they hear with the lives they are living. Over time, this dries up their spiritual lives. Thus, it is important to help them recognize not just what being a Christian means but how they might live it out in the digital world that is their native environment. Christians are called to love because God first loved us. Christians are called to be morally pure because God is morally pure. Christians are to be concerned for justice because God is concerned for justice. Christians are to be merciful because God is merciful.[1] Discipleship and mission being closely connected, it is important for the water of the Holy Spirit to flow through youth to those around them, thereby bringing Christ's touch to others. There is "no holiness but social holiness," John Wesley insists.[2] The relationship between discipleship and mission, i.e. between Christians and the community at large, is vital. Thus, the church, rather than merely training youth, may benefit from creating opportunities for youth to serve the society in creative and context-appropriate ways. Additionally, it is necessary for the church to raise awareness for mission among youth who are not familiar with mission and kindle the passion for it among those who are. By doing this, they can help youth to develop their own theology based on their own reflection within the community of faith, seeking to understand and respond to what it means to be accepted, sent, and called by God into the world, which is influenced and probably fragmented by digital technology.[3]

The literature review on the impacts of digital media in chapter 1 and the deeper discussion of digital media impacts on society in general and on youth in particular in chapter 2 have provided a description of the social context in which theologians take up the task of formulating a theology for youth discipleship. Digital culture has a profound influence on the formation of personal identity among the youth of Gens Y and Z. The literature review of Christian responses in chapter 1 has highlighted the need to discuss the

---

1. Botton, King, and Venugopal, "Educating for Spirituality," 45.
2. Wesley, *Works of John Wesley*, 321.
3. Seymour and Miller, "Openings to God," 24.

theology required for youth discipleship in the digital age. Chapter 3 has concluded that spiritual formation is encountering Christ in the context of community and personal daily life. This is the work of the Holy Spirit, who engrafts us into the mystical union with Christ. This process requires solitude, which means opening our lives to God and listening to his voice. The question remains: What does it mean for youth to follow Christ today? In answering this question, this chapter will propose the theologies needed for youth discipleship. It will analyze the impacts of digital media on discipleship and construct a subsequent theology of discipleship of youth in the Christian community. It will focus on the convergence between the topics of digital media and discipleship and then the convergence between the topics of discipleship and youth.

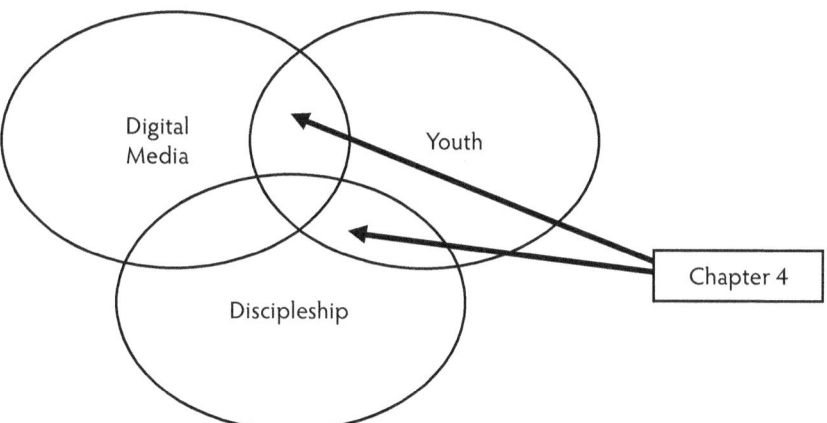

Figure 4.1. The convergence of digital media, youth, and discipleship

After discussing the impacts of digital media on the gospel, this chapter will discuss a theology of self-identity and the theology of discipleship, community, and youth. The main point presented here is that the arrival of the digital age has profound implications for culture, self-identity, and the gospel. There is a need for listening to and understanding the world's viewpoints, beliefs, and needs; contextualizing the message; representing the Scripture in the language of youth; and finally, bridging the generational gaps arising in digital culture. To disciple youth in the digital age, the church should be prepared to build a theology of self-identity that enables this generation to respond adequately to the negative impacts of digital media and to come to know Christ as their personal Savior. The theology of discipleship is the key guide for discipling the youth of this age. This will then lead to a theology of community, which defines the context for discipling youth. Last but not least, a theology of youth is helpful in appropriating the place of youth in Christian community.

1. Digital Media and the Gospel

In *Letters and Papers from Prison*, Bonhoeffer asks the question of what Christianity – or who Jesus Christ – actually is for us today.[4] His question is still relevant for us in this digital age.[5] The coming of the digital age brings profound changes to the culture – people's self-identities into which the gospel must speak. It changes both the way we think and act as well as how we look at ourselves, others, and the world.[6] Digital communication technologies have changed our relationships with information and other people from static structures to dynamic connections.[7] They create new forms of social connection and information sharing, and they promote individual choice and freedom.[8] The media, with its words, sounds, and visual images engulfing our lives, informs us of the way life is. Morality is redefined in accordance with the rules demanded by digital media: efficiency is the highest good; technology defines society; the fittest survive; humans are basically good; happiness consists of limitless material acquisition; happiness is the chief end of life. It turns the gift of sexuality into a commodity, the value of self-respect into pride, etc.[9]

How, then, should Christians interpret the gospel in this digital age? In the classic book *Christ and Culture*, H. Richard Niebuhr proposes five categories of the ways that Christians have historically understood culture in relation to Christianity: Christ Against Culture, Christ of Culture, Christ Above Culture,

---

4. Bonhoeffer, *Letters and Papers*, 362.

5. Much of this section has also appeared in: Vo, "What is Good about Digital Technology," 223–227.

6. Fortner, "Gospel in a Digital Age," 7.

7. Campbell, *Networked Theology*, 3.

8. Campbell, 9.

9. Fore, *Mythmakers*, 52–55.

Christ and Culture in Paradox, and Christ the Transformer of Culture.[10] The book is outdated now, to an extent, but still provides a useful lens through which to consider cultural issues as it places Christ in different positions in relation to culture. Exploring the ways that Christians view digital culture in relation to Christianity, William F. Fore suggests that there are three dominant responses among contemporary Christians: understanding media, using media, and reforming media. On the basis of the Christian commitment to helping set humans free from every kind of bondage, Fore opts for the reform position: Christians need to reform the media by impregnating it with gospel values.[11] Christianity offers a distinctive worldview and vision of who human beings are, what we should do, and what we value. Christians are called to learn how to live in the present world and yet not be of it, to discern both the signs of the times and the signs of God's reign. Therefore, we need to analyze digital culture in order to better communicate the gospel in this day and age.

According to Shane A. Hipps, who also aligns with the "reform" option, in the digital age, there is a shift from a modern, individualistic, and highly rational concept of the gospel to a postmodern, communal, holistic, and experiential one. The gospel message is no longer "an abstract, fixed idea but rather an unfolding, incarnational drama in which God is working to bring the world back into a reconciled relationship with Himself."[12] Hipps observes,

> Like it or not, our theology and interpretation of Scripture have a long history of mirroring our forms of media, a fact most easily seen in the way modern approaches to faith mirror the linear, rational, and abstract attributes of the printed word . . . I believe some of our methods, and thus our message *should* change and evolve – this is part of God's ongoing creation and relationship to God's people.[13]

Every time and place/culture provides a different hermeneutical lens through which Christians read the Bible and view life. Therefore, the youth of this generation are reading Scripture through the new interpretive lens created by digital media.

---

10. Niebuhr, *Christ and Culture*.
11. Fore, *Mythmakers*, 122–123.
12. Hipps, *Hidden Power*, 88–89.
13. Hipps, 88.

Hipps proposes that Jesus saw the close relationship between the medium and the message long before Marshal McLuhan said that "the medium is the message."[14] He quotes Matthew 9:16–17, where Jesus said that new wine has to be put into fresh wineskins. And the most important thing is that Jesus is the new wine.[15] We should share the good news about him with this generation with the fresh wineskins that they can understand. The gospel's essence and value are unchanging, and Jesus remains the only way through which we can get to heaven, but Hipps warns of the dangers of boasting about our knowledge of the gospel and refusing to make the effort to deliver the gospel message in a way that is relevant to youth. "When we claim the gospel message is unchanging, we risk boasting of a kind of omniscience in which we presume to know the totality of God's inexhaustible mysteries."[16] Scripture stories tell us about the continuing work of the Holy Spirit in revealing God to his people in ways that were relevant to them in a particular context in history. This suggests that our generation is bound to rediscover anew God's voice in the context of the digital age. The faithful Christian posture should be one of humbleness and faithfulness in rediscovering the mystery and wonder of God's grace for this, which means trying new ways and repenting when failures arise.[17]

Heidi A. Campbell and Stephen Garner also align with this "reform" option. They observe that digital technologies prompt Christians to experiment with new forms of worship and discipleship. Many churches see the internet as an essential tool for ministry.[18] They see the need for contextualizing the gospel in the digital age. "We must learn to express our understanding of the Christian faith in a language that is intelligible and credible in that contemporary context."[19] They suggest that Christians should seek "to love God and love neighbor with all hearts, minds and bodies in a way that helps us to live well in media culture and also to shape that culture for the sake of the

---

14. McLuhan, *Understanding Media*. McLuhan asserts that the form of a message, such as print, visual, musical, and electronic, determines the ways in which that message will be perceived.

15. McLuhan, 89.

16. McLuhan, 90.

17. McLuhan, 91.

18. Campbell and Garner, *Networked Theology*, 1–2.

19. Campbell and Garner, 11.

gospel of Christ"[20] However, they did not explain further how to do this. Jim McDonnell points out that there is a need to promote the values of the gospel, which respects and celebrates humanity: identifying those elements in the media that are points of contact with gospel values and teaching true personhood and wholeness of spirit to a generation living in fragmented societies rendered incoherent by the forces at work in digital media.[21] It is important for the gospel of wholeness or "oneness" to make connection with the heart and soul in an age when people are trying to project "multiple selves" in cyberspace.[22] More than ever, youth need to be part of a community where people are welcomed into redemptive relationship and can engage one another with the hope of the gospel. The main alternative will today always be the virtual community with all its dangers of disembodied interaction and emotional promiscuity.[23] This is not, however, a dismissal of the potential that may exist for employing virtual relationships as a means of spiritual formation to help people renew their faith or strengthen their relationship with God and live out his word in everyday life.[24]

The main narrative of the Bible provides a basis to construct the digital theology needed to provide practical guidelines for discipleship to the youth of this digital age.

> *The creation story:* The Old Testament begins with an affirmation of the goodness of God's creation. Genesis affirms the fundamental value of each human life (*imago Dei*). It demands that we are good stewards of creation, rather than its exploiters. This view of creation stands in sharp contrast to our cultures' frequent affirmation of consumption.
>
> *The Fall:* Evil can come into the world through the self-centeredness of individuals. We need to be careful not to let the media fragment our community.

---

20. Campbell and Garner, 15.
21. McDonnell, "Mass Media," 159–181.
22. McDonnell, 159–181.
23. McDonnell, 103–118.
24. Meadows, "Mission and Discipleship," 173.

> *Salvation:* Jesus came to save us. He taught us the values of the kingdom of heaven, which is very different from the value promoted by media such as wealth and possession, self-centeredness, etc.[25]

The "end times" are also an important part of this narrative since Christians should hold on to the eschatological hope that sustains the faithful. We are called to proclaim the gospel in our time. The gospel always comes wrapped in a cultural context. During the past two millennia, the church has been interpreting it in different cultural settings throughout the world.[26]

In summary, the impacts digital media has on discipleship are apparently insurmountable. Since the arrival of the digital age brings about profound implications for culture, self-identity, and the gospel, there is a need to communicate the gospel in a way that youth can comprehend and appreciate. It is important to help youth answer the question, "What does it mean to follow Christ today?" Even if the content and value of the gospel remain unchanged, its fruit is the life-changing experience here on earth and the promised eternal life. Youth need to be supported and guided toward this eternal life in their daily lives, in both the physical and the virtual world. This is the core task of Christian discipleship. To disciple youth in the digital age, the church should be prepared to build a theology of self-identity that enables this generation to respond adequately to the negative impacts of digital media and to come to know Christ as their personal savior. This leads us to the next section.

2. Theology of Self-Identity

Chapter 2 surveyed the consensus of recent social studies that the arrival of the digital age has profoundly reshaped contemporary youths' processes of developing a stable and healthy self-identity. The concept of *imago Dei* mentioned in the segment *Conformed to the Image or Character of Christ* in chapter 3 will also be discussed deeper here. This section presents a theology of self-identity, which will serve as a foundation for discipling youth in the digital age. As discussed previously, Buckingham observes that there is

---

25. Fore, *Mythmakers*, 56–59.
26. Fore, 16–17.

a tension between biographical identity and social identity.[27] This project takes Buckingham's review of the development theory and social theory as a guide and views that there is an inner identity but that it is also shaped by the cultural and social environment. The participation of youth in online relationships has profound effects on the processes by which their "inner" identity is formed. At this juncture, it is important to define personal identity and cultural identity from a theological viewpoint.

In the poem *Who Am I?* written in prison, Bonhoeffer expresses the tension between personal identity and cultural identity and resolves it from a theological viewpoint:

> . . . Who am I? This or the other?
> Am I one person today and tomorrow another?
> Am I both at once? A hypocrite before others,
> and before myself a contemptible woebegone weakling?
> Or is something within me still like a beaten army,
> Fleeing in disorder from victory already achieved?
>
> Who am I? They mock me, these lonely questions of mine.
> Whoever I am, thou knowest, O God, I am thine.[28]

In Michael Northcott's interpretation of this poem, Bonhoeffer acknowledges the outward face of dignity that he shows to the public world and at the same time laments the inward sense of isolation and weakness. In the same way as it is for the Davidic Psalmist (Pss 40; 139), this tension is resolved in the acknowledgment of God's knowledge of him, which is superior to his own knowledge of his inner self or of the social identity that others claim from him.[29] In light of *Sanctorum Communio*, as Northcott observes, Bonhoeffer set himself to repair Hegel's account of the self and in particular Hegel's overidentification of the individual with society, which submerses the individual in the mass society. This overidentification of the individual is shown in totalitarian societies, including Germany under the Third Reich, and more recently in modern consumer societies. Northcott elaborates,

---

27. Buckingham, 2.
28. Northcott, "'Who Am I?'" 13.
29. Northcott, 16.

> For Bonhoeffer, the reconciled self is located within the social world of the Church, and not of society as a whole, thus repairing the Hegelian error. It is in the form of the restored image of God, latent in the dignity of the human person, that the individual in the world becomes a responsible agent. And it is precisely the substantive nature of the restored self in Bonhoeffer that provides the continuity between the Church and those other creation mandates – work, family, state – where the grace of God is also at work.[30]

Bonhoeffer sets the personal self in the "Spirit-sanctified community" in which the true identity is reconciled and restored in Christ. In this community, "the moral encounter with other selves becomes redemptive rather than alienating."[31] Bonhoeffer is helpful in setting the personal self in the context of the faith community, where it is redeemed by Christ and restored into relationship with God and others. However, it is necessary to expound what this personal self is.

Peter Sedgwick suggests the factors that must be accounted for in any theological engagement with the ideas of personal identity, cultural identity, and personhood:

> The concept of personality, or personhood as it is sometimes called, has been much studied in contemporary theology. There is, however, a great deal of complexity in this area. My concern here is the grey area that occurs as we move from the theological account of personhood to giving an account of the cultural significance of "being a person" . . . It is the relationship of personal identity, cultural identity and personhood which concerns me. Personal identity is who we are here and now. Character is the same concept expressed as values and beliefs, or personal traits, over time, so it describes the enduring qualities of a person. Cultural identity is what contextualizes that. Personhood is the

---

30. Northcott, 18.
31. Northcott, 19.

basic substratum of a person's being, which can be described in secular or theological terms.[32]

Sedgwick observes that there is a defense of the unity between body and soul in a theological account of personhood. Body and soul are not two distinct forms. The soul is not the determining principle of body or the essential form of the body. The soul is described in Genesis 2:7 as the *nephesh haya* or the living soul. This rejects the dualism of body and soul. Described as *nephesh haya,* a human being is "oriented to meeting the desires which her body presents to herself."[33] To satisfy this desire, she needs to live in harmony with the spirit of God, which brings a person to life. Therefore, the person or "self" is relational. It is shaped by the patterns of communication and response in which human beings are engaged. At the heart of this is the divine, trinitarian communication.[34]

Sedgwick observes that in recent years, several theologians have proposed personhood grounded in *perichoresis*.[35] Therefore, relationships define personhood rather than substance being the ontologically prior category.[36] Furthermore,

> It is not as though one could be a complete person and then enter into a relationship. Since persons are embodied, their relationships to others are as important as one's relationship to oneself. Nevertheless, one must be careful here. Persons are defined by relationships but are not to be defined as relationships . . . The Christian account of a person is that she is a communicative agent in a covenantal relationship, called by a being named in the Judeo-Christian tradition as God. We are drawn by this being into a vocation to live out our lives as creatures who desire the truth of God's creation, and as we respond to this call so we fashion ourselves in the image of God. In this life we take responsibility by communications with others.[37]

---

32. Peter Sedgwick, "Who Am I Now?" 196.
33. Sedgwick, 198.
34. Sedgwick, 198.
35. Sedgwick, 197.
36. Sedgwick, 199.
37. Sedgwick, 199.

It is undeniable that the doctrine of the image of God is one of the basic principles of Christian morality and the concept of personhood and identity. There are, however, a range of ways in which theologians have understood the biblical, image-of-God language.

Paul Ramsey summarizes that there are two types of theory regarding the image of God. The first rests on an analogy with sculpture or painting. There is something within the makeup of man himself that may be said to be modeled in the image of God. The second draws an analogy with a mirror and its reflection. Nothing within the makeup of man has the form of being in the image of God. The image of God is understood as man obediently reflects God's will in his life and actions.[38] These two options bear further scrutiny.

a. Type 1: Sculpture or Painting

The first account of the image of God, as Ramsey observes, assumes that human beings have some faculty or capacity that distinguishes them from animals. This theory may be criticized for its proneness to blur the distinction between man and God. Aristotle's definition of "man as a rational animal" may be cited as the outstanding example of this view. Christians who follow Aristotle's view say that the *imago Dei* in man is his reason, which sets him apart from the rest of "living nature."[39] This is problematic since some humans may not have rational capacity due to sickness or impairment – for example, a person with dementia or mental sickness. Immanuel Kant proposed the ethics of equal regard, which played a large role in the modern era's loss of the biblical grammar of the term. This leads to the contemporary usage of the term in modern political anthropology: "We should respect all people because they bear God's image." However, this is just a fiction since it is only a modification of the biblical account of the *imago Dei*, which has to be rooted in faith in God.[40]

b. Type 2: Mirror

As observed by Ramsey, this theory was well shared by influential Christian theologians such as St. Augustine, Soren Kierkegaard, and Karl Barth. Behind

---

38. Ramsey, *Basic Christian Ethics*, 249–250.
39. Ramsey, 250–251.
40. Ramsey, 251–252.

them all lies the theology of St. Paul.[41] Ramsey provides a useful summary of this tradition in Christian thinking about the image of God as it applies to Christian ethical thinking. Augustine's Neoplatonic leanings led him to conceive of the soul as a substance. For him, being in the image of God requires not only unique intellectual powers but the spirit of obedience to God.[42] According to Kierkegaard, the image of God does not exist in man; man only exists in the image of God whenever he consents "to be nothing through the act of worship."[43] Karl Barth interprets the *imago Dei* as a person's appointed position vis-à-vis God and their response to God.[44] St. Paul makes it clear that Jesus Christ "is the image of the invisible God." (Col. 1:15) Ramsey concludes that the term *image of God* cannot be defined by probing deeply into the nature of man but that it is defined by human relationship with God made possible through Christ. It is through this relationship that humans reflect Christ's obedience to God and love for their neighbors.[45]

Ramsey's observation on the two types of theory regarding the image of God is helpful, and his conclusion is reasonable. It is clear that the "mirror" type has more truth than the "sculpture" type. However, "mirroring" or reflection cannot fully describe the relationship between humans, created in God's image, and God, the Creator. At this juncture, Bonhoeffer and Ian McFarland can shed more light on the discussion. Bonhoeffer's aim is to interpret the *imago Dei* in a manner that preserves the freedom of the human being to conform or not, which becomes impossible in accounts of the *imago* that understand it as a permanent attribute of human beings created in the image of God:

> To say that in humankind God creates God's own image on earth means that humankind is like the Creator in that it is free. To be sure, it is free only through God's creation, through the word of God; it is free for the worship of the Creator. For in the language of the Bible freedom is not something that people have for themselves but something they have for others. No one is free

---

41. Ramsey, 255.
42. Ramsey, 256–257.
43. Ramsey, 257–258.
44. Ramsey, 258.
45. Ramsey, 258–259.

> 'in herself' or 'in himself' ['an sich'] – free as it were in a vacuum or free in the same way that a person may be musical, intelligent, or blind in herself or in himself. Freedom is not a quality a human being has; it is not an ability, a capacity, an attribute of being that may be deeply hidden in a person but can somehow be uncovered. Anyone who scrutinizes human beings in order to find freedom finds nothing of it. Why? Because freedom is not a quality that can be uncovered; it is not a possession, something to hand, an object; nor is it a form of something to hand; instead it is a relation and nothing else. To be more precise, freedom is a relation between two persons. Being free means 'being-free-for-the-other', because I am bound to the other. Only by being in relation with the other am I free.[46]

Bonhoeffer asserts that humans can image God only when they receive true freedom "through the incarnation and the cross, through the sacraments and through the neighbour."[47]

Ian McFarland clarifies the biblical basis of Bonhoeffer's position. He observes that there is a lack of *imago* references in the Old Testament but that it is used most regularly in the New Testament in reference to Christ.[48] Jesus Christ is the image of God, while all humans are only "in" the image of God and bear it eschatologically. God's image is first to be identified with Jesus Christ.[49] McFarland concludes, "Christology governs anthropology."[50] The problem is how to position ourselves to discern this image in people.[51] McFarland suggests discerning the *imago Dei* in the poor, the disabled, and the canonized saint as an important resource for imagining the body of Christ because these people are good examples of dependence on Christ.[52] He also recognizes personal means such as chastity and, in particular, its manifestation in marriage as important loci for discerning the image of God encountered in

---

46. Bonhoeffer, *Creation and Fall*, 62–63.
47. Bonhoeffer, 71.
48. McFarland, *Divine Image*, 1–4.
49. McFarland, 6.
50. McFarland, 9.
51. McFarland, 60–64.
52. McFarland, 81.

our daily lives.[53] Finally, he points to the sacraments as principles for discerning the *imago Dei*, especially the Eucharist, because at it the body of Christ is simultaneously present with the church as a whole.[54]

In short, nothing within the makeup of humans has the form of being in the image of God. The *imago Dei* is present in humans to the degree that we are members in the body of Christ. This view of *imago Dei* contributes to the discussion of personhood. As discussed so far, personhood is defined not by ontological substance but by relationship with the Trinitarian God and his creatures. However, human beings are living in a society that demands certain kinds of personal identity and social identity. Theological traditions have also reinforced some patterns of gender identity and social roles. Sedgwick observes that there are two accounts of identity given in the theological literature:

> One is that personal identity is the self-sameness of being, where a person has a set of properties such as cognition, emotions and memory. The person lives through time with these attributes . . . A second way of speaking of self-identity is rather by way of one's constancy in relationships. All action presupposes the identity of those who act – the longer the period of action, the more constant the identity must be if the goal is to be reached. Nevertheless, this is a symbiotic relationship in which identity is formed through action during the entire life history.[55]

Sedgwick explains the reason behind this. The first account comes from an Arminian and Platonist account of the self as a being with feelings and sensibilities, while the second originates in the Calvinist account of self as the elect being who responds to the will of God in daily life.[56]

Sedgwick observes that in recent years, there is a focus on the first account, prompted by consumerism, which emphasizes the uniqueness of personal identity, and perceives that the self has innate powers for self-expression. It is fueled by a desire to experience, in reality, the pleasures created in the imagination. However, this self-imagery often becomes narcissistic, visual,

---

53. McFarland, 106–107, 118–121.
54. McFarland, 128–130.
55. Sedgwick, "Who Am I Now?" 200.
56. Sedgwick, 200.

and determinative of our reality.[57] In our age, digital media also boost the effect of consumerism, especially among young people. In the search for identity, as Sedgwick conceives it, the consumerism orchestrating our desires may gratify us temporarily, but it cannot give us any real sense of identity.[58] There is a need to redeem our lost "souls" by practicing spiritual disciplines such as worship and charity in order to let go of our possessed image of the self and strive instead to attain God's imagery for our lives.[59]

The theological account of relational personhood rooted in the Trinitarian God sets solid foundations for theological understanding of self-identity. Identity is described not by some substances that we possess but by a worshipping relationship with the Trinitarian God who also initiates us into communication and relationship with other people and his creation. It is worth pausing to reflect here: How can the theology of identity be applied to the youth of this digital age? As chapter 2 highlighted, digital media is having a significant influence on the socio-emotional development of youth. It can give youth opportunities for connecting with peers, improving self-esteem, practicing self-presentation, and exploring identity. It can also lead to a lack of self-control and the collapse of traditional communities. Developmental theories show the significance of the adolescent period in forming an inner identity, which is now strongly affected by the "Network Society" as suggested by social theories. Social media can enhance peer communications, which is crucial for youth identity formation, but it can also enslave youth in the "hive" and take away the solitude and resources needed for them to cultivate their inner identity. The theological account shows that this inner identity is defined in a worshipping relationship with God. The question to ask is, "how do we help youth build an intimate relationship with the relational God in this digital age?"

In the book *Faith for Exiles* (discussed in chapter 1), David Kinnaman, Mark Matlock, and Aly Hawkins describe the human search for identity.

> Human beings are unique among creation in part because we undergo a constant search for identity. We all want to know, Who am I, really? It is one of humanity's timeless questions; the

---

57. Sedgwick, 201.
58. Sedgwick, 201.
59. Sedgwick, 201–202.

search for answers has driven men and women from the very beginning. It is also an ageless question; that is, we return to the search on and off throughout our lives.[60]

The authors suggest that in order to form a resilient identity in the "digital Babylon," we need to practice experiencing intimacy with Jesus. They observe that not many who call themselves Christian can find deep joy in Jesus. This means that we need to clear religious clutter in order to experience closeness with and joy in Christ. This, the authors suggest, is a crucial part of any successful human search for identity.[61]

Digital technologies and media are now playing increasingly significant roles in this search for identity among youth. Digital technology and media provide youth with many identity-forming tools, communities, and adventures. Digital algorithms keep presenting youth with information, media, and social networks for them to join, consume, and identify themselves with. Facebook and YouTube suggest new feeds and video clips that youth will find interesting based on their past behavior. Artificial intelligence is used to secretly gather user information and behavior for marketers to sell their products, which in turn influence youths' identity because they consume and identify themselves with these products. Though promising to connect people, social networking sites constantly force youth to present a self-selected, carefully filtered, curated version of themselves to friends and followers on Facebook, Twitter, and Instagram. Every day, the message of social media tells youth to define their personal brand name just like all the marketers advertising their brand names.[62]

Today, social media not only force youth to define who they are but also suggest what will count as a correct answer to the question of who they are.[63] For example, Facebook profiles allow users to define their flexible gender identity. Kinnaman, Matlock, and Hawkins used the study of Gen Z conducted by Barna to find that today's teenagers are much more open to the idea that gender is determined by how one feels – not by his or her birth sex.[64]

---

60. Kinnaman, Matlock, and Hawkins, *Faith for Exiles*, Kindle locations 482–484.
61. Kinnaman, Matlock, and Hawkins, Kindle locations 423–425.
62. Kinnaman, Matlock, and Hawkins, Kindle locations 492–530.
63. Kinnaman, Matlock, and Hawkins, Kindle locations 492–530.
64. Kinnaman, Matlock, and Hawkins, Kindle locations 531–535.

Though these authors do draw clearly the link between this gender openness and social media, it is reasonable to say that the interface setup, algorithms, and contents of social media play a significant part in this.

The authors observe the response of the church to this phenomenon:

> The church has responded to the identity pressures of our culture by offering young people a Jesus "brand experience" rather than facilitating a transformational experience to find their identity in the person and work of Jesus . . . The church is one of the least demanding environments for young people, in terms of what they are asked to do mentally and emotionally and of what is expected of them when it comes to serving and giving. We're just so happy to have them there![65]

As brands don't ask all that much from their fans, the church just offers youth a happy experience without asking them to commit their whole lives to Jesus. However, the research conducted by Kinnaman, Matlock, and Hawkins shows that Christian youth are willing to be challenged for more commitment. Indeed, youth are fascinated by mission trips that require everything of them, perhaps even their lives. Giving youth more opportunities to serve is very significant to their spiritual growth.[66] The story of Daniel and his young Hebrew friends on exile in Babylon is a relevant and helpful lesson about identity formation in a time of challenges. They refused to compromise their faith in the face of pressure to conform.[67] From the story of Daniel, the authors define discipleship as "developing Jesus followers who are resiliently faithful in the face of cultural coercion and who live a vibrant life in the Spirit."[68]

To nurture a resilient identity in Christian disciples, it is necessary for youth to experience Jesus together with the faith community, family, friends, and other people who love and experience Jesus.[69] The authors suggest,

> Following Jesus means finding the ultimate answer to these questions in the person and work of Jesus. To be more precise,

---

65. Kinnaman, Matlock, and Hawkins, Kindle locations 554–556, 562–563.
66. Kinnaman, Matlock, and Hawkins, Kindle locations 561–567.
67. Kinnaman, Matlock, and Hawkins, Kindle locations 590–595.
68. Kinnaman, Matlock, and Hawkins, Kindle locations 600–601.
69. Kinnaman, Matlock, and Hawkins, Kindle locations 604–605.

in the Trinity. If there is a real Father, Son, and Holy Spirit, their life anchors our search for truth – especially the search for truth about ourselves. But the entire process begins by creating space where fellow Christians feel they have permission to ask the big questions. Questions of identity: Who am I, really? Where do I find my truest self? We are children of God, adopted into his family through Jesus. What the Scriptures say about us is the truest thing about us. Questions about how to live: How should I live in today's world? Do my choices matter? The Holy Spirit willingly and cheerfully gives wisdom and discernment to those who ask. Following Jesus redefines the search for how to live.[70]

We need to support youth in answering big questions of life and in finding the answer in Jesus.

There are also questions about intimacy and relationships since we are part of the community of Jesus, who calls us to bear one another's burdens and experience love and intimacy. We need to help youth answer questions of meaning and purpose since God the Creator made us in his image to love and serve him, other people, and creation. Since we are both physical and spiritual beings created by God, we can participate with him in blessing the world both physically and spiritually (Eph. 2:10).[71] To form a resilient identity, youth have to stay in a worshipping relationship with God and experience his presence in every moment of their lives by observing spiritual practices. This includes listening to God attentively and praying to him intimately.

The authors conclude on the practice of building a resilient identity through experiencing intimacy with Christ,

> Following Jesus is more than just believing the right things or feeling warm fuzzies about him. Being Christian is more than being on "team Jesus." It means we find the very essence of ourselves at his feet. Experiencing Jesus is entering into a dynamic relationship with him as the author and perfecter of our faith. Experiencing the real Jesus is the starting point and the ending

---

70. Kinnaman, Matlock, and Hawkins, Kindle locations 652–659.
71. Kinnaman, Matlock, and Hawkins, Kindle locations 659–680.

point – the Alpha and the Omega – of resilient faithfulness in digital Babylon.[72]

Kinnaman, Matlock, and Hawkins have done a practical job in suggesting that we need to support the youth of the "digital Babylon" to build a resilient identity by maintaining an intimate relationship with Jesus. However, since their theologies of discipleship, community, and youth have not been solidly established, it is important to revisit these theologies in the sections to come of this chapter.

To recap, the arrival of the digital age has profoundly reshaped contemporary youths' processes of developing a stable and healthy self-identities. It is important to define personal identity from a theological viewpoint. This section has suggested that a theological account of identity rests in a worshipping relationship with the Trinitarian God who restores the believer's identity as well as his or her relationship with God and with others. In order to help youth, whose identity is fragmented by digital culture, to form a resilient self-identity, churches should be prepared to guide them in their spiritual practice of experiencing intimacy with Jesus. This is the task of discipleship, which is helping youth to encounter Christ. This starts with the practice of solitude as discussed in chapter 3.3. The theology of discipleship discussed in the next section elaborates how this works in practical terms.

3. Theology of Discipleship

In this section, we will discuss what true discipleship is, especially in the context of discipling youth in the digital age.[73] We will expound Bonhoeffer's theology of discipleship and then build up a theology of discipling youth in the digital age. As discussed in the segment *Accord to Biblical Standards* in chapter 3, for Bonhoeffer, the Bible played a central role in Christian youth discipleship. In his *Eight Theses on Youth Work,* Bonhoeffer proposes that the church committed to discipling youth will need to focus on preaching the word of God to youth regardless of the day and age.

---

72. Kinnaman, Matlock, and Hawkins, Kindle locations 781–784.

73. Much of this section has also appeared in: Vo, "What is Good about Digital Technology," 227–233.

> It is the task of youth not to reshape the church, but rather to listen to the Word of God; it is the task of the church not to capture the youth, but to teach and proclaim the Word of God. (Thesis 1)
>
> Church youth work is possible only on the basis of addressing young people concerning their baptism and with the exclusive goal of having them hear God's Word. (Thesis 6)[74]

Preaching the word of God to youth should be the main emphasis in caring for and discipling youth. True baptism removes the generational gap so that, in Christ, there is no longer the Net Generation and others. All are disciples because all are baptized in Christ to live with one another (Eph 2:5).[75]

In his book *Discipleship*, Bonhoeffer describes discipleship in contrast to cheap grace:

> Cheap grace means grace as doctrine, as principle, as system. It means forgiveness of sins as a general truth; it means God's love as merely a Christian idea of God.[76]
>
> Cheap grace is preaching forgiveness without repentance; it is baptism without the discipline of community; it is the Lord's Supper without confession of sin; it is absolution without personal confession. Cheap grace is grace without discipleship, grace without the cross, grace without the living, incarnate Jesus Christ.[77]

Grace is costly. It requires us to not only trust God but also obey him. Bonhoeffer mentions the story of the rich young ruler, who comes to Jesus with a theological question but is sent away with the demand for a life-changing action – one of obedience:

> The call to discipleship here has no other content than Jesus Christ himself, being bound to him, community with him. But the existence of a disciple does not consist in enthusiastic

---

74. Bonhoeffer, *Berlin*, 515–516.
75. Root, *Bonhoeffer as Youth Worker*, 132.
76. Bonhoeffer, *Discipleship*, 43.
77. Bonhoeffer, 44.

respect for a good master. Instead, it is obedience toward the Son of God.[78]

Discipleship is following Jesus in daily life, whether in the physical world or in the virtual one. "Such grace is costly, because it calls us to follow; and it is grace, because it calls us to follow Jesus Christ."[79] As discussed in the segment *Grace* in chapter 3, our responses to God's grace are repentance, the discipline of community, the confession of sin, discipleship, and bearing Jesus's cross.[80] For Bonhoeffer, the Bible is the central means of grace providing the standard for the practice of Christian spiritual formation.[81] The church should make youth disciples of Christ by proclaiming the word of God to them in the power of the Holy Spirit rather than just attracting them with modern technology, youthful activities, programs, or ideas. It is not about wielding the media as a tool but rather about the gospel at work in the lives of believers.[82]

As for those who appeal to divine providence, they believe that God has intended to use digital media to reach the whole world with the gospel. They argue that digital media is a different form of what has been done before, from writing the gospels to printing devotional materials and broadcasting worship services, and thus that it should be considered a neutral medium. It may be true that digital media can enhance the spiritual practices of prayer and searching the Scriptures as personal and corporate disciplines. Social media can serve to enhance and build on real relationships. Virtual relationships can also be used for spiritual formation in renewing the faith or growing in intimacy with God and obeying God in everyday life.[83] Many Christians who are active on digital media report anecdotally that they find that it is a contributor to their spiritual formation through the wide availability of Bible applications for reading or listening to daily devotions or sermons, walking through the Bible, or reading the interlinear English-Greek Bible. During the time I have been teaching the Sunday school class of children from eight to sixteen years old at a local church in the UK, I have found that most of the

---

78. Bonhoeffer, 74.
79. Bonhoeffer, 45.
80. Bonhoeffer, 44.
81. Dahill, *Reading from the Underside*, 101.
82. Root, *Bonhoeffer as Youth Worker*, 132.
83. Meadows, "Mission and Discipleship," 173.

children own an iPhone or iPad, and I encourage the children and parents to use Bible applications daily to read or listen to the Bible or to have family devotional times. Some of them have been using these applications regularly and have found them useful in learning the Bible.

Though these things can be true, we should be mindful of pitfalls while using digital technology in discipling youth. Christians in ministry should be wary of an "easy" online mission or ministry with no blood, sweat, or tears and that entails no personal relationship or personal commitment.[84] It is important to be aware of the possible repercussions associated with virtual freedom – virtual addictions and virtual idolization – all of which undermine the life of true discipleship.[85] These pitfalls will be discussed further as we build up the theology of discipleship.

Spiritual discipline can deepen our communion with God and expand our love for our neighbor. Spiritual disciplines should not be associated with only the works of piety for growing in the knowledge and love for God such as prayer, reading the Scriptures, participating in the Lord's Supper, and fasting or abstinence. They are also the works of mercy and expressing our love for God to our neighbor. True discipleship is helping youth to become recipients of saving grace and participants in God's mission of love to the world.[86] Utilizing digital technology in discipling youth, we can develop virtual works of piety, through the use of internet prayer guides, online lectionary, and mobile Bible study applications. Virtual works of mercy can be focused not only on spiritual care – using digital media for mutual prayer and spiritual conversation – but also on the simple act of building friendship. The Net Generation can find creative ways to do these things. Mobile technology, with applications created for listening to worship music and sermons and for the Bible and spiritual reading, makes it easy to craft spiritual disciplines into the routines of daily life. Our social media also make it possible to enhance the works of mercy in caring for others such as through online counseling or fundraising for charity.[87]

---

84. Meadows, 174.
85. Meadows, 170.
86. Meadows, 178.
87. Meadows, 178–179.

It is possible to use digital media as a means of spiritual formation, but we should be aware of its pitfalls. To disciple youth in the digital age, it is necessary to build a theology of "self" that enables the youth of this generation to respond adequately to the negative impacts of digital media and come to know Christ as their personal Savior. The church has been slow in responding to the changes of society until they affect its own members.[88] The theology of "self" will enable and equip youth to fight against addiction to "virtual reality," which brings harm to our relationships with God and with other people.[89] Addiction to online gaming, selfies, instant messaging, and other forms of immersive feedback stimulation can alienate us from those around us and adversely affect their well-being.[90] According to Philip R. Meadows, relationships and community can be expressed through both digital media and face-to-face contact. The development of digital technology has woven our virtual relationships into our physical lives. Devices with 4G functionality and wireless hotspots keep us constantly connected to the virtual world and the people using it.[91] He suggests, "From an everyday perspective, convergence is what happens as people navigate the flow of life at the interface of embodied and virtual realities: from the development of personal identity to our participation in community."[92]

Some theologians regard the internet as evil because it creates a space where we can be disembodied minds, ignoring our bodies. They claim that if we try to operate without our bodies in cyberspace, we are trying not to be human and therefore are trying to be God.[93] However, this is not true since humans were created with bodies and souls. It is thus impossible to operate in cyberspace without our bodies. Our bodies, minds, and souls are all at work when we use the internet. Even though we may try to project a different "self" in cyberspace, our bodies are still connected no matter how hard we try to hide it. From a convergent perspective, the reality of life in the physical world and cyberspace flow well into each other.

---

88. Fortner, "Gospel in a Digital Age," 5.
89. Fortner, 5.
90. Bennett, *Aquinas on the Web?*, 148–163.
91. Meadows, "Mission and Discipleship," 165.
92. Meadows, 164.
93. Bennett, *Aquinas on the Web?*, 17.

Once again, it is important to be aware of the possible repercussions resulting from virtual freedom, the harms of virtual addictions and virtual idolization, all of which undermine the life of true discipleship.[94] Jana M. Bennett points out some drawbacks of the internet such as addiction to online games, selfies, instant messaging, and pornography, which can alienate us from those around us and damage the wellness of our lives.[95] She concludes,

> The internet caters to practicing some virtues but not others (such as patience), and whatever virtues may be learned online always also stand the chance of becoming vices. Vice happens offline too, just as idolatry does. I have shown also some of the ways that online theologians make statements worth saying to Christians. The advantage offline Christian communities have, however, is long-established practices that have enabled Christians to live more virtuously, as well as a broader array of Christian practices. There are quite simply practices that humans cannot do online: fasting, even by avatar, might be a case in point. Yet the fullness of Christian life should not be arbitrarily truncated in favour of the mode of community.[96]

Bennett's conclusion is reasonable, but I want to press the point that we should take extra steps to reach out to the youth who are already surrounded by digital media. The gospel of Jesus Christ is always incarnate. It always requires dynamic interaction with the Christian community within a concrete context.[97]

As Jesus was born into the cultural realities of his day, we should pursue a convergent and holistic discipleship that weaves together the physical and virtual realms of everyday life. As Jesus was in the world but not of the world, we must be careful of the dangers of allowing the virtual realm to hinder authentic relationships with God and the community.[98] In the words of Meadows,

---

94. Meadows, "Mission and Discipleship," 170.
95. Bennett, *Aquinas on the Web?*, 148–163.
96. Bennett, 173.
97. Ward, *God at the Mall*, 33–34; Schreiter, *Constructing Local Theologies*.
98. Meadows, "Mission and Discipleship," 177.

As Jesus was in the world, but not of the world, we must also adopt a critical stance towards the disembodying and compartmentalizing effects of digital culture on whole-life discipleship, as well as the danger of exchanging authenticity for hyper-reality. As Jesus was sent to be a transforming presence in the world, so whole-life disciples will intentionally extend their embodied witness into the virtual realm.[99]

Indeed, true discipleship is the foundation for witnessing in cyberspace, provided that its benefits are discerned and its dangers, withstood.[100]

The missional principle of contextualization requires us to find creative ways to engage youth in their own language. The idea of incarnation requires us to be present in digital spaces in order to connect with them and, in turn, connect them with God.[101] We should stay away from the temptation of just doing an "easy" online mission or ministry.[102] Similarly to physical mission and ministry, virtual mission and ministry should focus on transforming life, which starts with the difficult work of investing in the relationship. As digital natives, the Net Generation can find creative ways to achieve this, and we can benefit much by learning from them. Virtual mission and ministry can still bring about true transformation as long as we partner with the Holy Spirit and the Christian community. Online mission and ministry should be not an end in itself but rather a part of the joint effort with the church in bringing people to Christ and nurturing them in the faith.

God is, by nature, a communicator, who has been communicating himself to humanity from the creation of the world. The gospel itself is the story of God's communication with his people.[103] God's chosen medium for relating to the world is through the formation of a holy people, set apart from the surrounding nations, whose lives together are intended to display the reality and beauty of his presence, in the flesh. This story is recapitulated in the life of Jesus, through whom the church was born, is set apart by the Spirit,

---

99. Meadows, 177.
100. Meadows, 176.
101. Meadows, 173.
102. Meadows, 174.
103. Sogaard, *Media in Church*, 12–13.

and is sent as salt and light into a dark world.[104] The church is called to "declare [God's] power to the next generation, [God's] might to all who are to come." (Ps 71:8) This is the ultimate reason for youth discipleship, in spite of the changing world with its modern technologies and revolving ideas of community living. Knowing that Jesus Christ is – and will always be – the only relevant and redeeming presence that a person could ever experience is essential for doing youth discipleship.[105] For Christians, God's incarnation and redemptive activity through Jesus Christ color every aspect of how we understand and relate to culture and how we understand and minister to youth in this digital age.[106]

It is important to keep first things first. Chap Clark suggests the following biblical truths as anchor points for a faithful practice of youth discipleship.

> There is a Creator-God who is on the move to find those who are lost (Luke 15:1f).
>
> God's heart is decisively compassionate toward children (Mark 10:13f).
>
> God loves people enough to invade human history via the Incarnation (Philippians 2:5–11).
>
> Followers of Jesus Christ are likewise called to love and pursue those whom God loves, and therefore called to "go" into the world of the young people (John 17:18).
>
> The message of the gospel focused on the Incarnate Word brings hope and healing to every person regardless of culture, ethnicity, or age (Romans 10:12–13).[107]

From these, Clark concludes that our task is to connect God's story to the stories of youth. There is a need for the whole body of the church to care for a specific group.[108] It is the call of the church to pass on true knowledge of God to the youth in any cultural or environmental setting.[109]

---

104. Meadows, "Mission and Discipleship," 171.
105. Clark, "Changing Face," 42–43.
106. Richter, "Growing Up Postmodern," 63.
107. Clark, "Changing Face," 60–61.
108. Clark, 60–61.
109. Clark, 42–43.

So far, we have established that discipleship is following Jesus in daily life in both the physical and the virtual world. The church should make youth disciples of Christ by proclaiming the word to them in the power of the Holy Spirit rather than just attracting them with modern technology, youthful activities, programs, or ideas. It is not about wielding the media as a tool but rather about the gospel at work in the lives of believers. We have discussed how the theology of "self" plays an important role in affirming youths' embrace of their full selves while also encouraging them to resist the urge to disembody themselves via the cyber world within the culture already so fragmented. Alongside this, the theology of communication and the theology of incarnation further strengthen the resolve of the church to better equip youth for being truly present in both the physical and the virtual world. The theology of community, then, needs to be substantiated in order to allow youth to authenticate the gospel message in an environment defined and established by Christ.

4. Theology of Community

As discussed in the segment *In the Context of the Faith Community*, discipleship needs to be done in the context of the authentic community, the church. Hipps says that "community is the soil out of which the flower of discipleship grows."[110] The church community can serve as "networks for faith formation."[111] Therefore, it is important for the church to build a solid theology of community for discipling youth. Stanley Grenz presents a comprehensive theological foundation, which is helpful in undergirding the task of the faith community as it disciples the youth of the digital age. This foundation is presented in four central themes: God the Creator, humans before God, the center of Christian life, and the direction of ethical life. The theology of community needs to be rooted in the persons of the Trinitarian God and manifest through the Christian community where the authentic gospel is communicated.[112] Bonhoeffer suggests that the true church community is defined and established by Christ. It includes people saved by Christ. It

---

110. Hipps, *Hidden Power*, 120.
111. Emery-Wright and Mackenzie, *Networks for Faith Formation*, xv.
112. Grenz, *Moral Quest*, 271–275.

is through sharing life in sacrifice, intercession, and confession that people encounter the living Christ.[113]

a. A True Community

The church is a community of people sharing the same faith in Jesus regardless of their backgrounds. It is one of the important loci for their spiritual growth. However, in reality, the church is not always a real community, when people extend their individualism to spirituality. As Kinnaman observes,

> "Solo discipleship" may as well be an oxymoron, because those two words are completely antithetical, like pretty ugly, jumbo shrimp, a deafening silence, or acting naturally. Yet so often church is created for the individual. Songs are sung vertically to God; we no longer sing "horizontally" to one another. Even sacraments like baptism are often described in terms of individual spiritual journeys, disembodied from the corporate experience of the body of Christ. Both the vertical and the horizontal are important.[114]

Social networking sites such as Facebook and LinkedIn, on the surface, have rekindled our interest in community and renewed our quest for meaningful connections even though, in reality, it has increased our mobility, isolation, and individualism.[115] The quest for a true community still remains elusive. What, then, is a true community? Hipps suggests that the true community should move beyond screens to the sharing of everyday life. It means "becoming the people of God and the body of Christ."[116]

Jean Vanier defines true community as one that breaks down barriers to welcome differences.[117] Each person belongs to "the vast family of humanity."[118] It seems that Vanier proposes a universal community, which embraces everyone as part of the body. However, this is difficult in practice since each human being is born with innate selfishness and self-centeredness that prevents us

---

113. Bonhoeffer, *Discipleship*, 43–44; Root, *Bonhoeffer as Youth Worker*, 123.
114. Kinnaman, *Faith for Exiles*, Kindle locations 1392–1396.
115. Hipps, *Hidden Power*, 121.
116. Hipps, 122.
117. Vanier, *Community and Growth*, 20.
118. Vanier, 16; Bonhoeffer, *Discipleship*, 43–44.

from accepting those who are different from us.[119] Therefore, we need Christ's redemption for our lives and our communities. It is Christ who establishes the true community that is the church, as Bonhoeffer states in theses 2 and 3 of his *Eight Theses on Youth Work*:

> Our question is not: What is youth and what rights does it have, but rather: What is the church-community and what is the place of youth within it? (Thesis 2)

> The church-community includes those on earth whom God's dominion has torn away from the dominion of death and evil, those who hear the Word concerning the establishment of God's dominion among human beings in Jesus Christ and who obediently assemble around this Word in faith. The church-community is Christ's presence as the true Lord and Brother. Being in the church-community means being in Christ; being in Christ means being in the church-community. Sacrifice, intercession, and confession are the acts of fellowship in the church-community. It is only within the church-community that one can pass judgment on the church-community. By nature the church-community cannot be judged from the outside. (Thesis 3)[120]

Bonhoeffer asserts that the true church community is defined and established by Christ. It includes people saved by Christ. It is through sharing life in sacrifice, intercession, and confession that people encounter the living Christ.[121]

The church is not defined by any one person or any particular group. The church is not defined by youth or youthful spirit or activities. This point is once again emphasized in his *Sanctorum Communio*:

> The church does not come into being by people coming together (genetic sociology), rather than its existence is sustained by the Spirit who is a reality within the church-community; therefore, it cannot be derived from individual wills.[122]

---

119. Hare, *Why Bother Being Good?*, 28.
120. Bonhoeffer, *Berlin*, 516.
121. Bonhoeffer, *Discipleship*, 43–44; Root, *Bonhoeffer as Youth Worker*, 123.
122. Bonhoeffer, *Sanctorum Communio*, 160.

It is interesting to know that Bonhoeffer wrote his dissertation, *Sanctorum Communio,* while he was doing his first youth ministry at the church in Grunewald in 1927.[123] Andrew Root points out that it was his ministry with young people that moved Bonhoeffer to see the church as the locality for experiencing the living Christ.[124] He saw them in relation to the whole picture of the church community established by Christ. Youth can be saved by Christ and subsequently be part of the community, where we can experience Christ through sharing life with them as well as with people from other age groups.

In *Act and Being*, written in 1929–30, Bonhoeffer continues to expand on the notion that people can experience the revelation of God in the church community:

> The community in question is visible concretely; it is the Christian church that hears the preaching and believes it. The word of this community is preaching and sacrament; its action is believing and loving. The being of revelation, "Christ existing as community," has to be thought of in this concreteness.[125]

Regardless of youth culture in the digital age, youth remain part of the church community where they can experience Christ through the preaching of God's word, the sacraments, and acts of love. Youth belong to the community not because of their youthful spirit, ideas or activities but because of Christ.

Continuing the theme of *community,* Bonhoeffer elaborates this idea more in *Life Together,* which was written eleven years after *Sanctorum Communio*:

> Christianity means community through Jesus Christ and in Jesus Christ. No Christian community is more or less than this. Whether it be a brief, single encounter or the daily fellowship of years, Christian community is only this. We belong to one another only through and in Jesus Christ.[126]

An authentic community is a community where people are welcomed to redemptive relationships and where they engage one another with the hope

---

123. Root, *Bonhoeffer as Youth Worker*, 123.
124. Root, 45.
125. Bonhoeffer, *Act and Being*, 115.
126. Bonhoeffer, *Life Together*, 11.

of the gospel. The possible danger is that this community may be threatened by the virtual community with the disembodied interaction and emotional promiscuity.[127] Our task is to be aware of its pitfalls and use digital media as a means of spiritual formation and witness to strengthen our community. What, then, is the place of youth in the church community? Bonhoeffer writes in thesis 4 of *Eight Theses on Youth Work*, "[youth] is to serve the church-community by hearing, learning, and practicing the Word." It is important to recognize that young people can assist the church in contextualizing itself in a rapidly changing culture of the digital age. The church is a conservative institution that can easily become out of touch with society and culture if youth are not empowered to exercise their gifts.

To recap, Bonhoeffer asserts that the true church community is defined and established by Christ. It includes people saved by Christ. It is through sharing life in sacrifice, intercession, and confession that people encounter the living Christ. The church is not defined by any one person or any particular group. It is not defined by youth or youthful spirit or activities. Regardless of youth culture in the digital age, youth remain part of the church community where they can experience Christ through the preaching of God's word, the sacraments, and acts of love. An authentic community is a community where people are welcomed to redemptive relationships and where they engage one another with the hope of the gospel. The possible danger is that this community may be threatened by the virtual community with the disembodied interaction and emotional promiscuity. Our task is to be aware of its pitfalls and use digital media as a means of spiritual formation and witness to strengthen our community.

b. Participation

It is important to note that the blogging revolution and social networking sites also promote a theology of participation and community. The transparency on display in the blogosphere and social networking sites should remind us that the church must be a place where people are transparent before the Lord as well as among the redeemed community (Jas 5:16). John reminds us that confession of sin preludes walking in the light, which in turn leads to true fellowship with God and neighbors (1 John 1:6–10). The prevalence of online

---

127. Hipps, *Hidden Power*, 21–26.

diary communities and posting on social networking sites is an indication that people are longing for fellowship and need a place for honest confession.[128] Moreover, with a medium that places such an emphasis on participation in conversations, we need to ask whether the users are guilty of "always learning but never able to acknowledge the truth" (2 Tim 3:7). The purpose of dialogue is to arrive at truth, not simply to listen to each other speak. Yet, in postmodern fashion, users shy away from objective truth claims. The value of a true statement is lessened in the blogosphere and social networking sites because it is just an opinion that can always be retracted or modified later. In the cyber community or even the cyber church, there is no authority that determines what is good or bad.[129]

How shall we, as Christians, engage an increasingly participatory culture while maintaining a healthy sense of respect for the authority of Scripture and tradition? What we need is a theology of participation and community. We need to be reminded of what it means to be the church. Paul gave the Corinthians the picture of a human body, where each member has no life or purpose except in relationship with other members and with Christ, who is the head of the body. Scripture also describes the church as a Spirit-built temple, a kingdom of priests, and a holy nation. From the biblical viewpoint, participation means much more than entering into conversation with one another. It means serving, suffering, and sacrificing for each other's sake. Scripture's view of participation goes beyond the shallowness of cyberspace and calls us to the biblical standard of being priests to one another.[130] As Bonhoeffer says in *Act and Being* that people can experience the revelation of Christ in the church community,[131] Christians need to help the youth who are immersed in digital culture to be at home in an authentic community where real living for Christ is shared face to face. It is helpful to be aware of the temptation to avoid the risk for fear of exposure, insecurity, and awkwardness of dealing with someone face to face.[132] Participation means building true friendship with one another.

---

128. Bailey, "Welcome to the Blogosphere," 184.
129. Bailey, 186.
130. Bailey, 186.
131. Bonhoeffer, *Act and Being*, 115.
132. Bailey, "Welcome to the Blogosphere," 187.

Friendship is a significant mark of a true community. Jesus calls us friends (John 15:15). He came to befriend people from different backgrounds. Friendship is not just a context for love; it is all about love. We can observe and learn this from youth. For youth, friends seem to be "everything" to them. They are willing to do many things for their friends. It is quite easy for them to understand Jesus as their True Friend who laid down his life for his friends. In fact, young people are much more likely to be saved or converted than adults; Jesus said that the kingdom of heaven belongs to those who are like little children (Matt 19:4). Kenda Creasy Dean observes that youth are more open to Christ and to others since they have no "hardened self" to lose.[133] Therefore, our Christian practices should align the passions of youth with God's self-giving passion.[134]

Digital technology can serve as a means to deepen friendships, but it cannot do the same things that "physical" friendships do, which include hugging, playing, laughing, eating with each other, etc. The true community is the community that cares for each member in everyday life as well as in cyberspace. Vanier asserts, "If community is belonging and openness, it is also a loving concern for each person. In other words, we could say it is *caring, bonding and mission.* These three elements define it."[135] The God we worship is the Trinitarian God – and each member of the Trinity is in mutual love and eternal fellowship with one another and his love is overflowing to us, his creation.[136] None of us is isolated, but we are part of a community that God has placed us into. The Apostle Paul reminds us to use our gifts for the benefit of others. This requires us to sharpen our skills and maximize our talents in order to care for people not only in our community but also beyond it.[137] We need to encourage youth to care for each other not only in the virtual world but also in the physical world with home visitation, meal fellowship, and praying with each other. We also need to involve youth in caring for the needy beyond our community.

---

133. Dean, *Practicing Passion*, 64.
134. Dean, 65.
135. Vanier, *Community and Growth*, 20.
136. Grenz, *Moral Quest*, 263–267.
137. Lovin, *Christian Ethics*, 29–32.

In this subsection, we have discussed that social media rekindle the concepts of participation and community. Participation calls us to be true friends to one another. The question to ask is whether true participation and community can be expressed online in the virtual church.

c. Virtual Church

With the rise of digital technology, the church is evolving from the real world into the virtual world. A number of churches have created worship experiences in the virtual world. In the book *SimChurch: Being the Church in the Virtual World*, Douglas Estes presents what it means to "do" church in the virtual world.[138] He seeks to discuss the theology and ecclesiology of virtual churches. He perceives that a number of people will be members, not just of a real-world church but also of a virtual church, since virtual churches offer the sense of flexibility, transparency, and diversity.[139] He shares his experience of joining a virtual church where he could walk around, read the info boards, find his own seat, greet his neighbors, experience valid Christian worship, and fellowship with people after the service. He did everything he would have done if he had visited most any other Protestant church service. The only difference was that the church was in a virtual world. However, it was a real experience.[140] Estes argues, "If the virtual world is an aspect or extension of the real world, as I believe, and if this idea is both rational and defendable, then we may argue logically that it is possible for an authentic church to exist in the virtual world."[141]

In the New Testament, the word for "church" is *ekklesia*, which means a gathering, an assembly, or a town-hall meeting of citizens, and in a biblical sense, it refers to citizens of the kingdom of God.[142] However, the Bible never delimits the concept of an *ekklesia* but speaks of it using a large variety of metaphors, such as "the body of Christ" or "community of the Holy Spirit." As a result, it gives space for discussion of a new form of church in the virtual world.[143] A church is not a building or place, a ritualized institution, or a

---

138. Estes, *SimChurch*.
139. Estes, 27–28.
140. Estes, 33.
141. Estes, 35.
142. Estes, 36.
143. Estes, 36.

fellowship or activity; it is "a localized assembly of the people of God dwelling in a meaningful community with the task of building the kingdom."[144] In the same way, the author states that a virtual church is not a website, a podcast, or a blog. He defines, "A virtual church is a place where people professing to have faith in Jesus Christ gather regularly to be a meaningful community appointed to build up the kingdom – or more specifically, a virtual church *is* the confessing people gathering in a synthetic world."[145]

The author investigates the validity of virtual church in light of biblical accounts of the church: Christian community in the gospels, the early Jerusalem church in Acts, and the church in New Testaments epistles.[146] He starts with Jesus's popular statements about his involvement with his gathered followers: "For where two or three come together in my name, there am I with them." (Matt 18:20) From Jesus's statement, the church is a gathering of disciples under the authority of Jesus (Eph 4:15, 23–24), and a church cannot be the church without the presence of God (Eph 2:22).[147] Therefore, a virtual church "must gather together for Christ, with Christ present," if it claims to be a real church.[148] The story of Jesus meeting the Samaritan woman in John 4 is relevant to the discussion of the place to worship. Jesus told her, "A time is coming when you will worship the Father neither on this mountain nor in Jerusalem . . . a time is coming and has now come when true worshipers will worship the Father in spirit and truth, for they are the kind of worshipers the Father seeks." (4:21–23) Therefore, true worship of God will hinge not on a geographic location but on the Spirit's presence in the midst of worshippers (Matt 18:20). This can argue for the validity of virtual churches since a true biblical church is not defined by location, except for being in the Spirit.[149]

Acts 2:43–47 describes the church as *koinonia*, an intimate community. The virtual world does not prevent us from being an intimate community or from loving others unselfishly. Of course, there are trade-offs; while some aspects of the virtual world can hinder certain types of community experiences that only face-to-face contact can provide, some aspects of the virtual

---

144. Estes, 37.
145. Estes, 37.
146. Estes, 41.
147. Estes, 41.
148. Estes, 42.
149. Estes, 42–43.

world can encourage other types of community experiences, such as more regular meeting and contacts enabled by digital technology.[150] In the New Testament epistles, the most important metaphors for the church are "the body of Christ" and "the people of God," which are compatible with a virtual church. Paul writes to the church in Colossae, "For though I am absent from you in body, I am present with you in spirit and delight to see how disciplined you are and how firm your faith in Christ is." (Col 2:5) He also writes similarly to the church in Corinth (1 Cor 5:3–5). Even though he is not physically present, he still engages with both these churches in worship practices and church discipline. Paul views that geography cannot limit his participation in the church.[151] Biblical texts can support the validity of virtual churches as the church is not defined by spatial or geographical terms.[152]

Estes also argues that church history and tradition can support the validity of virtual churches. In his letter to the church in Smyrna, which is one of the earliest discussions about the church, Ignatius, the late-first-century bishop of Antioch, defines the church: "Where the overseer may appear, there let the people [of God] be; where Jesus Christ is, there is the whole church."[153] In his letter to the church in Philippi, Polycarp, the early-second-century bishop of Smyrna, reminds the church that it is "residing as an alien" in that city and that it transcends the physical world.[154] Irenaeus depicts the church solely in terms of its union with the Holy Spirit, while Tertullian writes that "where three are, the church is, even if they are just lay people." In the same way, Origen describes the church as the "gathering of all saints" and says that it "is [made] from the sum of many believers," and Cyprian explains that while the church will exist in different parts, all of the parts work together to make the true church of Christ. Estes observes,

> In fact, the church fathers chose to place a tremendous emphasis on the church as a place of good doctrine, true spirituality, and apostolic authority – not on location or structures. To them the

---

150. Estes, 43–44.
151. Estes, 45–46.
152. Estes, 46.
153. Estes, 48.
154. Estes, 48.

church was much more of a spiritual gathering than a physical meeting.[155]

Therefore, in light of the church fathers' descriptions of the church, it can be argued that a virtual church can be a viable church. In regard to the creeds, which are frequently used as a mark of a true church throughout Christian history, the idea of virtual churches does not contradict them. The Apostles' Creed defines the church only as "holy" as it focuses mostly on Jesus, while the Nicene Creed portrays the church with four characteristics: one, holy, catholic, and apostolic. A virtual church could be united with other churches, sanctified by the Spirit, catholic by representing the whole of God's plan, and apostolic in its mission to conquer the world for Christ.[156]

Thoughts from key theologians on the definition of the church can be supportive to the validity of a virtual church. Augustine perceived the church to be a society of redemption and divine love, while Martin Luther sees the church as a gathering of believers "who hear the voice of the Shepherd and [prefer] the terms *community* or *assembly* to the term *church*." Luther's idea of the priesthood of all believers led to the development of atypical church communities, including virtual churches.[157] Barth's definition of the church, "the church is when it takes place," recognizes that the church is not bound to geographic locale, while Han Küng contends that the church is a communion of pilgrims in a fallen world and calls for the empowerment of everyone in the body of Christ to use their spiritual gifts. Estes asserts that virtual churches may be able to fulfill Küng's vision for the church in ways that real-world churches could not do thanks to the collaborative nature of the virtual world.[158] However, Estes does not elaborate on this point.

Estes summarizes that in terms of theology and ecclesiology, a virtual church can be an authentic church. However, he raises a practical question:

> But – and it's a big but – the fact that a virtual-world church can be a real church doesn't mean that just *any* virtual group or virtual building calling itself a church is a real, authentic, biblical church. As in the real world, there is more to being a church than

---

155. Estes, 48.
156. Estes, 49.
157. Estes, 49–50.
158. Estes, 50–51.

just the name . . . We need to explore this a bit more deeply. Just what does it mean to *be* a church in the virtual world?[159]

A virtual church needs to have a real fellowship and community in order to be an authentic church. The question to ask is whether virtual community can work. For a community to be authentic, presence of its members is required.[160] Presence does not have to be physical. It can be telepresence. God can be fully present during our worship even though he is not physically present (Eph 2:22). Digital technology has challenged the traditional meaning of presence.[161]

Presence no longer requires to be physical, and we can be present in the virtual world. P2P (peer-to-peer) communication allows us to connect with one or more people online. People can come together and be present in the same place in the virtual world, and this can create a real community, and this real community can be a real church where a real God can be present with us. It doesn't matter whether we use avatars, chat rooms, or holographic virtual reality; what matters is that we are present and united in community under the lordship of Christ for the purpose of worship, fellowship, discipleship, ministry, and evangelism. We can become the church, the community, the people of God, when we are present together in the presence of God even in the virtual world.[162] Just as earlier communications technologies such as the telephone "brought people together," it is possible that the internet can bring the church together. Studies show that people who use the virtual world to worship seem to grow in community, whereas people who use the virtual world for sinful pursuits tend to become more isolated.[163] Creating community requires a lot of effort, whether in the real or in the virtual world. The church should not just rely on digital communication to build community. Community is about people, and it builds upon people.

Estes mentions some possible negative aspects of the virtual church. The danger of virtual connection is that it may create an imaginary community. One can log into a virtual community where it is just an empty space

---

159. Estes, 53.
160. Estes, 58.
161. Estes, 63–64.
162. Estes, 64–65.
163. Estes, 71.

because that person is the only one present at the time.[164] It is important for a virtual church to create more participation and engagement to keep people away from multitasking or distractions during worship. More participation will keep people from being isolated and individualized.[165] There are some other disadvantages for the online communities, such as the fact that virtual churches seem to favor short sermons and messages due to technical limits and short attention spans, and they also lack the depth of praise that can occur in churches in the real world.[166]

There will be something lost, even if something is gained, in the transition from physical gathering to online church. In terms of the sacraments, virtual churches will never do the same work as a church that is physically gathered. It is a real loss to not be able to gather physically and receive, by hand, the bread and cup. But there is also benefit from not having to do it physically, which can free a worshipper from the peer pressure inherent in real-world contexts in order to better examine themselves before participating or choosing not to participate.[167] Virtual churches do not have to do or appropriate everything that a physical church does, but they should create new online practices of worship. As visual possibilities for virtual churches are boundless, an online worshipper can meditate on icons in 3D virtual space.[168] Virtual churches eliminate geography, as people do not have to commute long distances to go to a small group.[169]

Virtual churches can be the renewed church in reaching many hard-to-reach parts of the real world. Estes concludes,

> I'm not suggesting that the virtual communities can or should replace real-world communities. That's not the issue. Rather, virtual churches are just another type of local church within the greater body of Christ. And just like any community, they have

---

164. Estes, 72.
165. Estes, 75.
166. Estes, 110–111.
167. Estes, 130–131.
168. Estes, 114.
169. Estes, 207.

strengths and weaknesses. But when tele-present people come together as a church, God is there.[170]

Estes is reasonable in saying that virtual churches are just another type of local church and do not stand exclusively by themselves but stand in the body of Christ together with other real-life churches. His argument of biblical text, church history, and theology for the validity of the virtual church is helpful. However, he does not discuss the theology of community, which is required in answering whether the virtual church can foster a meaningful and authentic community. He does not explore how a virtual church can be a meaningful community in practice. He also does not explore in depth the reasons why people build online churches and why people join these churches instead of joining a physical church near where they live. From an ecclesiological viewpoint, there is much to contemplate about the meaning of *koinonia* in light of the emerging virtual churches. If the church is understood as a formal gathering of people in a particular space for worship, the proper place for cyber fellowship needs to be considered and evaluated. Meadows reminds us of the dangers facing the virtual church: a gospel as an easy commodity, the truth based on personal preference, reducing spirituality to the pursuit of inner and private religious experience, etc.[171]

Some people can argue that the traditional church also faces some of the dangers mentioned above or the same challenges of consumerism and individualism, which have long plagued discipleship in general.[172] However, equating the two is completely unacceptable. Obviously, there are things that the cyber church cannot do. Members of a cyber church can never receive the sacraments or lay hands on someone. They cannot enjoy or appreciate the beauty and meaning of these sacraments bound up in our physical presence, either to perform or to receive them. The Apostle John reminds us that the incarnation, as well as incarnational relationships, is rooted in physicality: The Word became flesh and dwelled among us. Therefore, we should be aware of the limitations of cyberspace and employ moderation and wisdom in its use.[173]

---

170. Estes, 76.
171. Meadows, "Mission and Discipleship," 174.
172. Meadows, 174.
173. Bailey, "Welcome to the Blogosphere," 188.

The church is the holy people of God, the body of Christ, and the temple of the Spirit. It is essentially a real, embodied presence in the world. Among other things, the biblical church is essentially a community of people who "break bread" together, "wash one another's feet," and "stir up one another to love and good works."[174] This cannot be fully expressed in virtual form alone, as Meadows asserts:

> In a digital culture, being set apart means remembering that the physical virtues of incarnation are to be continued in the church, as a community of disciples, and this cannot be disembodied without compromising the truth of biblical Christianity.[175]

As previously discussed in the literature review in chapter 1, Jesse Rice states that a true community is a community that is responsible for others.[176] This poses more challenges for the online community in being accountable for one another, taking care of the physical needs of each other, caring for the sick, rejoicing with one another at weddings, crying with others at funerals, and burying the dead.

Furthermore, we should be aware of the "digital sin" added on by the use of the internet. Digital media can promote a kind of "virtual atheism" in which we can be tempted to think of cyberspace as a "God-free zone" that has no bearing on our spiritual lives or daily discipleship. Again, it is inevitable to find it hard to stay away from digital media, especially for youth who are born with it.[177] It is also fair to say that we are also tempted with other things outside of cyberspace. From a convergent perspective, there is no such thing as a virtual church but only a church of Christ with real people saved by grace through faith who are challenged to take up the cross to follow Jesus in both physical life and in cyberspace. Meadows assesses fairly by pointing out that the challenge of disembodying the church does not just affect cyberspace. In truth, face-to-face presence does not always mean the "real" presence of sharing life, loving, and sacrificing. Sin affects us both online and off-line.[178]

---

174. Meadows, "Mission and Discipleship in a Digital Culture," 171–172.
175. Meadows, 172.
176. Rice, *Church of Facebook*, 176.
177. Meadows, "Mission and Discipleship," 172.
178. Meadows, 172.

The church should know how youth understand true community. To those who were born in the postmodern world, their main concern is the authenticity preceding any kind of institutional commitment. The church is not fundamentally defined by organizational structures of either the traditional or the virtual kind. The church is defined by Christ. It is the community of people who have real relationships with Christ and with one another regardless of being off-line or online. Church emerges whenever two or three Christians gather in Jesus's name to worship him and to have fellowship with one another at home, in a built sanctuary, in a meeting place like Starbucks, or on a virtual network like Facebook, Skype, Zoom, or Microsoft Teams.

Personally, I have enjoyed Bible studies where some members joined us via Skype due to distance. Recently, due to COVID-19, many churches live stream their services. Many Bible study groups and prayer groups in many churches have gone online also. I also conduct Bible study for students on Microsoft Teams and Sunday schools for children on Zoom at my church in the UK. This phenomenon is new and needs more time to be observed and reflected upon. However, it can be said that digital technology can provide "connective spaces" where real people can make and sustain transforming relationships with God and one another. Church can exist between these spaces, and spiritual friendships can be embedded into everyday life regardless of being off-line or online. Discipleship in Christian community is incarnational and can flow between the physical life and cyberspace.[179] However, Meadows suggests,

> We should be careful not to let digital technology and social media redefine what we mean by friendship and community, and diminish the very quality of our face-to-face relationships. The danger of our digital culture is not that we will become less personal, but that we become hyperpersonal, living a kind of perpetual "out of body experience" in the midst of everyday life; having one face for our neighbors and another for our "always on" relationships.[180]

---

179. Meadows, 175.
180. Meadows, 175–176.

We should be aware not to let digital culture undermine our true community.

To recap, it is important for discipleship to be done in the context of the church community, which can serve as "networks for faith formation." As Grenz proposes, the theology of community is rooted in the persons of the Trinitarian God and manifested through the Christian community where the authentic gospel is communicated. Bonhoeffer suggests that the true church community is defined and established by Christ. It includes people saved by Christ. It is through sharing life in sacrifice, intercession, and confession that people encounter the living Christ. Regardless of youth culture in the digital age, youth remain part of the church community where they can experience Christ through the preaching of God's word, the sacraments, and acts of love. Social media rekindle the concepts of participation and community. Participation calls us be true friends to one another. However, the possible danger in the digital age is that this community may be threatened by the virtual community with its disembodied interaction and emotional promiscuity. Our task is to be aware of its pitfalls and use digital media as a means of spiritual formation and witness to strengthen our community. Having discussed the theologies of self-identity, discipleship, and community, let us move on to discuss the theology of youth proposed by Bonhoeffer, which is beneficial for us in discipling youth.

5. Theology of Youth

In this section, we will discuss Bonhoeffer's theology of youth in order to inform our work of discipling youth in this digital age. This theology will help appropriate the proper place of youth in the church – one in which their youthfulness is embraced fully. It is important for the church to be humble in listening to youth and letting them bring their gifts to the table. However, the church should be careful not to divinize youth.

a. The Divinization of Youth

Since youth are more adept in the world of the digital age, leading to the change in power and authority, this can lead the church to what Bonhoeffer refers to as the divinization of youth. His thesis 1 of *Eight Theses on Youth Work* reads:

> Since the days of the youth movement, church youth work has often lacked that element of Christian sobriety that alone might enable it to recognize that the spirit of youth is not the Holy Spirit and that the future of the church is not youth itself but rather the Lord Jesus Christ alone. It is the task of youth not to reshape the church, but rather to listen to the Word of God; it is the task of the church not to capture the youth, but to teach and proclaim the Word of God.[181]

Thesis 1 mentions the youth movement that negatively affected the church's view of youth during Bonhoeffer's time. The German youth movement sprang from the discontent of the middle-class youth protesting against the culture of their time. When compared to the American youth movement of the 1960s, it was not so much rebellion but romanticism.[182] However, both these movements affected not only national awareness but also the church's view of youth.[183] Protestant and Catholic youth groups were strongly influenced by the youth movement. The only difference was that they put an emphasis on religious motives in their cultural activities.[184] The divinization of youth led the church to replace the Holy Spirit with a youthful spirit, to overemphasize the role of youth in the future of the church, and to focus on cultural activities to attract youth rather than the word of God. It is the culture that instills the idea of youth being the future of the church. However, as stated by Bonhoeffer, the future of the church depends on Christ alone.

As Root observes, Bonhoeffer himself was once actively involved with the German youth movement when he was thirteen years old. He joined the Scouts but then gave up after one year, likely because he thought that the marching and drilling were a waste of time or that radicalization may have affected his group.[185] However, in later years, he showed appreciation for some aspects of the youth movement with the aim "to attack a cultural environment that has lost its inner truth, to loosen shackles of truth."[186]

---

181. Bonhoeffer, *Berlin*, 515.
182. Root, *Bonhoeffer as Youth Worker*, 23.
183. Root, 25.
184. Root, 27.
185. Root, 27; Bethge, *Dietrich Bonhoeffer*, 18–19. It is helpful to take note that the German youth movement was later enveloped into the Nazi's own agenda.
186. Bethge, 18–19.

Bonhoeffer's own youth ministry also had its origin in the romantic youth movement of the 1920s.[187] Therefore, Bonhoeffer knew, firsthand, both the positive and the negative effects of the youth movement. He did not reject it totally but reminded the church of its lacking "Christian sobriety" when approaching youth.

Perhaps Bonhoeffer shares the view of Karl Barth regarding the youth movement:

> A true youth movement can exist only in the form of being moved by a cause which has nothing to do with youth and age. It can exist only in the relation to an object in which we continue to live, as young people certainly, but above all in which we continue to live, not thinking that we can or should rejoice in our youth as such according to the motto: "Stay, you are so beautiful."[188]

Barth does not reject the youthful spirit either. Instead of seeing it as an end in itself, he says that it should be directed toward a bigger purpose for God. According to Barth, age is a "component of the calling in which we stand before God."[189] In the same way, Bonhoeffer does not discard youthful activities, but he reminds the church to keep "first thing first!"[190] Both Bonhoeffer and Barth make an important contribution to keeping the balance of acknowledging youth as being part of the body of Christ while not divinizing them for any reason. Youth have many gifts to offer the church, such as their passion, energy, and adeptness with technology. The church should model and train youth to listen to God while youth bring the renewing energy of commitment and continually call the church to be culturally relevant. The church should receive youth as part of the body of Christ (1 Cor 12). It is more than preaching the word of God at them or providing opportunities for youth to be shaped by the word, it is allowing their experiences of the word in their digital culture to also teach and renew us. However, it is important to keep *"first thing first."*

---

187. Root, *Bonhoeffer as Youth Worker*, 27.
188. Barth, *Ethics*, 196–197.
189. Barth, 196.
190. Dean, "Theological Rocks," 15. Dean proposes keeping "first thing first," thinking of "theological rocks" of youth ministry.

b. First Thing First

"*First thing first,*" in Bonhoeffer's teaching, entails this two-sided claim: youth need to listen to the word of God, and the church needs to proclaim the word of God. Bonhoeffer made "the first thing" clear in his *Ethics*:

> The church confesses that it is guilty of the breakdown of parental authority. The church has not opposed contempt for age and the divinization of youth because it feared losing the youth and therefore the future as if its future depended on the young! It has not dared to proclaim the God-given dignity of parents against revolutionary youth and has made a very worldly-minded attempt "go along with youth." Thus it is guilty of destroying countless families, for children's betraying their parents, of the self-divinizing of youth, and therefore of abandoning them to fall away from Christ.[191]

Root calls this a "theological turn," which is the move away from idolizing the youthful spirit and culture, or focusing on just the technical things in doing youth ministry, to focusing on the personal relationship with Christ. Again, Bonhoeffer asserts that "youth ministry is first and foremost a theological task – a ministry that seeks the encounter of the divine with the human."[192] However, this idea cannot be just a task to accomplish; but rather it needs to be a mindset and posture to be embraced by the whole church. According to Bonhoeffer, the church needs to remain true in preaching the word of God not just to youth but to all people. In his days, Bonhoeffer preached the word to youth in a creative way by engaging them with "heavy conversation," respecting their thoughts and ideas.[193]

In the same way, there are creative ways, including – but not limited to – games, movies, meal fellowship, and home visitations, through which the church can preach the word to youth in this digital age. However, it is important to keep the right focus, as James K. A. Smith reminds:

> And the sad fact is that our youth ministries have treated them as thinking things that need to be entertained when, in fact,

---

191. Bonhoeffer, *Ethics*, 139.
192. Root, *Bonhoeffer as Youth Worker*, 120.
193. Root, 57–58.

what they really crave is not liberation from ritual but rather liberating rituals. Have we failed to realize that while we're trying to entertain them, our young people are waiting for us to form them?"[194]

He suggests that the church should "invite young people into a wider repertoire of Christian disciplines as rhythms of the Spirit . . . Introducing young people to ancient disciplines of prayer, attention, discernment, fasting, and worship is like giving them rafts to make their way into the river of grace."[195] The church is not to entertain youth but to help them encounter Christ. In this regard, spiritual practices encourage youth to seek personal encounters with Christ.

Bonhoeffer's warning against the divinization of youth is not intended to absolve the church of its responsibility to youth. On the contrary, it is necessary for the church to care for youth while resisting slipping into an overemphasis on the role of youth or of the youthful spirit. Root emphasizes that Bonhoeffer's goal for youth and children's ministry is to carry children "into the center of life of the church-community."[196] Indeed, Bonhoeffer demonstrated his dedication to youth through his teaching youth in Sunday school, giving pastoral care to young adults at technical college, teaching confirmation class, running a youth club, being secretary to youth in the ecumenical movement, and writing about youth. This flurry of activities and his dedication to youth helped him realize the overemphasis of the church on youth and the need for the church to proclaim the word of God to youth in the correct way. It was precisely at this juncture that his writing became a practical response to the contemporary issue of overemphasis on youth. As youth grow up surrounded by digital media, the church should preach the word in a way that is more relevant to them. The church should also be prepared to empower them with the word and set them free to use their gifts of technology to enrich the church in return. In short, while training youth in the hermeneutical task, the church should, in turn, listen to their hermeneutic, not dismissing their role in the communal life of the church. While keeping first thing first, it is important to have a proper view of youth based on the Bible.

---

194. Smith, *You Are What*, Calibre page 130/188.
195. Smith, 132.
196. Smith, 56–57.

c. View of Youth in the Bible

Bonhoeffer asserts that there is no special privilege for youth in the church community. Youth have to serve the church community by learning and practicing the word of God. Bonhoeffer rejects the label "Christian youth," since it makes the youth a special Christian when compared to other Christians.[197] Root explicates further, "To label the young 'Christian youth,' Bonhoeffer believes, is to make faith bound not in their humanity and eschatological work of Christ, not in the wrestling of their being, but in the episodic time of 'special privilege' created by culture."[198] According to Bonhoeffer, there is no such thing as "Christian youth" but only Christians who are part of the church. By removing the label, there is hope for narrowing the generational gap. In *Ethics,* Barth considers that age or youthfulness is not something special in itself but that it needs to be directed toward God's purpose:

> The special seriousness of each age does not consist of a special attitude that we should take to life in that age, but of the seriousness with which we try to live and move toward the Lord of life in every age, as though for the very first time and as though there were no other age than the one which is now ours.[199]

Bonhoeffer states that youth are to be embraced fully in their form of youthfulness.[200] Deuteronomy 6:6–9, Proverbs 22:6, and Ecclesiastes 12:1 provide the basis for this conviction. Youth are not inherently more important or more loved, but they should receive special attention because of their developmental stage, especially in this digital culture. Furthermore, Bonhoeffer discusses, in thesis 5, the view of youth in the Bible, in which youthfulness is recognized and judged quite soberly.[201] The Bible does not divinize youth or a youthful spirit but sees "youth" as they are: "man's heart *is* evil from his youth" (Gen 8:21) and "youth *are* vanity" (Eccl 11:10).

Bonhoeffer wrote *Creation and Fall* while ministering to young people from the summer of 1931 to mid-1933. Witnessing firsthand the fallen nature of youth and their vulnerability to youthful folly prompted him to write

---

197. Bonhoeffer, *Berlin*, 516.
198. Root, *Bonhoeffer as Youth Worker*, 130–131.
199. Barth, *Ethics*, 196–197.
200. Root, *Bonhoeffer as Youth Worker*, 129.
201. Bonhoeffer, *Berlin*, 516.

"God's new action with humankind is to uphold and preserve humankind in its fallen world, in its fallen orders, for death – for the resurrection, for the new creation, for Christ."[202] Youth are fallen humans who are in need of God's salvation in the same ways as the adults. It is quite apparent that youth are more vulnerable to folly as they certainly do not always act wisely or with restraint – for example, Genesis 34:1–2.[203] The Bible makes it clear; "rejoice, O young man, in thy youth . . . but know thou, that for all these things God will bring thee into judgment" (Eccl 11:9). The church should be prepared to faithfully proclaim the word of God to youth lest we tumble into the mistake Bonhoeffer points out in *Ethics*: "The church has become guilty, therefore, of the loss of purity and wholesomeness among youth. It has not known how to proclaim strongly that our bodies are members of the body of Christ."[204]

The biblical mandate dictates that youth be humble and submissive to elders (1 Pet 5:5). This speaks to the "rebellious" tendency for which youth are quite known. Bonhoeffer offers his teaching regarding the act of honoring God and community:

> Honor, Christianity, young people who are 16 or 17 years old – how can these be brought together? . . . As God's creation, the individual human exists in the context of social life. From this observation follows first the honor of the social community and second the will of God that humans live in the community.[205]

As digital media is flooded with worldly values and ideas such as consumerism and individualism, the tasks of the church are to disciple youth with the word of God and to keep them away from the temptations of both cyberspace and everyday life. At the same time, it is important for the church to be humble in listening to the "prophetic voice" of youth.

d. Prophetic Voice

Youth are more adept in the world of the digital age, which can lead to a change in power and authority. Bonhoeffer's thesis 7 of *Eight Theses on Youth Work* mentions the right to protest, but it must be done in love. Root says that

---

202. Bonhoeffer, *Creation and Fall*, 140.
203. Kelly, "A Theology of Youth," 17.
204. Bonhoeffer, *Ethics*, 140.
205. Bonhoeffer, *Young Bonhoeffer*, 529–530.

theses 1–6 move youth ministry to unity with the church, whereas theses 7 and 8 need critique.[206] However, it can be argued that Bonhoeffer presents quite a balanced view, especially during a time when the church was corrupt and the youth spirit was idolized. Youth can be a voice of change to the church, but their protest must be in love. The prophetic voice should move youth closer to the church. Once again, Root observes this "children's/youth ministry is the sustaining force that moved Bonhoeffer to continue to see the church as the locale for experiencing the living Christ."[207] Young people can minister to the church. Bonhoeffer attests to being ministered to by the children in their prayer, which awoke his spiritual life and brought prayer to life in the church community.[208]

At this point, we see the special characteristic of this "protesting." In his own experience, Bonhoeffer pushed the church elders to take action against the Nazis. At youth conferences he likewise pressed young people to speak for peace and refuse violence – to be a prophetic voice in their church communities. However, this prophetic voice must come not from the rebellious and proud spirit of youth but from their solidarity – from their willingness to share in guilt with the church community.[209] Bonhoeffer observed the concept of *Führer* that negatively affected the young generation of his time as young people sought leadership for their own sake:

> The image of the "leader", as it arose in the youth movement . . . has ultimately become the only common denominator for the youth in all their desires, the symbol of the younger generation . . . The health and rectitude of young people are at risk.[210]

Bonhoeffer is right about the protest, the prophetic voice, and the leadership attitude of young people, but he does not explain why youth may have these attributes. This may come from the distinct characteristic of their age as expounded in popular development theories. Paul G. Kelly observes that,

---

206. Bonhoeffer, 134.
207. Bonhoeffer, 45.
208. Bonhoeffer, 60.
209. Bonhoeffer, 133–134.
210. Bonhoeffer, *Berlin*, 267–268.

from a biblical perspective, youth can have the responsibility and authority of adults.[211]

Bonhoeffer says that youth can protest but that it should come from a pure, loving, and humble heart for the Lord and the community. In *Life Together*, Bonhoeffer mentions the ministry of meekness: "He who would learn to serve must learn to think little of himself."[212] The church, first and foremost, must set an example of humbleness in listening to the voices of youth, including those raised in cyberspace. The youth, though having more freedom to protest due to the digital culture, should learn to protest with love and humility. The apostle Paul encapsulates this point in 1 Timothy 4:12: "Don't let anyone look down on you because you are young, but set an example for the believers. . ."

Bonhoeffer also reminds youth that protest needs authorization: "Ethical discourse does not merely depend on the correct content of what is said, but also on the speaker being authorized to say it."[213] As discussed earlier, the notion of authority is misconstrued among youth in this digital age. They presume authority from their gaining power over their parents in maneuvering the maze of knowledge made available at their fingertips. This newfound freedom, while invigorating and useful in many ways, also puts them at odds with the traditional authority figures in their lives. It is helpful that we are taught to know that even if something can be said, it is not made valid simply by being voiced. In fact, the authorization comes from actualizing their places within the church community, an act rendered impossible without first submitting to the authority God has placed in their lives.

In this chapter, we have analyzed impacts of digital media on discipleship, upon which to construe a workable theology of discipleship of youth in the Christian community. With the profound implications digital media has on our culture, self-identity, and the gospel, the message communicated to youth is discerned and contextualized. The theological account of identity rests in the worshipping relationship with the Trinitarian God who restores the believer's identity and his or her relationship to God and others. In order to help youth, whose identity is fragmented by digital culture, to form resilient self-identity, churches should be prepared to guide them in their spiritual

---

211. Kelly, "A Theology of Youth," 17.
212. Bonhoeffer, *Life Together*, 84.
213. Bonhoeffer, *Ethics*, 137.

practices of experiencing intimacy with Jesus. This is the task of discipleship, which is helping youth to encounter Christ. Discipleship is following Jesus in the daily life in both the physical and the virtual world. The church should make youth disciples of Christ by proclaiming the word of God to them in the power of the Holy Spirit rather than just attracting them with modern technology, youthful activities, programs, or ideas. We have discussed how the theology of "self" plays an important role in affirming youths' embrace of their full selves while also encouraging them to resist the urge to disembody themselves via the cyber world within a culture already so fragmented. Concurrently, the theology of communication and the theology of incarnation are equally crucial in teaching youth how to be truly present both online and off-line. Next, the theology of community, rooted in the persons of the Trinitarian God and manifested through the Christian community, assures youth of the need to be embraced, accepted, and loved, while encouraging them to extend that same hope to those around. The true church community is defined and established by Christ. Regardless of youth culture in the digital age, youth remain part of the church community where they can experience Christ through the preaching of God's word, the sacraments, and acts of love. The theology of youth, which lays the groundwork for mentoring youth in the digital age, suggests that the church should proclaim the word to the youth and appropriate the proper place of youth in the church, one in which their youthfulness is embraced fully. It points to a church that is humble in listening to youth and so serves their bringing their gifts into the body of Christ. The main claim of this project until now is that youth discipleship is teaching youth, whose personal identity is profoundly influenced by the digital culture, to practice experiencing intimacy with Christ in the context of the faith community and personal daily life.

CHAPTER 5

Youth Discipleship in the Digital Age

Digital technology has permeated our everyday lives, especially the lives of the young people who grow up surrounded by it. Recent studies in the West have shown the "evil" of digital technology, such as replacing real community, causing cyber addiction, and promoting "self" publication.[1] In the context of the post-colonial, communist, Asian country of Vietnam, the majority of the generation of people who are currently parents of teenagers assume that digital media is inherently evil. Parents and church leaders often tell children or young people to stay away from digital media since it can cause addiction, contains dangerous information, and is a waste of time. Even in what has been called the postmodern present under communist rule, social relations in Vietnam remain very hierarchical. As historian Jeffrey Hays observes,

> As with most group-orientated societies there are also hierarchical structures. In Vietnam these are very much based upon age and status. This derives from Confucianism, which emphasizes social order. Everyone is seen as having a distinct place and role within the hierarchical structure, be it the family or workplace. An obvious example is seen in social situations where the oldest person in a group is greeted or served first. Within the family the head would be responsible for making decisions and approving marriages.[2]

---

1. Watson, "Digital Media and Society," 31–37.
2. Hays, "Society in Vietnam,".

Within this hierarchical culture, Christian parents typically enjoin their children to stay away from digital media and focus on their studies and the Bible. With this approach, of course they never succeed, since young people can never stay away from the excitement on offer in the online environment. How should the church of Christ respond to such dynamics and disciple this generation?

We have discussed the social context for discipling youth in the digital age in chapter 1 and chapter 2, the theology of discipleship and spiritual formation in chapter 3, and the theologies needed for youth discipleship in chapter 4. This last chapter will contextualize the theology of discipleship in the setting of youth ministry in the digital age. It will focus on the convergence between the three topics of digital media, discipleship, and youth.

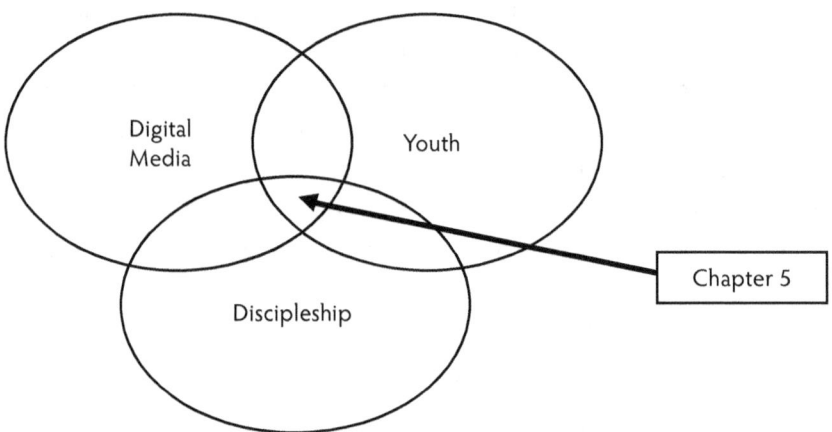

Figure 5.1. The convergence of digital media, youth, and discipleship

This chapter discusses the gains to be had from digital technology as well as the ways it can contribute positively to the discipling of youth in the digital age. How might discipleship faithfully proceed in the context of youth ministry? The main task of youth ministry is helping youth come to know and live out the Christian life, especially knowing what it means to be Christians in today's world, surrounded by digital media.[3] The essence of Christian life is relationship – relationship first with God as Father and with other members

---

3. Smallbones, "Educating People," 56.

in Christian faith communities.[4] Discipleship must be the central concern of the church, for it undergirds all the other tasks of the church such as worship, fellowship, mission, and evangelism.[5] Discipleship is effective when it leads to youth participation in the total life of the church where their learning can last the longest.[6] Discipleship must keep a balance of the three aspects of spirituality: affection, activity, and cognition.[7] After discussing the theology of youth ministry, this chapter will also draw implications for the whole project together and issue a call to the church to be "all things to all people," engaging practically in discipling the youth of the digital age. Finally, it will contextualize the theology of discipleship among young people in Vietnam. Spiritual disciplines in the digital age such as solitude, silence, and prayer will be displayed in one concrete setting.

1. What Aspects of Digital Technology Are Really Helpful?

In the digital age, information is delivered faster and more effectively than ever before.[8] This enables people to receive information from others quickly across long distances. Even though I study far away from my home country, sometimes I learn what is going on in the lives of the youth at my home church even more quickly than those who live nearer to them because they choose to inform me first via social media. In some ways, digital technology can shorten geographical distance. A very important feature of the digital age is how networking technologies move us toward a network society.[9] Digital technology enables telecommunication or "telepresence." Though this is not the same thing as embodied friendship in the flesh that can be "smelled" and "touched," keeping this digitally mediated connection can still sustain relationship in substantive ways.[10]

---

4. Smallbones, 60–62.
5. Smallbones, 55; Aleshire, "Christian Education and Theology," 17–19.
6. Jordan, "Role of the Pastor," 301–302.
7. Botton, "Educating for Spirituality," 34–35.
8. Fortner, "Gospel in a Digital Age," 10.
9. Meadows, "Mission and Discipleship," 165.
10. Meadows, 169.

Thus, social media stands as a challenge to the traditional concept of community and its insistence on physical presence. Social networking sites facilitate the formation of virtual communities of fan clubs or groups of like-minded people.[11] Of course, this cannot solve the issue of "echo chambers," where we only engage with people like us, which is not conducive for diversity and true inclusivity. However, this issue happens in physical life too. The premise of social media is that physical presence is not required. These online communities have much to offer in providing ways to share knowledge, personal experiences, and interests with people across the globe. People can make friends with someone they have never met before. Facebook provides the platform for people to gather online and form online communities. People can argue about the positive or negative effects of this. However, it is clear that digital technology makes it possible to care for your loved ones and to be there for them in a new way when physical presence is not possible. The apostle Paul uses the latest technology of his day – writing letters (Col 2:1, 5) – to share the word of God and to be there for other Christians.[12] Digital technology gives us creative and dynamic ways to connect with, care for, and reach out to others. Parents can watch over their little children in school through cameras, and neighbors can record video proof when somebody mistreats a child. Digital monitoring can locate people with Alzheimer's during an episode of wandering.[13]

All such forms of surveillance must be practiced with special care, as Eric Stoddart emphasizes:

> Surveillance of people has dominated our culture of technologised risk and eager claims to isolating privacy. As one who knew its gaze, suffered its harsh consequences, and now watches over us that we might flourish and not wither, the crucified God reorientates our perspective. Surveillance ought first and foremost be for people, and only as we, individuals and groups, lay and expert, keep holding it to account can we claim to be practising it carefully.[14]

---

11. Meadows, 170.
12. Brock, *Christian Ethics*, 274.
13. Stoddart, *Theological Perspectives*, Kindle locations 372–374.
14. Stoddart, Kindle locations 3915–3918.

According to Philip R. Meadows (discussed in chapter 2), relationships and community can be expressed through both digital media and face-to-face contact.[15] Previous chapters have presented, in some depth, the impacts of digital media on society in general and on youth in particular. It is certainly true that the internet can have both positive and negative influences on youth, but it is also a fact that they will have to grow up surrounded by digital media. The sheer inescapability of digital technology means that it is important for churches and youth leaders to learn not only to recognize but even to take advantage of the good aspects of digital technology in discipling youth. Online spaces can be a window through which adults get to know more about young people since often youth are much more open in sharing their lives online. There is a huge potential for adults to befriend young people in cyberspace, where the generational gap quickly appears to be much smaller when adults engage there in a caring way and know how to befriend young people. This is especially helpful in the context of countries that have hierarchical structure like Vietnam, where there is a huge distance between parents and children as compared to parent-child relationships in the West. Parents and children can be friends with each other on social media. More and more parents in Vietnam find that Facebook can help them connect better with their children and get to know more about them as compared to face-to-face interactions communication, which is bound to hierarchical structure, hindering them from talking with each other. Many young people in Vietnam now are open to sharing their lives with their parents on Facebook. This, in turn, strengthens parent-child relationships in real life. Of course, it is important to take into consideration the pitfalls of digital media discussed so far in this thesis.

During my time serving as a youth worker at a local church in Vietnam, I found that Facebook gave me a good opportunity to get to know more and interact with the young people. Online space can be a window to befriend the youth who are in need. During this time, I also ministered to some young people who were addicted to online games to the extent that they dropped out of school. Besides befriending them at the youth service, small group Bible study, and other face-to-face activities, I also befriended and accompanied them on Facebook. Though I am now on another continent to pursue my studies, I still keep in touch with them via Facebook in order to share in their

---

15. Meadows, "Mission and Discipleship," 165.

life journeys and give them advice when necessary. One boy came to know the Lord through a youth in our youth group. This boy came from a broken and poor family. He dropped out of school after grade 4 and was addicted to online games. I tried to help him by befriending him both off-line and online. I also found another school for him. He joined the youth group regularly and enjoyed the Bible study and fellowship. I noticed that he became less addicted to online games as he enjoyed fellowship with the youth group. However, due to my being away for my studies, I have had to leave my home country and home church, so I could not continue to take care of him face to face.

The boy in question successfully finished fifth grade – and with good results. Unfortunately, however, a paperwork tangle blocked his way to continuing into secondary school.[16] I found out about this during my short trip home in summer 2017 and managed to enroll him in a secondary school to study in sixth grade despite it being halfway through the term. Unfortunately, a few months later, he informed me via Facebook that the school had not let him continue to study because of his absence from many classes due to sickness and forgetting to go to school, which may well have been an effect of a return of online addiction. He also told me that he had skipped church for a while. I was sad but kept encouraging him to continue his studies next year. I also asked my coworkers in youth ministry to take him to the doctor and look after him.

I wanted to do more for him, but I could not because of the distance. I could only pray for him and encourage him via Facebook Messenger. Through this, I also knew that his "sanctuary" was cyberspace, where he could escape from his home, where he was constantly verbally abused by his family members who had a different faith and saw him as a "useless" teenager. My pastoral journey with this boy had revealed that there are indeed ministerial contacts that can be pursued online. There remain important pastoral lines of connection in the digital realm that can be utilized to care for young people and befriend them via digital technology. This is not to suggest that there are not also pastoral engagements that need to be face to face. It is important to be aware of these different modalities and for youth ministers to take advantage of what digital technology can do to help us disciple young people.

---

16. In Vietnam, secondary school starts from sixth grade.

There is a huge potential for adults to befriend youth in cyberspace. Digital technology makes it possible to reach out to and care for the young people who are immersed in cyberspace. The church is called to "declare [God's] power to the next generation, [God's] might to all who are to come" (Ps 71:8). As Christ goes into the far countries to seek the outcasts, the church is called to reach out to the outcasts too. Looking back on my ministry, I see how Christ has changed my ministry focus from the "bright" or "well-mannered" youth to those with more difficulties in life. I also see that the internet makes it possible for these young people to raise their voices or get some attention. In this changing world with its modern technologies and revolving ideas of community living, there is a constant challenge to the church to be "all things to all people." Having discussed the helpful aspects of digital technology while carefully discerning its risks, I will propose a theology of youth ministry which serves as the context for youth discipleship.

2. Youth Ministry

Youth ministry in the digital age is helping youth come to know and live out the Christian life, especially in today's world surrounded by digital media.[17] The essence of Christian life is relationship.[18] Discipleship must be the central concern of the church,[19] and it must lead to youth participation in the total life of the church.[20] Discipleship must keep a balance of the three aspects of spirituality – affection, activity, and cognition.[21]

a. Relationship

Youth ministry should reflect the purpose of God for his church, which is to build a community of people in communion with him and with one another. Relationship (communion) is at the center of the being of the Trinitarian God, whom we know as Father, Son, and Holy Spirit – or Creator, Redeemer, and Sustainer. It is this God who calls us and inspires us to reach out to young

---

17. Smallbones, "Educating People," 56.
18. Smallbones, 60–62.
19. Smallbones, 55.
20. Jordan, "The Role of the Pastor in Christian Education," 301–302.
21. Botton, "Educating for Spirituality," 34–35.

people. Therefore, the practice of church youth workers finds its true rationale in the God who calls believers to share about him with young people.[22] As discussed in the subsection "*Education*" in chapter 2, digital media change the way that youth learn in school and beyond. More interaction and collaboration in learning should be provided. Teachers should utilize digital platforms to bridge the gap between teacher and student, to know each student, to befriend them, and to accompany them in their studies and in their lives beyond the classroom. With the change in education in the digital age, what should the church, Sunday school teachers, and youth workers do to educate youth in their faith?

Discipleship is more than holding Sunday school classes and having children and youth memorize Bible verses. Its calling is to form and shape people as they discover their faith in God through Jesus Christ and learn to live their lives in light of that faith.[23] Discipleship, in short, is educating people to be Christians.[24] Being a Christian means more than knowing and understanding Scripture.[25] It means living life in all its fullness, as God intended it to be lived (John 10:10). It means developing a Father-child relationship with God and sibling relationships with the members of the church.[26] It is these images of fullness and familial relationships, when applied to the church, that suggest that the schooling or instructional model is not sufficient for conceiving youth discipleship but requires being changed or supplemented.[27] Jesus set the best example of the socialization model of teaching.[28] He taught his disciples, but he also lived with them and let them see him in various situations. He was completely open and honest with them. He modeled the godly way of life for them. This socialization supplements the schooling or instructional model as it provides a way of teaching the word of God as a lifestyle of relationship.[29]

Stanley Hauerwas points out the importance of sharing life with youth in discipling them:

---

22. Ward, God at the Mall, 33–34.
23. Good, "Celebrating Varieties," 1.
24. Smallbones, "Educating People," 56.
25. Smallbones, 58–59.
26. Smallbones 58–59.
27. Smallbones, 58.
28. Smallbones, 60–62.
29. Smallbones, 60–62.

> Recent studies suggest that, in most mainline, Protestant churches, our congregations have become the last stop for youth on the way out of church. We are doing a poor job of retaining our young. Of course, the sources of the problem are many. Yet we believe that a renewed sense of the unique way the church makes Christians through example is an essential part of any response to our young. We shall have to break our habit of having church in such a way that people are deceived into thinking that they can be Christians and remain strangers.[30]

He shares how his church conducted a confirmation class for teenagers with the goals of producing "people who more closely resemble, in their life-style, beliefs, and values, disciples of Jesus." Believing that "the manner in which most of us became Christian was by looking over someone else's shoulder," the church assigned adult "mentors" to pair up with the teenagers to do joint activities for three months, such as reading the Gospel of Luke, attending Sunday service, doing volunteer works for at least fifteen hours together, and so on.[31] This procedure of conducting confirmation edifies not only the teenagers but also the pastor, the mentors, and the whole congregation since it shows them "what it means to be the church."[32] Hauerwas concludes, "The church needs to see that one of its greatest resources is its ability to bring generations of disciples together . . . Ethics does not get much more Christian than this – an ordinary person living the Christian life before other ordinary people."[33] Therefore, it is important for the church to build networks of intergenerational relationships where people can share their lives with one another, especially with youth, whose faith is confirmed through real-life examples.

Steven Emery-Wright and Ed Mackenzie suggest the importance of the network of relationships for faith formation:

> The Scripture, theology, and sociological studies reveal the importance of a range of networks for growing faith. God has created us as relational beings, and this means that spiritual growth

---

30. Hauerwas, Willimon, *Resident Aliens*, chap. 5.
31. Willimon, Chap. 5.
32. Willimon, Chap. 5.
33. Willimon, Chap. 5.

requires relational bonds and social connections . . . While networks are necessary for growing in holiness at every stage of life, they are particularly important for young people, those between eleven and twenty years of age. During adolescence, teenagers undergo massive physical, emotional, and intellectual changes while also exploring issues of identity and purpose.[34]

Therefore, church leaders, youth workers, and parents need to create and maintain a healthy network of God-centered relationships to support youth.[35] In the digital age, where the youth are seeking cooperation, networking, and experiencing, socialization will come easily for them, albeit much guidance and discernment are needed. As discussed in the previous section, "*What Aspects of Digital Technology Are Really Helpful?*" digital technology gives us creative and dynamic ways to connect with, care for, and reach out to youth. There is a huge potential for church leaders, youth workers, and parents to befriend young people in cyberspace, where the generational gap quickly appears to be much smaller.

Having recognized these important points, my church has been successful in applying the socialization model for the past few years. In addition to offering Sunday school classes, which follow the typical form of the schooling or instructional model, Bible study groups or classes have also been transformed into cell groups. The youth are divided into smaller groups according to their age and have the opportunity not only to study the Bible through discussion but also to encourage one another to grow in their spiritual lives through worship, eating together, evangelizing, visiting one another, and sharing their life experiences. In addition, the church also has youth meeting every Sunday with various interactive activities for the youth such as small group discussions, games, movies, contemporary worship, and interactive Bible studies. Retreats and camps are also available in which church members can stay together for a few days to meditate on God's words and strengthen their relationships with God and with one another. There is also a youth ministry Facebook group to help youth stay connected with the church, youth workers, and other youth. Youth workers connect with and care for the youth both online and off-line. Online Bible study and other online activities such as doing

---

34. Emery-Wright and Mackenzie, *Networks for Faith Formation*, xvi.
35. Emery-Wright and Mackenzie, xvi.

some real-life challenges, online devotion or mediation were also conducted during the lockdown due to COVID-19. These activities have helped many members to grow in their spiritual lives. To recap, youth ministry should reflect the purpose of God for his church, which is to build a community of people in communion with him and with one another. Relationship (communion) is at the center of the being of the Trinitarian God, whom we know as Father, Son, and Holy Spirit – or Creator, Redeemer, and Sustainer. It is this God who calls us and inspires us to share life with young people.

b. Central Concern

According to Daniel Aleshire, while the church gathers for worship, fellowship, mission, evangelism, and discipleship, the distinctive task of discipleship undergirds all the others. For example, before people can mature in their worship, they must understand what worship is and how believers engage in it. Before people engage in missions, they must understand the task and methods of missions.[36] Therefore, discipleship must be the central concern of the church. In Christian discipleship, it is important for teachers and youth workers to examine the call to teach or serve since it is the particular call from God, not an additional work.[37] It is the work of transforming lives. It is leading youth forth into lives of faith and committed discipleship. At the same time, teachers and youth workers need to be properly trained to teach the Bible to youth in the way that is best for them. They need to understand how the youth who were born in the digital age view the gospel. They need access to a theology that enables them as they disciple the youth. Such ministry must also be faithful to the Bible while at the same time presenting it as the word of God in a manner that youth can understand and relate to. One fruitful way to do this is to let youth express their needs and discuss the activities that might be most engaging to them. Observing how they respond to youth programs in church can also help us create and adjust the curriculum in a way that suits them best.[38]

---

36. Aleshire, "Christian Education and Theology," 17–19.
37. Harris, "Teaching," 240.
38. Harris, 243.

c. Participation

In the section "Theology of Community" in chapter 4, we discussed how social media rekindle the concepts of participation and community. Participation calls us to be true friends to one another. The very neurological patterns of youth in the digital age have become especially attuned to interactive activities. In the digital native population, learning will be deepest and most long lasting when they are deeply immersed in the total life of the church.[39] Because the church is the community of faith called into being by Jesus Christ, it is a community that must, by definition, be fully inclusive. Its membership is not self-determined but established by Christ. It is on these grounds that youth need to be engaged in every possible aspect of church life since they are no less a part of God's people than anyone else in the church. They need worship that they can learn from, and in turn, they need to contribute to the worship experience.[40] It is best to involve youth in serving and caring for other youth, setting good examples to others, and also serving the whole church with their gifts of technology, music, arts, and so on.

d. Balance

Spirituality has three main components: affection, activity, and cognition. Affection transpires as God and worshipper meet and interact in the inner person. Activity takes place in acts of loving God with all one's strength as we serve others like Jesus did – binding wounds, feeding the hungry, etc. Cognition is enacted in the gaining of a deep understanding of biblical data that shapes a believer's spiritual experience. It is important that these three aspects be represented and strengthened in the spiritual life of the church.[41] The three main components of spirituality are mentioned in the epistle of the Apostle Paul to Christians in Philippi:

> And this is my prayer: that your love may abound more and more in knowledge and depth of insight, so that you may be able to discern what is best and may be pure and blameless for the day of Christ, filled with the fruit of righteousness that

---

39. Jordan, "Role of the Pastor," 301–302.
40. Ng, "Children in the Worshipping Community," 233.
41. Botton, "Educating for Spirituality," 35.

comes through Jesus Christ – to the glory and praise of God. (Phil 1:9–11)

James K. A. Smith shows how these three components are interrelated:

> In the dynamic relationship between love and knowledge, head and heart, the Scriptures paint a holistic picture of the human person. It's not only our minds that God redeems, but the whole person: head, heart, hands. Christ takes captive our minds but also our *kardia*, even what Paul calls our *splagchna*, our "inner parts" that are the seat of our "affections."[42]

Love (affection) is the condition for knowledge (cognition), and "learning to love [God] takes practice" (activity).[43] It is important for Christian youth discipleship to keep these three main components in the proper balance.

In this section, we have discussed that the task of youth ministry is helping youth to come to know and to live out the Christian life, especially in today's world surrounded by digital media. The essence of Christian life is relationship. It must keep a balance of the three aspects of spirituality – affection, activity, and cognition. Doing so properly, it will enable youth to participate in the total life of the church. Having discussed helpful aspects of digital technology and the theology of youth ministry, let us now draw practical implications of the whole project.

3. Implications for the Church's Practice of Discipling the Youth of the Digital Age

a. Being "All Things to All People"

Digital technology challenges the church and church workers to care for youth in a new way. If we want to disciple youth, we need to know their culture and use language that they can understand and relate to. Christians must discover anew what Paul was enjoining when he told the Corinthian church that he had become "all things to all people" in order to save them (1 Cor 9:19–23):

> Though I am free and belong to no one, I have made myself a slave to everyone, to win as many as possible. To the Jews I

---

42. Smith, *You Are What You Love*, chap. 1.
43. Smith, chap. ?.

became like a Jew, to win the Jews. To those under the law I became like one under the law (though I myself am not under the law), so as to win those under the law. To those not having the law I became like one not having the law (though I am not free from God's law but am under Christ's law), so as to win those not having the law. To the weak I became weak, to win the weak. I have become all things to all people so that by all possible means I might save some. I do all this for the sake of the gospel, that I may share in its blessings. (NIV)

Brian Brock and Bernd Wannenwetsch suggest that Paul cleared away any obstacles to the gospel by refusing "both itinerancy and patronage – the main markers of spiritual authorities of the day" – which might manipulate people's responses to the gospel.[44] They explain,

> Up to this point Paul has developed his apology for the kenotic apostolate he embodies by explaining why his renunciation of rights is necessary to preserve the freedom of the gospel in the course of his proclamation. In the famous passage now before us he describes with some precision how the kenotic character of his mission positions him within varying cultural and religious contexts.[45]

The gospel tells Paul about himself and the people to whom he is reaching out. In this way, the gospel brings Paul and the people together. The gospel is changing not only the people but also Paul himself:[46]

> Paul's discipline thus goes beyond asceticism in his pursuit of a thoroughgoing emptying of his own designs. This discipline consists in an active process of fighting those self-images and cultural habits, however ingrained and unconscious, that bar him from remaining faithful to the Christ who has appeared to him and bound him to other human beings.[47]

---

44. Brock and Wannenwetsch, *Malady of the Christian Body*, 209.
45. Brock and Wannenwetsch, 216.
46. Brock and Wannenwetsch, 212.
47. Brock and Wannenwetsch, 215.

Such a willingness to enter foreign cultural space, with all the embarrassment and powerlessness it will entail, is a prime example of the evangelistic kenosis Paul is commending. We must be prepared to become vulnerable by attempting to be "as" others in order to be "with" them.[48]

Following Paul's example, the church, youth workers, and parents are called to step out of their comfort zones to reach those in need, including young people who are lonely and lost in both cyberspace and physical life.

In this digital age, even though we are more technologically connected than ever before and even though there are truly wonderful elements to life in the modern world, the isolating conditions we face show no sign of letting up, as David Kinnaman, Mark Matlock, and Aly Hawkins observe: "An epidemic of loneliness sequesters tens of millions of people. Barna's data shows that adults are twice as likely to say they are lonely compared to a decade ago; about one out of five Americans say they feel lonely."[49] The solution to this kind of isolation is spending time together with youth.[50] This requires us to sacrifice our time and energy as we share our many talents and God-given gifts with others. We are called to reach the Net Generation for Christ. It will be the most joyful experience to bring other people to the kingdom of God, for our prize is not on earth but in heaven. As young people, they have strength, time, talents, and wisdom to pursue their interests, career, and reputation in both cyberspace and everyday life. We are called to share the gospel and bring it to them wherever they are. It is important that youth workers and parents remain present with young people, not as "police" but as friends and mentors, noticing their gifts and seeking to bring out the best in them. We need to teach them to live for Jesus and glorify his name in their daily lives, at school, at home, and everywhere they go.

What does it mean to "be all things" to the youth? It does not mean that we have to play online games like they do. In my experience as a youth worker, sometimes I felt out of place, because the young people were talking about online games that I knew nothing about. I found it helpful to privately ask one of them to tell me more about the game they were interested in when I

---

48. Brock and Wannenwetsch, 219.
49. Kinnaman, *Faith for Exiles*.
50. Kinnaman.

did a home visitation. Not only did my interest pay off in strengthening my relationship with that particular youth, but the information I gained helped me build relationships with other youth interested in similar games. It is always beneficial to put in the effort to get to know the youth more deeply and let them know that we really care for them and are interested in getting to know them more. This is not just about adopting a certain skill or mastering a certain technique. Rather, it is about cultivating a loving heart that cares enough to put in the effort to become "all things to all people."

Being "all things to all people" does require us to make some extra effort. A boy in the local church asked me to install Snapchat last year because most of the youth and students in the current local church where I am serving were using it more actively than Facebook. I installed it but did not make much effort to learn and use it because I found it uninteresting and difficult to use. Another young person asked me how it was that I never saw her story. Then she showed me how to use it. I tried but found it a bit boring, and I even uninstalled it later on. Recently, I found that several times, as they were talking about what other friends were doing while looking at Snapchat, I felt completely ignorant. Wanting to stay closer to the youth and get to know more about them, I decided to re-install it and spend a few hours learning how to use it. I started looking at their stories, sharing my story, and chatting with them more regularly. I find that at least I have gotten to know some more about the lives of the young people, and they have also gotten to know a bit more about me.

Some may argue that we do not need to go to cyberspace to share the gospel with or disciple youth. They prefer to stay "safe," even in this day and age. This argument is similar to the preachers, during Paul's time, who received payment when sharing the gospel while Paul himself decided not to. Paul cleared away any obstacles to the gospel by refusing "both itinerancy and patronage" that might manipulate people's responses to the gospel.[51] We should learn from Paul's zeal to clear away any obstruction to the gospel and bring the gospel to all people by making extra effort to reach those in need. This includes breaking down barriers with those who are different from us and making them feel welcome in our midst.[52] Since none of us are isolated but

---

51. Brock, *Malady of the Christian Body*, 198, 209.
52. Vanier, *Community and Growth*, 20.

are part of the community that God has placed us into, we need to encourage the young people to care for each other, not only in the virtual world but also in the physical world, and also to care for the needy beyond our community.

b. Practical Applications

1) Being True

As previously mentioned, in the digital age, there is a shift from a modern, individualistic, and highly rational concept of the gospel to a postmodern, communal, holistic, and experiential one. Hipps suggests that the practice of storytelling as a corporate spiritual discipline is one of the most powerful ways to deepen our connections with young people.[53] A cell group is a good place for youth to share their personal testimonies and life stories with one other. Youth ministry is a good place for youth workers to "be true" to youth, to open their lives to them, and to make apparent their own spiritual journeys, including their struggles and failings. When we work with young people or teach them, Rodger Nishioka suggests, some self-disclosure about our journeys with God is crucial because youth want to know whether the preacher really lives out the word of God.[54] Youth workers and preachers should not try to act like saints. Transparency is significant since youth want to see a true person from whom they can learn, not an elusive model to aspire to.

In my ministry experiences with youth, I often witness how encouraging my struggles, failures, or weaknesses are to the youth. They feel empowered when asked to pray for me. Their prayers, in turn, uplift my heart. Of course, I also share about how God saved me and the times when he led me through my failures or gave me success and blessings. One needs to strike a delicate balance so as not to overwhelm youth with the details of our lives. It is wise that we share the things about ourselves that are relevant and beneficial to youth while not causing unnecessary misunderstanding or unintended harm. Sharing how the gospel of Christ is at work in our lives keeps the focus on Jesus and not ourselves.

---

53. Hipps, *Hidden Power*, 117.
54. Nishioka, "Preaching and Youth," 42.

2) Gym Time

During my time serving as a youth worker at a local church in Vietnam, I had a chance to minister to some youth who were addicted to online games to the extent of dropping out of school. The good thing is that they enjoyed fellowship with other youth and with youth workers. They also regularly attended the youth service, small group Bible studies, and other youth group activities. They even responded very actively in Bible study at times. My concern was to find ways to help them with their game addictions. We are told in 1 Timothy 4:8, "For physical training is of some value, but godliness has value for all things." Thus, besides praying with them and giving them advice from the Bible regarding addictions, I also decided to ask them to join another youth worker to work out. This man, who is very good at power lifting, used to be a game addict himself when he was a teenager. He shared his testimony to the youth group – that when he was in junior high school, he used to skip classes to play computer game. One day, the teacher told his mom of his continual absences in class. When he reached home, he saw his mom in tears. She did not say anything, yet her tears helped him understand how much he had grieved her heart. Therefore, he decided to change his behavior from then on. He started to read the Bible, and he asked God for help. From that time on, God transformed his life. He started to serve in the youth group as one of the youth leaders and later on became a youth worker.

The youth addicted to games enjoyed the gym time with this youth worker as well as the conversations they had about school, sports, and other facets of life. There is no recipe for this process – no miracle cures or easy solutions – but an ongoing, long-term process. These youth continued to join the youth groups at church and eventually got back to school. As they grew in faith in Jesus and in fellowship with the other youth, their addictions lessened. Online games and cyberspace are still very attractive to them, and they still remain very active on it. However, they are attracted more to the fellowship that the youth group and Bible study time bring. The search for a meaningful community is inherent in youth, as it is in all humankind. Thus, it is important for the church to be a true community where youth and others can share their struggles, make friends, and encounter the saving grace of Jesus Christ. Since addiction to social media can be a critical challenge to youth, the church community should make an effort to help them overcome it. Just as with any other addiction, there is no onetime solution to this. The most important thing is to journey with them, meet their need, and give them plenty of support. We should learn more about the social interactions between youth and media, and the way youth form certain habits. This will better prepare us to disciple youth regardless of the rapidly changing world of technology.

3) Online Police?

It is interesting to see that there is an increasing number of parents joining social networking sites such as Facebook and making friends with their children. Many youth workers are also quite active on social networking sites. There is a temptation for these adults to monitor the online activities of youth like online police. They rebuke their children harshly when certain posts seem provocative or inappropriate. This is not helpful since children can always find ways to sneak around and thus remain unchanged in their actions. It is certainly not an easy task to navigate for the adults to be able to discipline youth without alienating them in the process. One time, a parent of a youth told me that she had seen a not-quite-appropriate photo of her son on Facebook. She wisely decided to not to force him to take it down. She shared with him during their daily Bible study and prayer time that she cannot watch over him all the time, but God can. She expected him to live a righteous life that flowed from a heart of obedience and love for God. She told me that he had already known what to do, and she expected that he would be obedient to God.

It is impossible for adults to act as online police toward young people since they cannot be online all the time. It is also difficult to restrict the online activity of their children. However, the alternative of leaving children to their own devices without any guidance at all in cyberspace is much worse. Between policing and giving up engagement at all, is the aspiration of parents and youth workers to act as digital mentors by modeling healthy ways of engaging in the online world.[55] Emery-Wright and Mackenzie suggest,

> Parents and churches need to help young people engage positively with the online world. The online world can be wonderful and stimulating place . . . Given the presence of young people on social media, it is also important that other Christians are

---

55. Emery-Wright and Mackenzie, *Networks for Faith Formation*, 122.

present with them and encourage them through that medium. While this does not mean that every parent or church leader needs to engage, this could be one way in which a youth minister remains present to the young people they serve.[56]

This approach keeps the lines of communication with youth open and remains engaged with them. Such an approach is an offer of support in the fight of youth against the negative aspects of the online world.[57]

There is a youth in my youth ministry who has a disability. She dropped out of school after first grade due to some family problems and the combination of her physical and intellectual disabilities. As a result, she can only read and write very little. I noticed, however, that she is quite "smart" and active on Facebook. She also offered some good answers during small group Bible study time at church. Upon these observations, I decided to find a way for her to get back to school. She has been studying well in that school since that point. Now she is in seventh grade. Observing that she likes cooking, I also encouraged her to learn baking so that she could earn money from this job in the future. She now can bake very nice cakes. It is also good to know that her knowledge, as well as her faith and fellowship with the youth group, is growing. She has also been serving actively in youth ministry such as by leading a youth service, sharing a Bible message, giving Bible quizzes, doing home visitations, encouraging younger youth to follow Christ, and baking delicious cakes for the youth group or to raise funds for youth camps. I am very encouraged when observing how she has been contributing her gifts to the church.

Brian Brock and Bernd Wannenwetsch observe the biblical basis of discerning the gifts of youth as they commentate on 1 Corinthians 12:4–7 that every member of the body is a "*revealer* of the Spirit to the body as a whole" and the Spirit is the "arranger" of the spiritual gifts, which need to be discovered in real time:

> The Spirit alone is the arranger of the gifts that make up the different parts of the body. This notion of revealing is closely connected to the *moment* of discovery. If respective fruits of the

---

56. Emery-Wright and Mackenzie, 123.
57. Emery-Wright and Mackenzie, 122.

Spirit are meant to reveal the Spirit to the body, we must speak in terms of a moment of discovery, since a revelation is never merely a deposit that can be known in advance but is an actual happening, an instance of recognition and reception. A *charisma* thus reveals the Holy Spirit to the body as each respective gift is embraced as God's gift. This is why the gifts are *energēma* – always *enacted* and always needing to be *discerned* in real time.[58]

Youth can contribute their gifts to the church if the church helps them discover their places in the body of Christ, as Brock and Wannenwetsch observe:

> Such moments of revelation in the embrace of a particular gift might occur in the life of young Christians, for instance, when members of the body help them to discover their proper places and roles in the community. Should a shy teenager be given some form of leadership role in a church's youth work, the discovery of her unique gift to the body as a whole will typically be prepared by an initial tentative grasp of that gift by those who encourage her to step forward in order to allow the full *phanerosis* of the gift to appear.[59]

Therefore, it is important that youth workers and parents remain present with young people, not as "police" but as friends and mentors, noticing the gifts in them and seeking to bring out the best in them.

Kinnaman's survey of the churches in North America shows the importance of mentoring in discipling youth: "Four out of ten resilient disciples (more than double of any of the other groups) have had an adult mentor at church – someone other than a staff member. More than half of resilient disciples look to an older person for advice when making difficult decisions."[60] He adds that mentoring youth requires intentional planning and consistent effort.[61] Therefore, the church should think of ways to provide mentorship to youth. My youth ministry has a tradition of having older youth take care of younger youth during their five years in youth ministry (13–18 years old). As

---

58. Brock and Wannenwetsch, *Therapy of the Christian Body*, 2:79. *Phanerosis* means "manifestation" (1 Cor 12:7).
59. Brock and Wannenwetsch, 2:79.
60. Kinnaman, *Faith for Exiles*.
61. Kinnaman.

youth grow older and become young adults, they still maintain their relationships with the youth that are younger than them. English club or tutoring and vocational training provide good environments for intergenerational mentorship. Serving groups, such as technical, worship, music, and decoration, with members of different ages also provide potential places for mentoring, not only in serving the church but also in Christian living.

During a Sunday school class of children aged eight to twelve at my current church in the UK, I asked them, "Are you addicted to digital media?" I received some honest affirmative answers. It is interesting to see that children realize their struggles. One boy said that it was very difficult for him to stay away from his iPhone. Another boy told me after class that he had no one to play with, so the iPad was his only friend at home. It is important to raise awareness regarding digital-device addiction among children. At the same time, Sunday school teachers, youth workers, and parents should join in an effort to support them with biblical truth, advice, care, and prayer. Instead of giving smart devices to children to play on by themselves, parents should endeavor to spend more quality time engaging with their children.

We have a practice of hosting a conference between youth workers and parents at least once a year to share updates about youth ministry, communicate with the parents the needs of the youth, listen to their concerns, and pray for the youth as well as for one another. It is most advisable for church workers and Sunday school teachers to build connections with the parents in order to more effectively care for youth. During a meeting between Sunday school teachers and parents, some parents shared their concerns about their children's addiction to digital devices and social media. One parent said that she had once decided to take all the digital devices away during her children's bedtime, to which her son had responded, "Aha! You don't trust me!" Though having no clear solution, it is encouraging that the parents care enough about their children to share their struggles with one another. The parents really put their hearts into praying for the children, for themselves, and for the church in ministering to the children. In short, it is important that youth workers and parents remain present with young people, not as "police" but as friends and mentors, noticing the gifts in them and seeking to bring out the best in them.

4) Living Word

One person told me that the youth in his church no longer want to attend Bible study class or Sunday school, so the church had to cancel them. This sad reality, unfortunately, happens in many other churches as well. This is not just the problem of youth workers; it represents a problem for the whole church. It is the problem of pastors, Sunday school teachers, youth workers, and parents. Young people need the living word of God that can transform their lives so that they can live life as a "living sacrifice" to God. In this, they need a community of faith with whom to journey. In this digital age, youth are requesting a change in the model of pedagogy, from a teacher-focused approach based on instruction to a student-focused model based on collaboration. Therefore, we need to work harder to bring the word of God to them in ways that they can understand and embrace. We can utilize games, movies, power points, music, crafts, food, skits, fashion shows, Bible apps, online devotionals, and other similarly innovative means to deliver the gospel message more effectively.

Nishioka points out that it is important to engage the senses as we seek to deliver the Bible's message to youth in our postmodern and digital age.[62] For example, youth would really enjoy it if we remade the Passover feast and they could wear Jewish costumes, dance, and eat the Passover meals. We can let them grill fish by the seaside, visit the vineyard or lighthouse, or make a clay pot, bringing to life the images presented in the Bible. We can make a simple meditation with just a pencil, a piece of paper, and a Bible passage, or we can make it into a prayer journey with tangible objects and experiences. Actually, we have implemented these activities in our youth ministry. They went well and the youth enjoyed them very much. Youth can certainly benefit from these activities in which careful preparations are made and the Holy Spirit is at work. Nishioka presents this as good news:

> More than you can possibly imagine, today's young people are yearning for the Word to grab hold of them and transform them. And they don't care if they look foolish to others. They yearn for the hope of the Gospel. They yearn for the Truth of Jesus Christ. They want to climb the ladder. They want to see forever![63]

---

62. Nishioka, "Preaching and Youth," 42.
63. Nishioka, 44.

We need to preach the message of hope to them since most young people are struggling to find reasons for sources of hope in their lives. Jesus Christ is our only hope, and the church is an ideal community in which we can experience that.[64]

5) Sharing the Gospel

We are created in God's image (Gen 1:27). Each of us is a uniquely designed and gifted masterpiece of the Creator.[65] Knowing that God is our only true source of security frees us from anxiously trying to save and secure ourselves. This is important, good news to share with youth who are confused and overwhelmed by the overload of information from social media.[66] It is essential for the church to make Christian hope the central doctrine of our ministry with youth. Emphasizing hope as a starting point for youth ministry offers youth an opportunity to confront the problems that they are facing in the digital age with the divine power necessary for living in the promises of God. It is important to nurture hope in youth so that they can serve as God's agents, bringing hope to all humanity.[67] The church is called to pass on the true knowledge of God to youth in the digital age. It is crucial that youth ministry commits to turning lost youth into fully committed disciples of Jesus. Youth ministry must be missional and educational, maintaining a balanced focus on both discipleship and evangelism.[68]

Chapter 4 outlined the profound implications for culture, self-identity, and the gospel that attend the coming of the digital age. Digital media can be used as a means for sharing the gospel, and at the same time, it must be recognized that it also presents a temptation. The main temptation is to see social media missional engagement as somehow easier than embodied mission – a route that does not demand blood, sweat, tears, or personal relationship and commitment.[69] As David Kinnaman emphasizes, God's countercultural mission means "living as a faithful presence by trusting God's power

---

64. Nishioka, 42.
65. Clark, "The Changing Face," 49.
66. Richter, "Growing Up Postmodern," 76.
67. Parker, "Theological Framework," 273–274.
68. Cannister, "Youth Ministry's Historical Context," 90.
69. Meadows, "Mission and Discipleship," 174.

and living differently from cultural norms."[70] Living as Jesus's disciples is countercultural because in certain respects, it runs in very different directions from the culture of the world. The faithful Christian community is distinct from the systems and structures of power, sexuality, and money of the world. Romans 12:2 says, "Don't copy the behaviour and customs of this world, but let God transform you into a new person by changing the way you think." (NLT) Mission is not just about going on mission trips or sharing the gospel verbally.[71] Kinnaman defines,

> But the idea of mission we're conveying here is that God is powerful, active, and intentional, and he wants his followers to play a part in redeeming people and restoring the world to himself. Biblically speaking, this includes a wide range of aspirations, including serving others, caring for creation, receiving God's blessing in order to bless others, and seeking to save the lost in Jesus's name.[72]

The good news is that God chooses to work his mission in part through his people. Of course, he doesn't need us to do his work, but he wants to give us the privilege of joining with him in the mission to reconcile the world to himself. He wants us to participate in his grand mission and live out his mission with others because he loves us and wants to work with us in showing his love to other people.[73] Counterchultural mission is the outward expression of living as a disciple of Christ. This is not an individual practice but a corporate practice of the whole body of Christ for the sake of the world. It is about the community of faith working together to influence the world toward God's good, original intentions.[74]

Practicing counterchultural mission requires believers to turn away from the self-centeredness that is promoted by digital media in order to develop the muscles of sacrifice and service. In the "digital Babylon" of self-promotion invited on sites like YouTube and Twitter, Christians must learn to be comfortable as outsiders like Jesus was. This requires practicing the spiritual

---

70. Kinnaman, *Faith for Exiles*.
71. Kinnaman.
72. Kinnaman.
73. Kinnaman.
74. Kinnaman.

disciplines of service, sacrifice, silence, solitude, letting go of control, thinking less about ourselves, and cultivating an engaged heart toward one another and for the sake of others.[75] One positive aspect of millennial and Gen Z Christians is that as they are trying to figure out how to navigate this digital culture, they can experience empathy for people who are different from themselves. This is a good and godly instinct as Paul wrote that he became "all things to all people" so that he might win some to Christ (1 Cor 9:21–22). He appealed to his Greek hearers by talking about the "Unknown God" (Acts 17:22–23) and advised his readers to have "gracious and attractive" conversations with nonbelievers (Col 4:6).[76] With the rising of online hate speech and the decreasing of the expression of mercy and forgiveness toward others in the "digital Babylon," Christians discover that they have both a responsibility and an opportunity to participate in God's mission by showing love to the world in the graciousness of their speech. Even in the relational tension of our times, we are called to express God's love through Jesus's work on the cross to a hurting world, regardless of political affiliation, sexual orientation, or religious affiliation.[77]

Besides showing love in speech, practicing countercultural mission also requires the faith community to work together to bless others, especially those in need. The church can play a significant role in helping youth understand the needs of the poor, both locally and globally, and in giving them real opportunities to serve the poor.[78] By participating in Jesus's countercultural mission in the world, we can make a difference in "digital Babylon," plagued as it is with a sense of entitlement, narcissism, self-centeredness, and consumerism. The church should disciple youth to put aside selfish ambition and reach out for others who are outside of their church's circles.[79] The church should exploit the collaborative nature of the virtual world and its sense of flexibility, transparency, and diversity in order to reach out into many hard-to-reach parts of our world.[80] Participating in Jesus's countercultural mission in the world means reaching out not only to physical contacts but also to online contacts.

---

75. Kinnaman.
76. Kinnaman.
77. Kinnaman.
78. Kinnaman.
79. Kinnaman.
80. Estes, *SimChurch*, 27–28, 76.

It is fascinating to see young people bringing their Facebook friends or online-game friends who are not believers to church. Young people are much better than adults at sharing the gospel through friendship. Witnessing for Christ encourages them to strengthen their own relationships with God and with the faith community. They "behave" themselves online and off-line because they know that God is watching them, and their nonbelieving friends are watching them too. In Vietnam, public proclamation of the Christian faith outside of the church is legally proscribed, but it is legal to proclaim the gospel through personal relationships and social action. And now young people have an online community where they can share faith or tag their friends on an invitation to a youth gospel event at church. It is encouraging to see non-Christian youth enjoy friendship with the youth at church and be able to learn more about Jesus and grow in their faith because of it.

Youth workers should encourage youth to share their faith with their friends. The church should not only care for its own youth but also care for and reach out to the youth outside of the church, bringing them into the church community. Digital and visual communication have exciting potential to allow young people who have not heard the gospel before or who are not familiar with the church to explore the faith without feeling preached to. The need to present a gospel message that is engaging to youth both inside and outside the church is real and challenging. Yet it is certainly rewarding and joyful to the church community to win souls for Christ. It is also important to remember that we are never alone in our effort because it is the Holy Spirit who prompts us to act and who faithfully works with and beside us.

4. Contextualizing the Theology of Spiritual Formation for Youth Ministry in Vietnam

Having discussed helpful aspects of digital technology, the theology of youth ministry, and practical implications for the church in general, in this section, I will contextualize the theology of spiritual formation for youth ministry in Vietnam. As mentioned earlier, in the *introduction*, I grew up in a local church under the denomination called the Evangelical Church of Vietnam and served there for a few years as a youth worker. Besides attending Sunday school and service on Sunday mornings, youth can gather for a youth worship service on Sunday afternoons, with mid-week youth Bible studies in addition.

Bible camp is organized once a year. Some years we have organized an action camp, emphasizing physical games, outdoor activities, sports, and community service. Other years we have put on silent camps, in which silent meditation, prayer journeying, and one-to-one counseling are the main activities.

In the prayer journey version of the summer camp, I have applied some methods of prayer offered in Richard Foster's *Celebration of Discipline*. The youth have tended to respond positively to this approach. Much to our surprise, some youth even gave us the feedback that they loved the silent camps more than the action camps. This response is interesting in that youth are normally considered very active and almost incapable of staying away from all the attractions offered in cyberspace let alone being silent. These experiences suggested to me that there may be something about spiritual disciplines that can enrich the practice of discipleship of the youth of today's generation, as Richard Foster claims:

> Superficiality is the curse of our age. The doctrine of instant satisfaction is a primary spiritual problem. The desperate need today is not for a greater number of intelligent people, or gifted people, but for deep people. The classical disciplines of the spiritual life call us to move beyond the surface loving into the depths. They invite us to explore the inner caverns of the spiritual realm. They urge us to answer to a hollow world.[81]

In light of the foregoing study of spiritual formation and spiritual disciplines discussed in chapter 3, I will define youth discipleship among young people in Vietnam:

> Youth discipleship is leading youth in Bible study, worship, fellowship, service, and evangelism in the context of the faith community and supporting them in their daily lives. The main goal is to bring spiritual transformation through God's grace and the power of the Holy Spirit in the lives of the youth, which in turn enables them to reflect the image of Christ and share his love with nonbelievers. In the context of a digital society, the spiritual practices, especially solitude, can encourage youth to seek personal encounter with Christ in their quiet times and in their mundane activities, both online and offline.

---

81. Foster, *Celebration of Discipline*, 1.

This section will draw out the applications for youth discipleship in the context of the faith community and the daily lives of youth. The table below shows the main connections between main themes in the theology of spiritual formation and the practical applications. Of course, there are other connections, for example, "grace" or "conformed to Christ's image" can be linked to all the applications. But for the sake of simplicity in the presentation, only direct connections will be drawn.

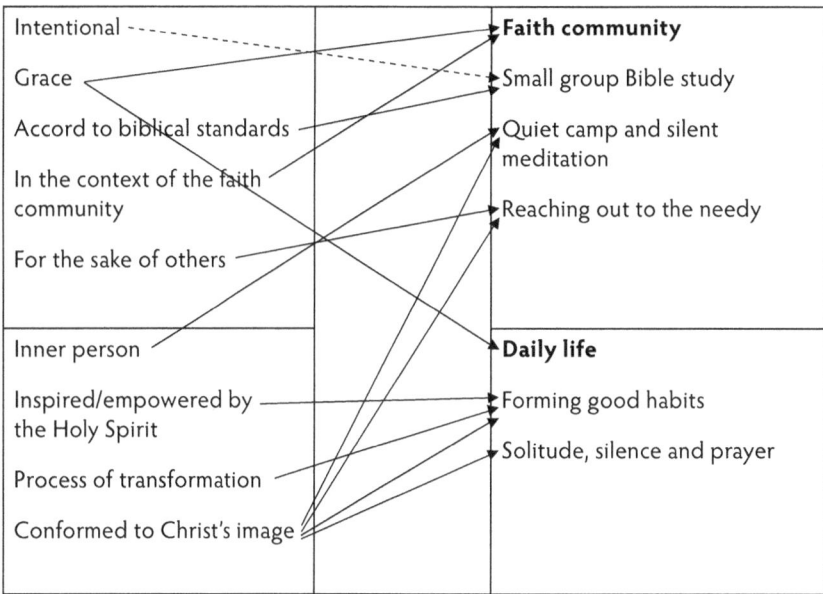

Figure 5.2. Mapping the themes of spiritual formation with practical applications

a. In the Faith Community

As discussed in the segment "In the Context of the Faith Community" in chapter 3, the faith community established by Christ is an important locus for spiritual formation. Christians can experience the revelation of God in the church community. In this subsection, I will discuss practical applications for spiritual formation in the faith community, prompted by my working experience with youth in the church in Vietnam.

1) Small Group Bible Study

The segment "Accord to Biblical Standards" in chapter 3 set out a theology of spiritual formation in which the Bible is the foundation for spiritual formation. The Bible is not only for personal devotion but also for corporate study. In my pastoral experience, small group Bible study has proved important in the work of discipling youth. It is an intentional program, but as the study of spiritual formation reminds us, we need to rely on God's grace and the power of the Holy Spirit. Without the work of the Holy Spirit, Bible study remains a dry program with no life in it. Only the Spirit can speak the word of God to the hearts of youth and bring about spiritual transformation.

In my own pastoral experience, I have found myself and the young people I ministered to regularly edified through small group Bible study where we shared our lives and what we learned from God with one another. In small groups, youth can share their interpretations of various passages in the Bible together, discuss their applications, and pray for one another. This is very beneficial in the spiritual life of youth. This corporate *lectio divina*, studying the Bible in the context of faith community, is significant to youths' spiritual transformation as discussed earlier in the subsection "Theology of Spiritual Formation: Dietrich Bonhoeffer" in chapter 3; the word of God and the Christian community are the loci for spiritual formation. In this practice, youths' trust in God has grown, and so has their knowledge of God's presence with them in daily life. I saw youth who were addicted to gaming be attracted to small group Bible study and transformed by the word of God. I have also found that the practices of Bible quizzes and the memorization of key verses in the youth service at my church are also helping young people store up wisdom and treasure for the spiritual life. Furthermore, David Helm suggests the method of one-to-one Bible reading, which is applicable to nonbelievers and believers at different levels of spiritual growth.[82] This is a claim that can be tested as it is applied to youth ministry.

2) Quiet Camp and Silent Meditation

The segments "*Inner Life*" and "*Conformed to the Image or Character of Christ*" in chapter 3 developed the claim that a theology of spiritual formation will have an important role for the spiritual practices of solitude, silence, and

---

82. Helm, *One-to-One Bible Reading*.

prayer. In this segment, I would like to indicate what I have discovered about the practices of solitude, silence, and prayer for youth ministry. My church has a policy of allowing no digital devices during youth camps. This started more than ten years ago and continues to this day. When away from home for five days at camp, the youth have to turn in their digital devices. It is helpful for the youth to have some time away from cyberspace in order to focus on God during Bible study, silent meditation, and prayer, as well as during fellowship with one another through games, fun activities, discussion, sharing, etc. Most of the youth leave their smart devices at home, but a few smuggle theirs in against the rules. Some are caught during the week, while others repentantly and voluntarily submit theirs during camp. In the end, most of them see the benefits of time away from digital media.

Emery-Wright suggests,

> Time away from the social network is important. It is important for parents to ensure their children spend significant periods of time offline, and to be positive role models for them too. This might involve agreeing on a "no screens" rule during mealtimes, or perhaps designating Sunday as digital Sabbath for the family.[83]

It turns out that recent brain research has shown similar results:

> After five days interacting face-to-face without the use of any screen-based media, preteens' recognition of nonverbal emotion cues improved significantly more than that of the control group for both facial expressions and videotaped scenes. Implications are that the short-term effects of increased opportunities for social interaction, combined with time away from screen-based media and digital communication tools, improves a preteen's understanding of nonverbal emotional cues.[84]

For a few years we have also applied silent meditation a few times per year in the youth service. The result was encouraging as the youth took these practices seriously and found them interesting and helpful. This gave them a pause from their noisy lives surrounded by digital media. They could have a time to quiet themselves before God, repent of their sins, cast their burdens

---

83. Emery-Wright and Mackenzie, *Networks for Faith Formation*, 123–124.
84. Uhls et al., "Five Days," 387.

on him, enjoy his presence, and listen to his word. The youth felt refreshed and recharged spiritually after the silent mediation and went back to their daily lives with fresh perspectives on God's presence and his will for their lives.

3) Reaching Out to the Needy

As we have discussed in the segment *"For the Sake of Others and the World"* in chapter 3, spiritual formation is not only for the sake of the individual Christian's life but also for the sake of others in the community and the world. We have seen how the Desert Fathers link loving the neighbor with solitude, silence, and prayer. Since spiritual formation cares for the whole life – spirit, emotions, relationships, intellect, vocation, physical health, and resource stewardship – as Diane J. Chandler suggests, we need to help youth in those aspects of life too. This is not an easy task since it requires much effort and commitment. I have been helping some youth who are dropping out of school or addicted to games. This requires extra effort, but the result is very encouraging. We need to have better knowledge or a better support network for youth in these aspects of life.

We are called by the Spirit to reach out to the needy. This also includes young people who are anxious, lonely, forgotten, and lost in both physical life and cyberspace as they are the generation who grew up surrounded by digital media. In my youth ministry, I have been often drawn to youth who have special circumstances such as living in a broken family, dropping out of school, having a certain disability, or being addicted to gaming. These youth and others who are coming from a good background also find themselves lonely and often go online to find friends or recognition. One boy often says hi to me via WhatsApp or Facebook Messenger, and I, as a youth worker, need to discover what this small gesture means within his digital culture so that I can understand what is being said to me and use appropriate language to respond pastorally. As Paul reminds us of being "all things to all people" in order to save them (1 Cor 9:19–23), there is a need for youth workers to step out of their comfort zones to reach those in need, including youth who are lonely and lost in both cyberspace and physical life.

In terms of the aspect of reaching the world for Christ, it seems a big thing for youth to imagine. Some youth do, however, bring their school friends or online-game friends to church with the outcome that their guest becomes a believer. The theological framework presented in chapters 3 and 4 suggests that the pastoral priority is to help the youth encounter Jesus Christ first at a youthful age, and then they can grow up and transform the world on bigger scales as they follow the leading of the Holy Spirit. Kenneth Boa observes that reaching out to others also leads to positive results in believers' spiritual lives:

> Nurturing spiritually relates to a lifestyle of evangelism and discipleship. When we are part of the process of introducing people to Jesus and encouraging them to grow after they have come to know him, we discover that our own passion and spiritual vitality enhanced.[85]

Therefore, it is important to teach youth to reach out to the needy, not only within but also beyond the Christian community. Spiritual formation is not only for the sake of individual Christians' lives but also for the sake of the world at large.

b. In Personal Daily Life

Since spiritual formation is a journey to become like Christ, it should happen in the daily lives of believers. In this subsection, I will suggest some of the practical applications that are relevant in youth ministry to helping youth encounter Christ in their personal daily lives.

1) Forming Good Habits

Spiritual formation is an ongoing encounter with Christ. It is about long-term relationship with Christ. It is living our lives as children of light. Therefore, cultivating the fruit of a new life such as patience and self-control in Christ is significant. In my several years of work with young people, I have found it helpful to give them some practical application for their daily lives, such as practicing breaking bad habits and creating new habits. The youth have often become excited about setting their own goals to have daily devotions, regulate their sleep patterns, or reduce online or game time to one or two hours per day. Some can last one to two weeks; some can last one to three days. Some fail and give up, but others try again. Some get better; others get worse. However, I find that this exercise is helpful for youth to at least break away from the unending cycle of bad habits, aiming toward a life of better

---

85. Boa, *Conformed to His Image*, 367.

self-control, being aware that human beings cannot do good things without the help of God. Here, Richard Foster's realism is a logical implication of the theology developed so far: "Many of these practices are useful, to be sure, and some are more useful than others. But none is essential. What is essential is personal encounter with Jesus, interactive relationship with the great God of the universe, inner transformation into Christlikeness."[86] The most important is personal encounter with Christ. This is a loving relationship which Christians need to cultivate.

James K. A. Smith states that "love is a habit" and "learning to love takes practice."[87] We can teach youth the practice of the presence of God from Brother Lawrence since they need to experience the presence of God in their everyday lives whether online or off-line. It is important to teach youth to form a habit of continually conversing with God – "That in order to form a habit of conversing with God continually, and referring all we do to Him; we must at first apply to Him with some diligence: but that after a little care we should find His love inwardly excite us to it without any difficulty."[88] Personally, I think this is not something so difficult to do if this habit is formed from an early age. I practiced this since I was a little boy and kept on doing it till now. I shared this with youth and children in church, and they were excited about it. However, we should be careful that forming good habits is not by our own effort. Jean-Pierre de Caussade says:

> To quench thirst, it is necessary to drink. Reading books about it only makes it worse. Thus, when we long for sanctity, speculation only drives it further from our grasp. We must humbly accept all that God's order requires us to do and suffer. What he ordains for us each moment is what is most holy, best, and most divine for us.[89]

It is not about a list of works to do, but it is enjoying each present moment with Christ, drinking from his living water.

We can also learn, from Nathan Foster, the practice of forming good habits in spiritual disciplines. He describes, "The disciplines go deep, very deep, and

---

86. Foster, "Ten Counsels."
87. Smith, *You Are What You Love*.
88. Brother Lawrence, *Practice of the Presence*, 4.
89. Caussade, "Present Moment."

deserve a lifetime of practice."[90] He takes up the spiritual disciplines from his father, Richard Foster, and locates them now in the context of modern, ordinary life. This approach is very helpful for our young generation as each person can practice the spiritual disciplines in his or her daily, ordinary life. He explains the significance of practice in forming habits: "Practice develops into habit, for better or, unfortunately, for worse . . . Here is another way to look at the topic: virtue is good habits we can rely upon to make our lives work well; vice is destructive habits we can rely upon to destroy our lives. Both are habits."[91] He concludes, "The concept of the spiritual disciplines is really quite simple: we do the practices that Jesus did. Over time these practices become habitual, thus enabling us to respond to life in a way more like Jesus would if he were to live our life."[92] Nathan Foster is helpful in giving practical application of being like Christ in daily life. He is correct that technology can take over the place of God in our lives, but there is a hope that Jesus can conquer the technology and use it for expanding his kingdom. There is a need to study what conforming to Christ is in the midst of the digital world. However, as for now, spiritual formation and spiritual disciplines do not talk much about this.

I appreciate Nathan Foster's experiment of practicing spiritual disciplines in this modern, ordinary life. There is a need to experiment with this among youth who are surrounded by digital media. There is also a need to come up with spiritual disciplines for the digital world, such as online mediation and devotions, online prayer, and online study. Personally, I found myself being encouraged spiritually by listening to *Our Daily Bread* online and reading through the Scriptures via applications on my smartphone. I also introduced these applications to youth and children in my church, and they eagerly received it. I know some of them continue to use them regularly. Thus, more research needs to be done in the future on the area of new spiritual disciplines for the digital world. The practice of forming good habits is very important as we help youth in their spiritual formation. We can learn from Brother Lawrence in the practicing of the presence of God and from Nathan Foster in forming good habits of spiritual discipline in modern daily life.

---

90. Foster, *Making of an Ordinary Saint*, 111.
91. Foster, 17–18.
92. Foster, 6.

2) Solitude, Silence, and Prayer

Conforming to Christ starts with solitude, which means opening our lives to Jesus and listening to his voice. This segment discusses how to present to youth two practices directly linked with solitude: silence and prayer. I found that one of the most important applications for me, after exploring spiritual formation, is the practice of silence demonstrated by the Desert Fathers. As discussed above with regards to the quiet camps and silent mediation in youth ministry, although the youth may like these activities, they are occasional; the main thing is helping youth to be disciples of Jesus in daily life – helping them have daily devotions and apply the Bible in their daily lives. It is important to explore the aspect of silence in our daily lives in the midst of all the noise and distractions from both the physical world and the virtual world. There is a need to explore the possibility of being online, staying connected to the world, and yet being able to stay connected to God and maintain an open heart to God.

Nathan Foster shares his story of success after spending a year practicing spiritual disciplines:

> I'm not enslaved to an electronic tether. I don't need to post anything online. I can celebrate without sharing it with the world. I don't need to be successful the way I used to. I don't fear boredom. I don't need to achieve or become. I am free to live, to love, and to be loved. Maybe the greatest and most surprising gift this process has facilitated is that I've become content and grateful with my portion. I'm learning to celebrate in the moment and in the daily routine of life.[93]

His story is very ideal. It seems that he disconnected from the world, or at least cyberspace, in order to stay connected to God. However, I have criticized this as a fragmented approach since believers are placed in the world and are connected to God at the same time. There are times when believers need to be in complete solitude, but there are other times when they need to be in the world – to stay connected to the world and to stay online and yet keep a solitude of heart that remains connected to God. This is a more difficult challenge than completely withdrawing from the world – or from the

---

93. Foster, 192.

digital world in particular. Nathan Foster's approach seems not to move as completely away from the monastic and mystical approach to the ordinary life as he claims.

Therefore, there is a huge need to test and explore more of the richness of spiritual disciplines in the context of the digital age. The Desert Fathers remind us to keep the true silence that is encounter with God.[94] While solitude leads to silence before God, which is an important step in spiritual formation, it cannot be complete without prayer.[95] It is important to teach youth that prayer is not prayer primarily as an activity of the mind, or else they may find that prayer is a burden or like a shopping list. "One of these demonic ruses is to make us think of prayer primarily as an activity of the mind that involves above all else our intellectual capacities. This prejudice reduces prayer to speaking with God or thinking about God."[96]

Youth should learn to find rest in God through prayer:

> The crisis of our prayer is that our mind may be filled with ideas of God while our heart remains far from him. Real prayer comes from the heart. It is about this prayer of the heart that the Desert Fathers teach us . . . The literal translation of the words "pray always" is "come to rest." The Greek word for rest is *hesychia*, and hesychasm is the term which refers to the spirituality of the desert.[97]

> Hesychastic prayer, which leads to that rest where the soul can dwell with God, is prayer of the heart.[98]

The prayer of the heart is about not just emotion but the inner being since in the Jewish-Christian tradition, it refers to the source of all physical, emotional, intellectual, volitional, and moral energies.[99] The prayer of the heart prompts us to surrender our all to Jesus.[100] It is the prayer of truth since it

---

94. Nouwen, *Way of the Heart*, 60.
95. Nouwen, 69.
96. Nouwen, 72.
97. Nouwen, 69.
98. Nouwen, 75.
99. Nouwen, 77.
100. Nouwen, 79.

reveals the truth about ourselves and about God and prompts us to find rest and salvation in Christ.[101]

However, how can we and youth practice the prayer of the heart in our everyday lives? The Desert Fathers give us a hint: "The prayer of the heart is nurtured by short, simple prayers. It is unceasing and all-inclusive."[102] Nouwen further explains,

> A word or sentence repeated frequently can help us to concentrate, to move to the center, to create an inner stillness and thus listen to the voice of God. When we simply try to sit silently and wait for God to speak to us, we find ourselves bombarded with endless conflicting thoughts and ideas. But when we use a very simple sentence such as "Oh God, come to my assistance," "Jesus, master, have mercy on me," or a word such as "Lord" or "Jesus," it is easier to let many distractions pass by without being misled by them. Such simple, easily repeated prayer can slowly empty out our crowded interior life and create the quiet space where we can dwell with God. It can be like a ladder along which we can descend into the heart and ascend to God. Our choice of words depends on our needs and the circumstances of the moment, but it is best to use words from the Scripture.[103]

Henri Nouwen brings this into our modern day. As we practice this way of simple prayer, we experience rest and God's active presence. Even while we are talking, studying, gardening, or building, this prayer keeps us aware of God's ever-present guidance.[104]

In short, it is helpful for youth to have their quiet time before God. As discussed in the segment "*Accord to Biblical Standards*" in chapter 3, Nouwen suggests practicing *lectio divina* coming from the Benedictine tradition. It is important for youth to start their day by reading the Bible attentively with deep faith that God has a word for them in their unique situation.[105] This does not have to be long, it can even be just five to ten minutes. Youth can

---

101. Nouwen, 79.
102. Nouwen, 80.
103. Nouwen, 82.
104. Nouwen, 82.
105. Nouwen, *Spiritual Formation*, xxiii.

read a short passage from the Bible, reflect on it, and pray. They can also use the verse-of-the-day feature of the Bible app *YouVersion* or some devotional material such as *Our Daily Bread*, which is available in an app or online. In Vietnam, our youth can also use Vietnamese devotionals such as *Live with the Bible* (*Sống với Thánh Kinh*) or *365 Rays* (*365 Tia Sáng*). Then youth can practice short prayer throughout the day as they study, play, or surf the internet. There is a prayer that I have prayed all the time, since I was young, in my daily life: "Lord, have mercy." Now I also teach the children and youth in my church to pray, "Lord, have mercy," or, "Lord, please protect me," as they go online or off-line. Adam Thomas also suggests good reflection and prayer based on St. Ignatius's "Examen":

> Step One. By writing the words, "Yes, Lord, you are here," I acknowledge God's presence around me and within me.
>
> Step Two. After opening myself up to God's presence, I give thanks for all the ways I felt blessed today.
>
> Step Three. I reflect on the events of the day and focus on one that brought me closer to or pushed me farther from God.
>
> Step Four. I reflect on a particular encounter or conversation with an individual during which I either did or did not fulfill my promises as a disciple of Jesus Christ.
>
> Step Five. I read what I have written and write a sentence about tomorrow in light of what happened today.
>
> And again, I listen and breathe. And something else detaches in the form of a prayer to God: "Lord, grant me focus for tomorrow," or "Lord, I need practice welcoming people," or "Lord, help me slow down."[106]

This is a very helpful way to close the day rather than ending it with digital media. Our youth ministry always encourages youth to start and end the day with devotion and prayer and to keep connecting with God throughout the day through short prayers. This is a very important lifestyle for youth to establish.

---

106. Thomas, *Digital Disciple*.

To conclude this chapter, digital technology gives us creative and dynamic ways to connect with, care for, and reach out to young people immersed in cyberspace. The online domain can be a window to be entered in which believers can learn more about youth since often there they are open to freely sharing their lives. There is huge potential for adults to befriend youth in cyberspace where the generational gap seems to be smaller. As Christ went into the far country to seek the outcasts, the church is called to reach out to the outcast young people of the digital age. The internet makes it possible for these young people to raise their voices and come to the church's attention. Digital technology can also serve as a new means for spiritual formation. Discipling youth of the digital age is helping them come to know and live out the Christian life, especially in today's world surrounded by digital media. The church is called to become "all things to all people" and to reach out to the youth who are surrounded by digital media. It is important that the church fosters the community with care and helps youth be disciples of Christ in both the physical and the digital worlds. In our modern life surrounded by digital technologies, the task of youth ministry is to teach youth to listen to God's voice and obey him. This can involve studying the Bible in church and in daily life, caring for the needy, and forming good habits. The spiritual practices of solitude, silence, and prayer can encourage youth to seek personal encounter with Christ in their quiet times and in their mundane activities both online and off-line. In short, youth discipleship in the digital age is helping youth, whose personal identities are profoundly influenced by the digital culture, encounter Christ mainly through the practice of solitude in the context of the faith community and personal daily life, which means opening oneself to the Spirit and letting him restore one's identity and relationships with God and others.

Conclusion

The average adult might claim to have evaded the worst effects of digital media to various degrees, but to young people who are native of this age, the impacts of digital media are all too obvious. Adolescence is a significant period in the formation of personal identity, and it is now strongly affected by the "Network Society." In response to the question, at the beginning of this project, of whether the contemporary church should use digital media in discipling youth, the conclusion has been drawn that the church cannot faithfully pursue its discipleship responsibilities without engaging it intentionally and thoughtfully. This position has been developed in both critical and constructive directions. The church should neither naively embrace digital culture nor stubbornly reject it. Rather, it should make the effort to be well informed and understanding, and it should critically process what it learns before forming the theology and discipleship that apply to the youth of this digital age. This thesis has taken the key question to be: How should the church of Christ disciple the youth of this generation?

First, this research has surveyed the best insights from various types of literature related to the social-scientific study of cultural changes in the digital age as well as Christian responses to these changes. Scholars are divided in their views of the effect of digital media on society. Manuel Castells takes a neutral view of information technology, seeing it as a variegated pattern of mutations taking place within the economic, social, and cultural domains that can be summarized under the heading of an emerging network society. Robert Hassan presents a picture of the same information society but emphasizes the "speeding-up" of time and the "shrinking" of space. Don Tapscott offers an optimistic view of the effects of these changes on the youth, whom he presents as smarter and better at collaboration than previous generations. Mark Bauerlein presents a far darker picture of the youth of the digital age, whom he calls the "dumbest generation." Hal Niedzviecki presents a similarly depressing portrait of people of all ages in the rise of "Peep culture." Howard Gardner and Katie Davis argue that the identity, creativity, and imagination of contemporary youth are indeed being fundamentally reshaped by digital applications and that this reshaping is, all told, more negative than positive. Adam Greenfield presents an updated account of this pessimistic take on radical digital technologies, which he takes to be reshaping the social landscape and our daily lives tremendously and in mostly negative ways. Shoshana Zuboff completes this dark picture by surveying the coalescence of a large set of subsystems to form the juggernaut that is surveillance capitalism.

Despite these higher-level disagreements among analysts of digital culture, this project takes the view that digital media can have both good and bad influences on youth. The more important thing is to discern how to help them navigate through these challenges. Tracking the divide between social-scientific analyses of digital culture, Christian responses to social changes caused by digital media also range from pessimistic to more balanced to optimistic. The Christian analysts all agree, however, that in the end there is a need for contextualization of the gospel for the digital age. William F. Fore, Robert S. Fortner, and Shane A. Hipps were from the earliest generation of Christians calling for the church to respond to the effects of digital media. More recent literature on digital theology by Jesse Rice, Leonard Sweet, Elizabeth Drescher, Tim Challies, Adam Thomas, Jana M. Bennett, Heidi A. Campbell, Stephen Garner, Stephen D. Lowe, Mary E. Lowe, and Chris Shirley offers a more supple criticism and more developed constructive proposals for how to engage with digital culture and its effects on society as well as the communication of the gospel. Among the latest authors, Bennett, Campbell, and Garner propose the richest theological case for engagement with digital theology in neither embracing nor fully rejecting digital technologies.

This project has taken, from these Christian responses, the call to develop a digital theology that takes into consideration both the positive and the negative influences of digital technologies as well as the need to find ways to communicate the gospel to youth where they are, both online and off-line. The literature on youth ministry and the theology of youth work are helpful for this work of communicating the gospel to youth in a digital culture. Pete Ward calls for the contextualization of the gospel for youth in their concrete context, while Kenda Creasy Dean suggests intentional reflection on the "theological rocks" of youth ministry. Andrew Root proposes an important role for Dietrich Bonhoeffer in forming a theology of discipleship, youth, and youth ministry. Steven Emery-Wright and Ed Mackenzie highlight the importance of Christian networks for the spiritual growth of youth. David Kinnaman, Mark Matlock, and Aly Hawkins suggest spiritual practices for discipling youth in the "digital Babylon." Despite all this good work, this thesis has argued that there remains a need to construct a theology for discipling youth in the digital age, which has been the central task undertaken here.

This project continued with investigating the impacts of digital media on society in general and on the youth of the digital age in particular. It concludes that the youth of Gens Y and Z are neither smarter nor dumber than the previous generations as each generation has its own set of challenges and opportunities. It is understandable that their facility with technology is born out of accessibility and familiarity. One main claim of this thesis is that digital culture has a profound influence on the formation of personal identity among the youth of Gens Y and Z. The "Network Society" has strongly affected the process of forming an inner identity, a significant task in the adolescent period. The design of digital media and apps can enslave youth in the "hive" and take away the solitude and resources needed for them to cultivate their inner identity. The conclusion drawn from social studies is that we need to teach them to engage with digital media with responsibility and discernment. In order to journey with them and bring out the best in them, it is necessary for institutions such as schools and families to reinvent better ways to accommodate youth. In this context, how should the church of Christ disciple the youth of this generation whose personal identities are profoundly influenced by digital culture?

To answer this question, the project then engaged the theology of spiritual formation by way of the ideas of two Reformed theologians, John Calvin and Dietrich Bonhoeffer, and filled out their theologies of spiritual formation by drawing on the influential writer on spirituality, Henri Nouwen. Modern authors on spiritual formation such as James C. Wilhoit, Michael Burer, Kenneth Boa, Jeffrey P. Greenman, Dallas Willard, Diane J. Chandler, Paul Pettit, Richard Foster, and Nathan Foster proposed nine common themes in the definition of spiritual formation. Some modern authors in the survey mention the aspects of intentionality, grace, and accordance to biblical standards in their definitions of spiritual formation, while other authors mention the aspects of the faith community and the sake of others and the world. Most of them mention the inner person, the Holy Spirit, and the process of transformation, and all authors in the survey mention that spiritual formation is conforming to Christ's image. Even though presented in separated segments, all these themes on spiritual formation overlap and are closely linked to one another.

Most of the definitions of spiritual formation offered in this literature, however, describe the what, who, why, and where of spiritual formation but give little answer to the how. The exceptions to this tendency are Richard Foster, who offers an account of the spiritual disciplines, and Nathan Foster, who seeks to apply these spiritual disciplines to modern, ordinary daily life. Though these modern writings seem weak in theology, this thesis suggested that the study of Calvin, Bonhoeffer, and Nouwen on spiritual formation can provide a solid theological backup for the modern accounts of spiritual formation. Calvin presents a theologically well-developed account of spiritual formation as encounter with Christ or being conformed to Christ. Bonhoeffer emphasizes the significant role of the Bible as a central means of grace in spiritual formation. According to Bonhoeffer, the gospel of Jesus Christ is the foundation for spiritual formation, which takes place in the context of the faith community. Nouwen adds that spiritual formation is not about tasks but about encountering Christ through spiritual practices, among which the practice of solidude is essentential. This discussion yielded the conclusion that spiritual formation is encountering Christ in the context of community and personal daily life, which starts with solitude in which we open our lives to God and listen to his voice. The question to ask is: What does it mean for youth to follow Christ or encounter Christ today?

In answering this question, this project, then, analyzed several theologies needed for youth discipleship. The main point presented here is that the arrival of the digital age has profound implications for culture, self-identity, and the gospel. It has reshaped contemporary processes of youth developing stable and healthy self-identities. The theological account of relational personhood rooted in the Trinitarian God sets solid foundations for a theological understanding of self-identity. Identity is described not by some substances that we possess but by a worshipping relationship with the Trinitarian God, who also sets us up for communication and relationship with other people and his creation. In order to help youth, whose identity is fragmented by digital culture, to form a resilient self-identity, churches should be prepared to guide them in their spiritual practice of experiencing intimacy with Jesus. There is a need to communicate the gospel in a way that youth can comprehend and appreciate. The unchangeable value of the gospel needs to come to fruit in life-changing experiences here on earth as the beginning of the promised eternal life as the youth follow Jesus in their daily lives, in both the physical and the virtual worlds. This is what "discipleship" is all about.

In discussing the theology of discipleship, first, we have discussed how the theology of "self" plays an important role in affirming youths' embrace of their full selves while also encouraging them to resist the urge to disembody themselves via the cyber world within a culture already so fragmented. Alongside this, the theology of communication and the theology of incarnation further strengthen the resolve of the church to better equip youth at being truly present in both the physical and the virtual worlds. Also, a theology of community allows youth to authenticate the gospel message in an environment defined and established by Christ. It is important for discipleship to be done in the context of the church community, which can serve as a network for faith formation. This theology of community is rooted in the persons of the Trinitarian God and manifested through the Christian community, where the authentic gospel is communicated. Bonhoeffer suggests that the true church community is defined and established by Christ. It includes people saved by Christ. It is through sharing life in sacrifice, intercession, and confession that people encounter the living Christ.

Last but not least, the theology of youth helps locate the proper place for youth in the church in this digital age. Bonhoeffer's theology of youth was valuable in constructing our work of discipling youth in this digital age. This theology helps appropriate the proper place of youth in the church – one in which their youthfulness is embraced fully. It is important for the church to be humble in listening to youth and for it to encourage them to bring their gifts to the table. The relationship between the church and its youth should always be one of giving and receiving, each strengthening the other in the joined effort to better proclaim the word of God and serve God's community regardless of the ever-changing current of the digital world. Throughout the discussion, the writings of Bonhoeffer played the most crucial role in undergirding several theologies including those of self-identity, discipleship, community, and youth. Bonhoeffer also contributes, through both his writings and his actions in life, to the absolute need of contextualizing the message to most effectively serve the people of a certain time and place. Overall, his insights help construct a digital theology in which to instruct the church on how best to disciple youth in this changing age of digital technology. The culminating claim of this thesis is that youth discipleship is teaching youth, whose personal identity is profoundly influenced by the digital culture, to practice experiencing intimacy with Christ in the context of the faith community and personal daily life.

Finally, this project has reflected on the theological implications ecclesiologically and culturally. In order to contextualize the theology of discipleship in the context of youth ministry in the wider world of this digital age, it has discussed helpful aspects of digital technology, the theology of youth ministry, and implications of the whole project taken together. Regardless of possible negative effects, digital technology opens a window for adults to step into the world of young people. It enables these young people to raise their voices or get some attention. There is huge potential for adults to befriend youth and mentor them in cyberspace. Digital technology makes it possible to reach out to and care for the young people using social media. Youth workers should utilize these helpful aspects of digital technologies while building a youth ministry that reflects the purpose of God for his church to build a community of people in communion with him and with one another. Relationship (communion) is at the center of the being of the Trinitarian God who calls us and inspires us to reach out to young people. Therefore, our practice as youth workers finds its true foundation in the God who calls us to share God with young people. Youth discipleship in the digital age is helping youth come to know and to live out the Christian life, especially knowing what it means to be Christians in today's world surrounded by digital media. The essence of Christian life is relationship, first with God as Father and then with other members in Christian faith communities. The main task of youth ministry is teaching youth to build an intimate relationship with Christ in the context of the faith community and personal daily life.

Discipleship must be the central concern of the church, for it undergirds all the other tasks of the church such as worship, fellowship, mission, and evangelism. Discipleship is effective when it leads to youth participation in the total life of the church where their learning can last the longest. With regards to reaching nonbelievers for the Lord, the church can take a cue from watching the youth, the way they interact with their peers, and how they cultivate friendships. Their way is the key to evangelism in this age and time. In this changing world, with its modern technologies and revolving ideas of community living, there is a constant challenge to the church to be "all things to all people." Digital technology challenges the church and church workers to care for youth, both in cyberspace and in physical life. If we want to disciple the youth, we need to know their culture and use language that they can understand and relate to. As Christ goes into the far countries to seek the outcasts, the church is called to reach out to the outcast young people of the digital age. Finally, practical applications for ministering to youth in this digital age, such as being true, gym time, mentoring, and sharing the living word of God and the gospel, have been born out of careful observations with a discerning yet open mind to the new world of digital media we are all living in. These applications, constructed from the aforementioned theologies, follow closely the cues laid out by youth immersed in the world of technology.

This project concludes with the contextualization of the theology of spiritual formation in youth ministry in Vietnam. In light of the foregoing study of spiritual formation and spiritual disciplines, I have defined youth discipleship among young people in Vietnam as follows.

> Youth discipleship is leading youth in Bible study, worship, fellowship, service, and evangelism in the context of the faith community and supporting them in their daily lives. The main goal is to bring spiritual transformation through God's grace and the power of the Holy Spirit in the life of the youth, which in turn enables them to reflect the image of Christ and share his love with nonbelievers. In the context of a digital society, the spiritual practices, especially, solitude can encourage youth to seek personal encounter with Christ in their quiet time and in their mundane activities both online and offline.

From this definition, I have drawn the applications for youth discipleship in the context of the faith community and the daily life of the youth in Vietnam. It is important that the church fosters the community with care and helps youth to be disciples of Christ in both the physical and the digital world. In our modern lives surrounded by digital technologies, the task of youth ministry is to teach youth to listen to God's voice and obey him. This can involve studying the Bible at church and in daily life, caring for the needy, and forming good habits. The spiritual practices of solitude, silence, and prayer can encourage youth to seek personal encounter with Christ in their quiet time and in their mundane activities both online and off-line.

In short, the assertion of how the content is never truly divorced from its medium has never been proven truer than in this digital age. Recognizing the power that medium has on its content prompts us to respond, with urgency, to the prevalent needs of a working theology and practical guidelines for the generation affected by it. Indeed, digital media bears the greatest impacts on the youth who were born in the digital age. The task is not to catch on to the hype or even to catch up with youth's adeptness to technology in order to make the church seem more up to date. The task is for the church to take initiative in ensuring first, that youth feel understood and accepted in their involvement with the digital world and second, that they are equipped to engage with technology with greater discernment and responsibility. The digital theology proposed in this project highlights the goal of discipleship in leading youth in this digital age to be faithful followers of Jesus.

The church is called to proclaim the word of God and inspire youth to live out the mandates of the Christian life in both the physical and the virtual worlds. Discipleship reaches its pinnacle when it leads to youth participating in the total life of the church, with all of the gifts they can bring as children of the digital age. It is important to let them know that they always have a seat at the table. With its feet firmly planted on the unchangeable word of God, the church should look into the world through the eyes of youth who were born in the digital age. Though the word of God remains unchanged, our understanding and applications to each age will continue to evolve, ready to adapt to the changing characteristics of culture, its affected people and the progressive technology that comes with it. There is a huge need to test and explore the richness of spiritual disciplines in the context of this digital age and, at the same time, to come up with new spiritual disciplines for youth to apply in both the virtual and physical worlds.

The unique contribution of this thesis is to have directly developed a theological account of discipling youth in the digital age. What the literature review presented in chapter 1 highlighted was the lack of an explicit theology of youth discipleship in both the theological literature engaging the church and the rise of the information age as well as contemporary youth discipleship literature. In this thesis I have drawn on the latest social-scientific analyses of digital culture and digital theology in order to fill this gap by discussing in detail how digital media is profoundly shaping the identity of today's youth. On the basis of this surveying of contemporary social-scientific studies I have drawn out how their new technological environment is reshaping the patterns of their spiritual growth. A nuanced understanding of the effects that modern technology has on youth discussed in this thesis promises to help the church disciple this generation with discernment, authenticity, and faithfulness.

This thesis also presented a robust theology of spiritual formation formed with the task of youth discipleship firmly in view, and in engagement with contemporary theologians in evangelical circles and beyond. Given the flatness of the world in the digital age and the disinterest of today's youth in the distinctives offered by different denominations, the contextualization of youth discipleship in the digital age can contribute to the task of the churches in the world in evangelical circles and beyond in discipling young people more adequately as well as empowering them to participate in and to bless the church through their gifts. This thesis should therefore resource the church's pastoral work of helping youth find a place both online and in an authentic community where real living for Christ is shared face to face and beyond. With the unique contextualization of the theology of spiritual formation in Vietnam, this thesis will also be beneficial for my home country, Vietnam, where the church has not built a theology for discipling youth in the digital age.

As I draw close to the end of my time working on this thesis, the COVID-19 pandemic is affecting the whole world. This pandemic offers a real picture of how the people of the world, while separated physically, can be digitally connected. Due to lockdowns, online activities are utilized more than ever before with online classes being offered to students, work-from-home arrangements to employees, educational apps – for free – to the public, drawing classes – by artists – to children, etc. People are doing all kinds of acts of kindness, using the internet to reach out to others in need. Many churches have made the decision to live stream or put services online. Online Bible studies are also conducted. While the church is rethinking its practices and ministries during this special time, it is important to keep in mind youth and children, who may be forgotten. Some churches are conducting youth meetings online, as well as Bible studies, children's addresses, and Sunday school. I also conduct Bible study for students on Microsoft Teams and Sunday schools for children on Zoom at my church in the UK.

Youth ministers today must be continually learning and testing ways to engage the children in online Sunday school through music, arts and crafts, crosswords, Bible quizzes, and games. Parents are encouraged to read the Bible and pray with their kids at home, to reduce their time online; and to increase family activities and other off-line activities since they are at home together most of the time. At my home church in Vietnam, youth workers are finding creative ways to encourage the youth to stay healthy, both physically and spiritually, during lockdown by posting, on their youth ministry's Facebook page, daily challenges for the youth such as cleaning up their room, cooking a meal for family, doing one form of physical exercise, sharing tips for online study or a wonderful memory with family, and praying for a friend. I can see, through their likes, shares, and comments on the Facebook page, that most of the youth enjoy these activities. This is also a good time for people to ponder how much they miss face-to-face contact with others as well as to more directly consider the value of the church gathering face to face and sharing the holy communion. Since this phenomenon is new, there is a need for social scientists and theologians to study the effects of online church and its online ministry to youth in pandemic times.

For now, it can be said that the tension between the physical and the virtual worlds has been an ongoing struggle for the church in general and for the church in its relationships with youth in particular. Yet in fact, most of the differences can be reconciled to bring about benefits for both. The goal of this research has been to bridge the two worlds, bringing them both into conversation. The question of the church's ministry to youth cannot be one in which the worlds of youth and adults are pitted against one another. The aim, rather, must be to seek ways to embrace the reality of the culture that all are living under – one that is heavily dictated by digital media and its attendant philosophies. Learning to navigate this new world is a combined effort of the church members – both youth and non-youth – working toward common understanding, appreciation, and cooperation. The main claim of this project is this: youth discipleship in the digital age is helping youth, whose personal identities are profoundly influenced by the digital culture, to encounter Christ mainly through the practice of solitude in the contexts of the faith community and of personal daily life, which means opening oneself to the Spirit and letting him restore their identities and relationships with God and others. Our hope is in the Lord!

APPENDIX

Definitions of Spiritual Formation

As compared to Christian literature that responds to social changes caused by digital media, the literature on spiritual formation has a longer history and is much more developed. The importance of spiritual formation is widely agreed upon by Christian churches. Modern Christian writers have defined spiritual formation in various ways but mostly agreed with one another in main themes. This appendix lists key definitions of spiritual formation proposed by them and then shows the reoccurrence of nine common emphases of spiritual formation across these definitions. The purpose of this survey is to secure a clearer picture of the definition of spiritual formation. This provides detailed information for the discussion of the theology of spiritual formation in chapter 3.

James C. Wilhoit

> Christian spiritual formation refers to the intentional communal process of growing in our relationship with God and becoming conformed to Christ through the power of the Holy Spirit.[1]

Michael Burer

> The intentional transformation of the inner person to the character of Christ.[2]

---

1. Wilhoit, *Spiritual Formation*, 23.
2. Burer, "Towards a Biblical Definition."

Kenneth Boa

> The grace-driven developmental process in which the soul grows in conformity to the image of Christ.[3]

Jeffrey P. Greenman

> Spiritual formation is our continuing response to the reality of God's grace shaping us into the likeness of Jesus Christ, through the work of the Holy Spirit, in the community of faith, for the sake of the world.[4]

Dallas Willard

> The Spirit-driven process of forming the inner world of the human self in such a way that it becomes like the inner being of Christ himself . . . the outer life of the individual becomes a natural expression or outflow of the character and teachings of Jesus.[5]

> Spiritual formation in the tradition of Jesus Christ is the process of transformation of the inmost dimension of the human being, the heart, which is the same as the spirit or will. It is being formed (really, transformed) in such a way that its natural expression comes to be the deeds of Christ done in the power of Christ.[6]

> Spiritual formation could become a term for those processes through which people are inwardly transformed in such a way that the personality and deeds of Jesus Christ naturally flow out from them when and wherever they are. In other words, it can be understood as the process by which true Christlikeness is established in the very depths of our being.[7]

---

3. Kenneth Boa, *Conformed to His Image*, 515.
4. Greenman and Kalantzis, *Life in the Spirit*, 24.
5. Willard, *Renovation of the Heart*, 22.
6. Willard, "Spiritual Formation"
7. Willard.

When we talk about spiritual formation we are talking about framing a progression of life in which people come to actually do all things that Jesus taught. So we are obviously going for the heart. We are aiming for change of the inner person, where what we do originates.[8]

Diane J. Chandler

Christian spiritual formation is defined as an interactive process by which God the Father fashions believers into the image of his Son, Jesus through the empowerment of the Holy Spirit by fostering development in seven primary life dimensions (spirit, emotions, relationships, intellect, vocation, physical health and resource stewardship).[9]

Portland Seminary, George Fox University

Christian spiritual formation is the process of being conformed to the image of Christ for the glory of God and for the sake of others (II Corinthians 3:17–18).

The focus of spiritual formation is the Holy Spirit, who guides the ongoing journey.

The response is submission. Formation is an organic, life-long, and holistic process involving right (ortho) thinking, right behaviors, and right feelings of individuals and communities.[10]

Renovare

We are all spiritual beings. We have physical bodies, but our lives are largely driven by an unseen part of us. There is an immaterial center in us that shapes the way we see the world and ourselves, directs the choices we make, and guides our actions. Our spirit is the most important part of who we are. And yet we

---

8. Willard.
9. Chandler, *Spiritual Formation*, 19.
10. Portland Seminary, "Spiritual Formation."

rarely spend time developing our inner life. That's what Spiritual Formation is all about.

Spiritual Formation is a process, but it is also a journey through which we open our hearts to a deeper connection with God. We are not bystanders in our spiritual lives, we are active participants with God, who is ever inviting us into relationship with him.

Spiritual Formation helps us reclaim our relationship with God as it was meant to be. It's not trying – it's training in eternal living, determined discipleship to Jesus Christ, and the way we discover the renewable source of spiritual energy we've been looking for (2 Cor 4:16).[11]

Paul Pettit

While spiritual formation means different things to different groups and definitions are agreeably difficult to arrive at, at the very least we can state the following two principles with conviction. First, spiritual formation is the holistic work of God in a believer's life whereby systematic change renders the individual continually closer to the image and actions of Jesus Christ. And second, the change or transformation that occurs in the believer's life happens best in the context of authentic, Christian community and is oriented as service toward God and others.[12]

Richard Foster

The Christian idea of spiritual formation is, very simply, the formation and conformation and transformation of the human personality—body, mind, and spirit—into the likeness of Jesus Christ.[13]

---

11. Renovare, "Spiritual Formation."
12. Pettit, *Foundations of Spiritual Formation*, 19.
13. Foster, "Ten Counsels."

Nathan Foster

> The concept of the spiritual disciplines is really quite simple: we do the practices that Jesus did. Over time these practices become habitual, thus enabling us to respond to life in a way more like Jesus would if he were to live our life. As we submit our will to spiritual practices, God's grace brings forth character transformation. This seems to be the dominant means God uses to bring about change in our lives. Christian spiritual formation is the process of becoming people formed into the likeness of Christ's character.[14]

Henri Nouwen

> Spiritual formation, I have come to believe, is not about steps or stages on the way to perfection. It's about the *movement* from the mind to the heart through prayer in its many forms that reunite us with God, each other, and our truest selves.[15]

> Thus to live the spiritual life and to let God's presence fill us takes constant prayer, and to move from illusions and isolation back to the place in the heart where God continues to form us in the likeness of Christ takes time and attention.[16]

> I will focus here on five practices that seem of special importance: *reflection* on the living documents of our own hearts and time, *lectio divina*, *silence*, *community* and *service*. Practiced together, especially with a spiritual director and community of faith, these areas of discipline help fashion our hearts for God.[17]

---

14. Foster, *Making of an Ordinary Saint*, 16.
15. Nouwen, *Spiritual Formation*, xvi.
16. Nouwen, xvii.
17. Nouwen, xxi–xxii.

The occurrence of the nine common themes in the definitions of spiritual formation

	Intentional	Grace	Bible Standard	Faith Community
James C. Wilhoit	Y		The gospel	Y
Michael Burer	Y			
Kenneth Boa		Y		
Jeffrey P Greenman		Y		Y
Dallas Willard			Do all things that Jesus taught	
Diane J. Chandler				
Portland Seminary				
Renovare				
Paul Pettit				Y
Richard Foster				
Nathan Foster		Y		
Henri Nouwen			Lectio Divina	Y

Definitions of Spiritual Formation

For Others	Inner Person	Holy Spirit	Process of Tranform.	Conform to Christ's Image
		Y	Y	Y
	Y			Y
	Y		Y	Y
Y		Y	Continuing response	Y
	Y	Y	Y	Y
	Y Whole Person theology	Y	Interactive process	Y
Y	Y Holistic	Y	Y	Y
	Y Heart connects with God		Y Journey	Determined discipleship to Jesus Christ
Y			Y Life change	Y
	Y Body, mind, and spirit		Y	Y
			Y	Y
	Y	Y The movements of the Spirit	The movement	Y

Bibliography

Social-Scientific Study on Digital Media and Technology

Borgmann, Albert. *Technology and the Character of Contemporary Life: A Philosophical Inquiry*. Chicago: University of Chicago Press, 1987.

Burstein, Daniel, and David Kline. *Road Warriors: Dreams and Nightmares along the Information Highway*. New York: Dutton, 1995.

Castells, Manuel. *The Information Age: Economy, Society, and Culture*, 2nd ed. Vol. 1 of *The Rise of the Network Society*. Malden, MA: Blackwell Publishing, 2000.

Czitrom, Daniel. *Media and the American Mind: From Morse to McLuhan*. Chapel Hill, NC: University of North Carolina Press, 1982.

Greenfield, Adam. *Radical Technologies: The Design of Everyday Life*. London: Verso, 2017.

Hassan, Robert. *The Information Society: Cyber Dreams and Digital Nightmares*. Digital Media and Society Series. Cambridge: Polity, 2008.

Jones, Steve, and Stephanie Kucker. "Computers, the Internet, and Virtual Cultures." In *Culture in the Communication Age,* edited by James Lull, 212–23. London: Routledge, 2001.

McLuhan, Marshall. "The Medium is the Message." In *Media and Cultural Studies: KeyWorks*, edited by Meenakshi Gigi Durham, 129–38. Malden, MA: Blackwell Publishers, 2001.

———. *Understanding Media: The Extensions of Man*. London: Routledge and Kegan, 1964.

Naisbitt, John. *High Tech/High Touch: Technology and Our Search for Meaning*. New York: Broadway Books, 1999.

Niedzviecki, Hal. *The Peep Diaries: How We're Learning to Love Watching Ourselves and Our Neighbors*. San Francisco: City Lights Books, 2009.

Postman, Neil. *Technopoly: The Surrender of Culture to Technology*. New York: Alfred A. Knopf, 1992.

Stoll, Clifford. "You Can't Live on the Internet." In *Minutes of the Lead Pencil Club*, edited by Bill Henderson, 54–59. Wainscott, NY: Pushcart Press, 1996.

Turkel, Sherry. *Life on the Screen: Identity in the Age of the Internet*. New York City, NY, 1995.

———. *The Second Self: Computers and the Human Spirit*. New York: Simon and Schuster, 1984.

Watson, Willis Towers. *Digital Media and Society: Implications in a Hyperconnected Era*. Geneva: World Economic Forum, 2016. http://www3.weforum.org/docs/WEFUSA_DigitalMediaAndSociety_Report2016.

Zuboff, Shoshana. *The Age of Surveillance Capitalism: The Fight for a Human Future at the New Frontier of Power*. London: Profile Books, 2019.

Youth Identity and Culture

Adams, Gerald R., and Michael D. Berzonsky, eds. *Blackwell Handbook of Adolescence*. Malden, MA: Blackwell Publishing, 2003.

Arnett, Jeffrey Jensen. "Emerging Adulthood: A Theory of Development from the Late Teens through the Twenties." *American Psychologist* 55, no. 5 (May 2000): 469–480. https://doi.org/10.1037/0003-066X.55.5.469.

———. *Emerging Adulthood: The Winding Road from the Late Teens through the Twenties*. 2nd ed. New York: Oxford University Press US, 2015.

Barna, George. *Generation Next: What You Need to Know About Today's Youth*. Grand Rapids: Baker Publishing Group, 1995.

Bauerlein, Mark. *The Dumbest Generation: How the Digital Age Stupefies Young Americans and Jeopardizes Our Future (Or, Don't Trust Anyone Under 30)*. New York: Jeremy P. Tarcher, 2009.

Buckingham, David. *After the Death of Childhood: Growing up in the Age of Electronic Media*. Cambridge: Polity, 2000.

———, ed. *Youth, Identity, and Digital Media*. Cambridge: MIT Press, 2008.

Buckingham, David, and Sara Bragg, eds. *Young People, Sex and the Media: The Facts of Life?* New York: Palgrave Macmillan, 2004.

Cherry, Kendra. "Freud vs. Erikson: Comparing Theories of Development." *Verywell Mind* (blog). Updated May 11, 2022. https://www.verywellmind.com/freud-and-erikson-compared-2795959.

Cover, Rob. *Digital Identities: Creating and Communicating the Online Self*. London: Academic Press, 2016.

Csikszentmihalyi, Mihaly, and Reed Larson. *Being Adolescent: Conflict and Growth in the Teenage Years*. New York: Basic Books, 1984.

Danby, Susan J., Marilyn Fleer, Christina Davidson, and Maria Hatzigianni, eds. *Digital Childhoods: Technologies and Children's Everyday Lives*. Vol. 22 of *International Perspectives on Early Childhood Education and Development*, edited by Marilyn Fleer and Ingrid Pramling. Samuelsson Singapore: Springer Nature, 2018.

Davis, Katie. "Young People's Digital Lives: The Impact of Interpersonal Relationships and Digital Media Use on Adolescents' Sense of Identity." *Computers in Human Behavior* 29, no. 6 (November 2013): 2281–93. https://doi.org/10.1016/j.chb.2013.05.022.

Eklund, Lina, and Sara Roman. "Do Adolescent Gamers Make Friends Offline? Identity and Friendship Formation in School." *Computers in Human Behavior* 73 (August 2017): 284–89. https://doi.org/10.1016/j.chb.2017.03.035.

Epstein, Jonathon S., ed. *Youth Culture: Identity in a Postmodern World*. Oxford: Blackwell, 1998.

Erikson, Erik H. *Identity: Youth and Crisis*. New York: Norton, 1968.

Faix, Tobias. "Hybrid Identity: Youth in Digital Networks." *Journal of Youth and Theology* 15, no. 1 (2016): 65–87. https://doi.org/10.1163/24055093-01501005.

Feldman, S. Shirley, and Glen R. Elliot, eds. *At the Threshold: The Developing Adolescent*. Cambridge: Harvard University Press, 1990.

Francis, Leslie J., and William K. Kay. *Teenage Religion and Values*. Leominster: Gracewing, 1995.

Gardner, Howard, and Katie Davis. *The App Generation*. London: Yale University Press, 2013.

Giedd, Jay N. "The Digital Revolution and Adolescent Brain Evolution." *Journal of Adolescent Health* 51, no.2 (2012): 101–5. https://doi.org/10.1016/j.jadohealth.2012.06.002.

Hall, G. Stanley. *Adolescence*. New York: Appleton, 1904.

———. *Youth: Its Education, Regimen, and Hygiene*. New York: Appleton, 1906.

Lerner, Richard M., and Laurence Steinberg, eds. *Individual Bases of Adolescent Development*, 2nd ed. Vol.1 of *Handbook of Adolescent Psychology*. Hoboken, NJ: John Wiley and Sons, 2004.

McLeod, Saul. "Freud's Psychosexual Stages of Development." *Simply Psychology* (blog). Updated 2019. https://www.simplypsychology.org/psychosexual.html.

Moshman, David. *Adolescent Psychological Development: Rationality, Morality, and Identity*. 2nd ed. Mahwah, NJ: Lawrence Erlbaum Associates, 2004.

Pini, Mónica, Sandra I. Musanti, and Teresa Cerratto Pargman. "Youth Digital Cultural Consumption and Education." *Designs for Learning* 7, no. 2 (2014): 58–79. https://doi.org/10.2478/dfl-2014-0063.

Powys, John Cowper. *The Meaning of Culture*. New York: W. W. Norton, 1992.

Pressley, Michael, and Christine B. McCormick. *Child and Adolescent Development for Educators*. New York: Guilford Press, 2006.

Rauch, Jonathan. "Generation Next." *The Economist Readership* (blog). Accessed June 23, 2020. Available from https://web.archive.org/web/20190313195431/http://te.tbr.fun/generation-next/.

Savina, Elena, Jennifer L. Mills, Kelly Atwood, and Jason Cha. "Digital Media and Youth: A Primer for School Psychologists." *Contemporary School Psychology* 21 (January 2017): 80–91. https://doi.org/10.1007/s40688-017-0119-0.

Schultze, Quentin J., Roy M. Anker, James D. Bratt, William D. Romanowski, John W. Worst, and Lambert Zuidervaart. *Dancing in the Dark: Youth, Popular Culture and the Electronic Media*. Grand Rapids: Eerdmans, 1991.

Seiter, Ellen. *The Internet Playground: Children's Access, Entertainment, and Mis-Education*. New York: Peter Lang, 2004.

Shantz, Carolyn Uhlinger, and Willard W. Hartup, eds. *Conflict in Child and Adolescent Development*. Cambridge: Cambridge University Press, 1992.

Tapscott, Don. "The Net Generation." *Don Tapscott* (website). Accessed August 15, 2017. http://dontapscott.com/speaking/net-generation/.

———. *Grown Up Digital: How the Net Generation Is Changing Your World*. New York: McGraw Hill, 2009.

———. *Growing up Digital: The Rise of the Net Generation*. New York: McGraw Hill, 1998.

Uhls, Yalda T, Minas Michikyan, Jordan Morris, Debra Garcia, Gary W. Small, Eleni Zgourou, and Patricia M. Greenfield. "Five Days at Outdoor Education Camp without Screens Improves Preteen Skills with Nonverbal Emotion Cues." *Computers in Human Behavior* 39 (October 2014): 387–92. https://doi.org/10.1016/j.chb.2014.05.036.

Weber, Sandra, and Shanly Dixon. *Growing Up Online: Young People and Digital Technologies*. New York: Palgrave Macmillan, 2007.

Williams, Alex. "Move Over, Millennials, Here Comes Generation Z," *New York Times* (online). September 18, 2015. https://www.nytimes.com/2015/09/20/fashion/move-over-millennials-here-comes-generation-z.html.

Willis, Paul. *Common Culture: Symbolic Work at Play in the Everyday Cultures of the Young*. New York: McGraw Hill Education, 1990.

———. *Moving Culture: An Enquiry into the Cultural Activities of Young People*. London: Calouste Gulbenkian Foundation, 1990.

Yust, Karen-Marie. "Digital Power: Exploring the Effects of Social Media on Children's Spirituality." *International Journal of Children's Spirituality* 19, no. 2 (2014), 133–43. https://doi.org/10.1080/1364436X.2014.924908.

Technology and Theology

Bailey, Justin A. "Welcome to the Blogosphere." In *Everyday Theology: How to Read Cultural Texts and Interpret Trends*, edited by Kevin J. Vanhoozer, Charles A. Anderson, and Michael J. Sleasman, 173–88. Grand Rapids: Baker Academic, 2007.

Bennett, Jana Marguerite. *Aquinas on the Web? Doing Theology in an Internet Age.* London: T and T Clark, 2012.

Borgmann, Albert. *Power Failure: Christianity in the Culture of Technology.* Ada: Barzos Press, 2003.

Brock, Brian. *Captive to Christ, Open to the World: On Doing Christian Ethics in Public.* Eugene, OR: Cascade Books, 2014.

———. *Christian Ethics in a Technological Age.* Grand Rapids: Eerdmans, 2010.

Campbell, Heidi A., ed. *Digital Religion: Understanding Religious Practice in New Media Worlds.* New York: Routledge, 2013.

———. *When Religion Meets New Media.* New York: Routledge, 2010.

Campbell, Heidi A., and Stephen Garner. *Networked Theology: Negotiating Faith in Digital Culture.* Grand Rapids: Baker Academic, 2016.

Campbell, Heidi A., and Gregory P. Grieve, eds. *Playing with Religion in Digital Games.* Bloomington, IN: Indiana University Press, 2014.

Challies, Tim. *The Next Story: Life and Faith after the Digital Explosion.* Grand Rapids: Zondervan, 2011. Calibre.

Drescher, Elizabeth. *Tweet If You Love Jesus: Practicing Church in the Digital Reformation.* Harrisburg, PA: Morehouse Publishing, 2011.

Estes, Douglas. *SimChurch: Being the Church in the Virtual World.* Grand Rapids: Zondervan, 2019.

Fore, William F. *Mythmakers: Gospel, Culture and the Media.* Cincinnati: Friendship Press, 1990.

Fortner, Robert S. *The Gospel in a Digital Age.* Accessed November 4, 2008. Available from https://web.archive.org/web/20050218214826/http://www.calvin.edu/academic/cas/faculty/pweb/gospel.pdf.

Garner, Stephen. "Imaging Christ in Digital Worlds: Continuity and Discontinuity in Discipleship." *Communication Research Trends* 38, no. 4 (2019): 21–30. https://search.proquest.com/docview/2353631548.

Harvey, Barry. *Taking Hold of the Real: Dietrich Bonhoeffer and the Profound Worldliness of Christianity.* Eugene, OR: Cascade Books, 2015.

Hess, Mary E. "A New Culture of Learning: Digital Storytelling and Faith Formation." *Dialog: A Journal of Theology* 53, no. 1 (March 2014): 12–22. https://doi.org/10.1111/dial.12084.

Hipps, Shane. *Flickering Pixels: How Technology Shapes Your Faith.* Grand Rapids: Zondervan, 2009.

———. *The Hidden Power of Electronic Culture: How Media Shapes Faith, the Gospel, and Church.* Grand Rapids: Zondervan, 2005.

Houston, Graham. *Virtual Morality: Christian Ethics in the Computer Age.* Leicester, UK: Apollos, 1998.

Hunt, Jodi G. "The Digital Way: Re-imagining Digital Discipleship in the Age of Social Media." *Journal of Youth and Theology* 18, no. 2 (December 2019): 91–112. https://doi.org/10.1163/24055093-01802003.

Hutchings, Tim. "On Digital Theology by @tim_hutchings." *The Big Bible Project* (website). Accessed August 14, 2017. http://archive.bigbible.uk/2012/07/on-digital-theology.

Le Duc, Anthony. "Cyber/Digital Theology: Rethinking about Our Relationship with God and Neighbour in the Digital Environment." *Religion and Social Communication* 13, no. 2 (2015): 132–58. https://ssrn.com/abstract=3057507.

Lowe, Stephen D., and Mary E. Lowe. *Ecologies of Faith in a Digital Age: Spiritual Growth through Online Education*. Downers Grove, IL: InterVarsity Press, 2018.

McDonnell, Jim. "Mass Media, British Culture, and Gospel Values." In *The Gospel and Contemporary Culture*, edited by Hugh Montefiore, 159–81. London: Mowbray, 1992.

Meadows, Philip R. "Mission and Discipleship in a Digital Culture." *Mission Studies* 29, no. 2 (2012): 163–82. https://doi.org/10.1163/15733831-12341235.

Pattison, George. *Thinking about God in an Age of Technology*. Oxford: Oxford University Press, 2005.

Rice, Jesse. *The Church of Facebook: How the Hyperconnected Are Redefining Community*. Colorado Springs: David C. Cook, 2009.

Shirley, Chris. "Overcoming Digital Distance: The Challenge of Developing Relational Disciples in the Internet Age." *Christian Education Journal* 14, no. 2 (2017): 376–90. http://search.ebscohost.com/login.aspx?direct=true&db=rfh&AN=ATLAiGFE171023000693&site=ehost-live.

Sogaard, Viggo. *Media in Church and Mission: Communicating the Gospel*. Pasadena, CA: William Carey Library: 1993.

Spadaro, Antonio. *Cybertheology: Thinking Christianity in the Era of the Internet*. New York: Fordham University Press, 2014.

Stoddart, Eric. *Theological Perspectives on a Surveillance Society: Watching and Being Watched*. Surrey: Ashgate, 2011. Kindle.

Sweet, Leonard. *Viral: How Social Networking Is Poised to Ignite Revival*. Colorado Springs: WaterBrook Press, 2012.

Thomas, Adam. *Digital Disciple: Real Christianity in a Virtual World*. Nashville: Abingdon, 2011. Calibre.

Ward, Pete. *Liquid Church*. Carlisle: Paternoster Press, 2002.

———. *Mass Culture: Eucharist and Mission in a Post-Modern World*. Oxford: The Bible Reading Fellowship, 1999.

Theology of Discipleship

Aleshire, Daniel. "Christian Education and Theology." In *Christian Education Handbook,* edited by Bruce P. Powers, 13–28. Nashville: Broadman and Holman, 1996.

Andrews, Alan, ed. *The Kingdom Life: A Practical Theology of Discipleship and Spiritual Formation.* Colorado Springs: NavPress, 2010.

Astley, Jeff, and Leslie Francis, eds. *Christian Perspectives on Faith Development: A Reader.* Leominster: Gracewing, 1992.

Athyal, Abraham P., and Dorothy Yoder Nyce, eds. *Mission Today: Challenges and Concerns.* Kilpauk, India: Gurukul Lutheran Theological College, 1998.

Augustine. Vol 1 of *Confessions.* Edited and translated by Carolyn J. B. Hammond. Cambridge: Harvard University Press, 2016.

Barna, George. *Growing True Disciples.* Ventura, CA: Issachar Resources, 2000.

Barth, Karl. *Ethics.* Edited by Dietrich Braun and translated by Geoffrey W. Bromiley. Eugene: Wipf and Stock, 2013.

Battles, Ford Lewis. *Analysis of the Institutes of the Christian Religion of John Calvin.* Phillipsburg: P&R, 2001.

Bethge, Eberhard. *Dietrich Bonhoeffer: Theologian, Christian, Contemporary.* London: Collins, 1970.

Bevans, Stephen B. *Models of Contextual Theology.* Maryknoll: Orbis Books, 1992.

Boa, Kenneth. *Conformed to His Image: Biblical and Practical Approaches to Spiritual Formation.* Grand Rapids: Zondervan, 2001.

———. *That I May Know God: Pathways to Spiritual Formation.* Colorado Springs: Multnomah Publishers, 1998.

Bonhoeffer, Dietrich. *Act and Being.* Translated by H. Mertin Rumscheidt and edited by Wayne Whitson Floyd. Vol. 2 of *Dietrich Bonhoeffer Works.* Minneapolis: Fortress Press, 1996.

———. *Berlin: 1932–1933.* Edited by Larry L. Rasmussen and translated by Isabel Best and David Higgins. Vol. 12 of *Dietrich Bonhoeffer Works.* Minneapolis: Fortress Press, 2009.

———. *Creation and Fall: A Theological Exposition of Genesis 1–3.* Edited by John W. de Gruchy and translated by Douglas Steven Bax. Vol. 3 of *Dietrich Bonhoeffer Works.* Minneapolis: Fortress Press, 1997.

———. *Discipleship.* Edited by John D. Godsey and Geffrey B. Kelly and translated by Barbara Green and Reinhard Krauss. Vol. 4 of *Dietrich Bonhoeffer Works.* Minneapolis: Fortress Press, 2001.

———. *Ethics.* Edited by Clifford J. Green and translated by Reinhard Krauss, Douglas W. Stott, and Charles C. West. Vol. 6 of *Dietrich Bonhoeffer Works.* Minneapolis: Fortress Press, 2005.

———. *Letters and Papers from Prison*. Edited by John W. De. Gruchy and translated by Isabel Best, Lisa E. Dahill, Reinhard Krauss, and Nancy Lukens. Vol. 8 of *Dietrich Bonhoeffer Works*. Minneapolis: Fortress Press, 2010.

———. *Life Together*. London: SCM Press, 1963.

———. *Sanctorum Communio: A Theological Study of the Sociology of the Church*. Edited by Clifford J. Green and translated by Reinhard Krauss and Nancy Lukens. Vol. 1 of *Dietrich Bonhoeffer Works*. Minneapolis: Fortress Press, 2009.

———. *The Young Bonhoeffer*. Edited by Clifford J. Green, Marshall D. Johnson, and Paul Duane Matheny and translated by Mary C. Nebelsick and Douglas W. Stott. Vol. 9 of *Dietrich Bonhoeffer Works*. Minneapolis: Fortress Press, 2002.

Bosch, David J. *Transforming Mission: Paradigm Shifts in Theology of Mission*. Maryknoll, NY: Orbis Books, 1992.

Botton, Ken, Chuck King, and Junias Venugopal. "Educating for Spirituality." *Christian Education Journal*, 1NS (1997): 33–48.

Brock, Brian, and Bernd Wannenwetsch. *The Malady of the Christian Body*. Vol. 1 of *A Theological Exposition of Paul's First Letter to the Corinthians*. Eugene, OR: Cascade Books, 2016.

———. *The Therapy of the Christian Body*. Vol. 2 of *A Theological Exposition of Paul's First Letter to the Corinthians*. Eugene, OR: Cascade Books, 2018.

Burer, Michael H. "Towards a Biblical Definition of Spiritual Formation: Romans 12:1–2." *Bible.org* (website). Accessed June 4, 2018. https://bible.org/seriespage/towards-biblical-definition-spiritual-formation-romans-121-2.

Calhoun, Adele Ahlberg. *Spiritual Disciplines Handbook: Practices That Transform Us*. Downers Grove, IL: InterVarsity Press, 2005.

Calvin, John. "Institutes of the Christian Religion." Translated by Henry Beveridge. *Christian Classics Ethereal Library* (website). Accessed April 26, 2008. http://www.ccel.org/ccel/calvin/institutes.toc.html.

———. *Institutes of the Christian Religion*. Edited by John T. McNeil and translated by Ford Lewis Battles. Vols. 20–21 of *Library of Christian Classics*. Louisville: Westminster John Knox Press, 1960.

Canlis, Julie. "Calvin's Institutes: Primer for Spiritual Formation." *CRUX* 47, no. 1 (Spring 2011): 16–29.

Caussade, Jean-Pierre de. "The Present Moment." *Renovaré* (website). Accessed November 29, 2018. https://renovare.org/articles/the-present-moment.

Chandler, Diane J. *Spiritual Formation: An Integrated Approach for Personal and Relational Wholeness*. Downers Grove, IL: InterVarsity Press, 2014.

Dahill, Lisa E. *Reading from the Underside of Selfhood: Bonhoeffer and Spiritual Formation*. Eugene, OR: Wipf and Stock, 2009.

Dettoni, John M. "What is Spiritual Formation?" In *The Christian Educator's Handbook on Spiritual Formation,* edited by Kenneth O. Gangel and James C. Wilhoit, 11–19. Wheaton: Victor Books, 1994.

Donahue, Bill. *The Willow Creek Guide to Leading Life-Changing Small Groups.* Grand Rapids: Zondervan, 1996.

Dorr, Donal. *Mission in Today's World.* Maryknoll, NY: Orbis Books, 2000.

Downs, Perry G. *Teaching for Spiritual Growth: An Introduction to Christian Education.* Grand Rapids: Zondervan Academic, 1994.

Dunn, Richard R., and Jana L. Sundene. *Shaping the Journey of Emerging Adults: Life-Giving Rhythms for Spiritual Transformation.* Downers Grove: InterVarsity Press, 2012.

Foster, Nathan. *The Making of an Ordinary Saint: My Journey from Frustration to Joy with the Spiritual Discipline.* Grand Rapids: Baker Books, 2014.

Foster, Richard. *Celebration of Discipline: The Path to Spiritual Growth.* London: Hodder and Stoughton, 1980.

———. "Ten Counsels: Richard Foster on Spiritual Formation." *Reformed Worship* (website). Accessed June 7, 2018. https://www.reformedworship.org/article/march-2008/ten-counsels-richard-foster-spiritual-formation.

Fowler, James W. *Faith Development and Pastoral Care.* Philadelphia: Fortress Press, 1987.

———. *Stages of Faith: The Psychology of Human Development and the Quest for Meaning.* New York: Harper and Row, 1981.

Gnanakan, Ken. *Kingdom Concerns: A Theology of Mission Today.* Leicester: InterVarsity Press, 1993.

Goggin, Jamin, and Kyle Strobel, eds. *Reading the Christian Spiritual Classics: A Guide for Evangelicals.* Downers Grove: InterVarsity Press, 2013.

Good, Raney. "Celebrating Varieties of Christian Formation Ministries." *Christians in Education* 5, no. 3 (Summer 1999): 1–14.

Greenman, Jeffrey P., and George Kalantzis, eds. *Life in the Spirit: Spiritual Formation in Theological Perspective.* Downers Grove: InterVarsity Press, 2010.

Greenway, Roger S. *Go and Make Disciples!: An Introduction to Christian Missions.* Phillipsburg, New Jersey: P and R, 1999.

Grenz, Stanley J. *The Moral Quest: Foundations of Christians Ethics.* Westmont, IL: InterVarsity Press, 1997.

Hagglund, Bengt. *History of Theology.* Saint Louis, Missouri: Concordia Publishing House, 1968.

Hare, John. *Why Bother Being Good?* Westmont, IL: InterVarsity Press, 2002.

Harris, Maria. "Teaching: Forming and Transforming Grace." In *Congregations: Their Power to Form and Transform,* edited by C. Ellis Nelson, 238–263. Atlanta: John Knox Press, 1988.

Hauerwas, Stanley, and William H. Willimon. *Resident Aliens: Life in the Christian Colony; A Provocative Christian Assessment of Culture and Ministry for People Who Know That Something Is Wrong*. Nashville: Abingdon Press, 1989. Available as a PDF at https://b-ok.cc/book/829157/32c2cb.

Hawkins, Don. *Master Discipleship: Jesus's Prayer and Plan for Every Believer*. Grand Rapids: Kregel, 2019.

Helm, David. *One-to-One Bible Reading: A Simple Guide for Every Christian*. Sydney: Matthias Media, 2012.

Hesselgrave, David J. *Communicating Christ Cross-culturally: An Introduction to Missionary Communication*. Grand Rapids: Zondervan, 1991.

Howard, Evan B. "Lectio Divina in the Evangelical Tradition." *Journal of Spiritual Formation and Soul Care* 5, no. 1 (Spring 2012): 56–77. http://search.ebscohost.com/login.aspx?direct=true&db=rfh&AN=ATLA0001899623&site=ehost-live.

Hull, Bill. *The Complete Book of Discipleship: On Being and Making Followers of Christ*. Colorado Springs: NavPress, 2006.

Hybels, Lynne, and Bill Hybels. *Rediscovering Church*. Grand Rapids: Zondervan, 1995.

Jonas, Robert A., ed. *The Essential Henri Nouwen*. Boston: Shambhala, 2009.

Jordan, C. Ferris. "The Role of the Pastor in Christian Education." In *Christian Education Handbook*, edited by Bruce P. Powers, 295–310. Nashville: Broadman and Holman, 1996.

Kort, Wesley. *Take, Read: Scripture, Textuality, and Cultural Practice*. University Park: Pennsylvania State University Press, 1996.

Kraft, Charles H. *Christianity in Culture: A Study in Dynamic Biblical Theologizing in Cross-cultural Perspective*. Maryknoll: Orbis Books 1979.

Kraft, Charles H. *Communication Theory for Christian Witness*. Nashville: Abingdon Press, 1983.

Lawrence, Brother. *The Practice of the Presence of God: The Best Rule of a Holy Life*. London: Epworth, n.d.

Lazareth, William H. *Christians in Society: Luther, the Bible, and Social Ethics*. Minneapolis: Augsburg Fortress, 2001.

Lovin, Robin W. *Christian Ethics: An Essential Guide*. Nashville: Abingdon Press, 2000.

McClung, Grant. *Globalbeliever.com: Connecting to God's Work in Your World*. Cleveland: Pathway Press, 2000.

McFarland, Ian A. *The Divine Image: Envisioning the Invisible God*. Minneapolis: Fortress Press, 2005.

McGrath, Alister E. *Christian Spirituality: An Introduction*. Malden: Blackwell Publishing, 1999.

———. *Christian Theology: An Introduction*. Malden: Blackwell Publishing, 2001.

Muller, Richard A. *Christ and the Decree*. Durham: Labyrinth Press, 1986.
Newbigin, Lesslie. *The Gospel in a Pluralist Society*. Grand Rapids: Eerdmans, 1989.
———. *Truth to Tell: The Gospel as Public Truth*. London: SPCK Publishing, 1991.
Niebuhr, H. Richard. *Christ and Culture*. New York: Harper and Row, 1951.
Northcott, Michael. "'Who Am I?': Human Identity and the Spiritual Disciplines in the Witness of Dietrich Bonhoeffer." In *Who Am I? Bonhoeffer's Theology through His Poetry*, edited by Bernd Wannenwetsch, 11–29. London: T and T Clark, 2009.
Nouwen, Henri J. M. *Adam: God's Beloved*. Maryknoll: Orbis Books, 1997.
———. *Spiritual Formation: Following the Movements of the Spirit*. London: SPCK, 2011.
———. *The Way of the Heart: Desert Spirituality and Contemporary Ministry*. London: Darton, Longman and Todd, 1981.
Ogden, Greg. *Transforming Discipleship: Making Disciples a Few at a Time*. Downers Grove, IL: InterVarsity Press, 2016.
Parker, T. H. L. *Calvin: An Introduction to His Thought*. London: Continuum, 1995.
Paul, Doug. "Why the difference between discipleship & spiritual formation matters." *100 Movements* (website). Accessed April 19, 2018. https://www.100movements.com/articles/why-the-difference-between-discipleship-spiritual-formation-matters.
Pettit, Paul. *Foundations of Spiritual Formation: A Community Approach to Becoming Like Christ*. Grand Rapids: Kregel, 2008.
Pobee, J. S., ed. *Religion in a Pluralistic Society*. Leiden: E. J. Brill, 1976.
Ramsey, Paul. *Basic Christian Ethics*. Chicago: University of Chicago Press, 1950.
Reist, Benjamin A. *A Reading of Calvin's Institutes*. Louisville: John Knox Press, 1991.
Schreiter, Robert J. *Constructing Local Theologies*. Mary Knoll: Orbis Books, 1985.
Schwanda, Tom. "Evangelical Spiritual Disciplines: Practices for Knowing God." *Journal of Spiritual Formation and Soul Care* 10, no. 2 (2017): 220–236. http://search.ebscohost.com/login.aspx?direct=true&db=rfh&AN=ATLAiAZI180131001559&site=ehost-live.
———. "'To Gaze on the Beauty of the Lord': The Evangelical Resistance and Retrieval of Contemplation." *Journal of Spiritual Formation and Soul Care* 7, no. 1 (Spring 2014): 62–84. http://search.ebscohost.com/login.aspx?direct=true&db=rfh&AN=ATLA0001982851&site=ehost-live.
Schwarz, Christian A. *Natural Church Development: A Guide to Eight Essential Qualities of Healthy Churches*. St. Charles, IL: ChurchSmart Resources, 1996.
Sedgwick, Peter. "Who Am I Now? Theology and Self-Identity." *Theology* 104, no. 819 (May 2001): 196–203. https://doi.org/10.1177/0040571X0110400306.
Sell, Alan P. F. *The Great Debate: Calvinism, Arminianism, and Salvation*. Grand Rapids: Baker Book House, 1982.

Seymour, Jack L. and Donald E. Miller. "Openings to God: Education and Theology in Dialogue." In *Theological Approaches to Christian Education*, edited by Jack L. Seymour and D. E. Miller, 7–24. Nashville: Abingdon Press, 1990.

Smallbones, Jackie L. "Educating People to be Christian." *Christian Education Journal* 10, no. 2 (Winter 1990): 55–63.

Smith, Gordon T. "Restoring Historic Monasticism? A Counter-Proposal." *Journal of Spiritual Formation and Soul Care* 10, no. 2 (2017): 265–71. http://search.ebscohost.com/login.aspx?direct=true&db=rfh&AN=ATLAi9KZ180131001562&site=ehost-live.

Smith, James Bryan, and Lynda Graybeal. *Spiritual formation Workbook: Small Group Resources for Nurturing Christian Growth*. London: HarperCollins, 1999.

Smith, James K. A. *Desiring the Kingdom: Worship, Worldview, and Cultural Formation*. Vol. 1 of Cultural Liturgies. Ada: Baker Academic, 2009.

———. *Imagining the Kingdom: How Worship Works*. Vol. 2 of Cultural Liturgies. Ada: Baker Academic, 2013.

———. *You Are What You Love: The Spiritual Power of Habit*. Grand Rapids: Brazos Press, 2016. Epub.

Stonehouse, Catherine. "After a Child's First Dance with God: Accompanying Children on a Protestant Spiritual Journey." In *Nurturing Child and Adolescent Spirituality: Perspectives from the World's Religious Traditions*, Edited by Karen-Marie Yust, Aostre N. Johnson, Sandy Eisenberg Sasso, and Eugene C. Roehlkepartain, 95–107. Lanham, MD: Rowman and Littlefield, 2006.

Tye, Karren B. *Basics of Christian Education*. St. Louis, MO: Chalice Press, 2000.

Vanier, Jean. *Community and Growth*. London: Darton, Longman and Todd, 2007.

Van Rheenen, Gailyn, and Anthony Parker. *Biblical Foundations and Contemporary Strategies*. Grand Rapids: Zondervan, 1996.

Warren, Rick. *The Purpose Driven Church: Every Church Is Big in God's Eyes*. Grand Rapids: Zondervan, 1995.

Wesley, John. Vol. 14 of *The Works of John Wesley*. Peabody, MA: Hendrickson Publishers 1991.

Wilhoit, James C. *Spiritual Formation as if the Church Mattered: Growing in Christ through Community*. Ada, MI: Baker Academic, 2008.

Willard, Dallas. *Renovation of the Heart: Putting on the Character of Christ*. Colorado Springs: NavPress, 2002.

———. "Spiritual Formation in Christ Is for the Whole Life and Whole Person." In *For All the Saints: Evangelical Theology and Christian Spirituality*, edited by Timothy George and Alister McGrath, 39–53. Louisville: Westminster John Knox Press, 2003.

———. "Spiritual Formation: What It Is, and How It Is Done." *Dallas Willard* (website). Accessed June 4, 2018. http://www.dwillard.org/articles/individual/spiritual-formation-what-it-is-and-how-it-is-done.

Williams, Rowan. *Being Disciples: Essentials of the Christian Life*. Grand Rapids: Eerdmans, 2016.

Woodward, James, Stephen Pattison, and John Patton, eds. *The Blackwell Reader in Pastoral and Practical Theology*. Oxford: Blackwell Publishers, 2000.

Yung, Hwa. *Mangoes or Bananas? The Quest for an Authentic Asian Christian Theology*. Oxford: Regnum Books, 1997.

Youth discipleship

Breen, Mike. *Outside In: Reaching Un-Churched Young People Today*. London: Scripture Union, 1993.

Brierley, Peter. *Reaching and Keeping Teenagers*. Grand Rapids: Monarch Books, 1993.

Buckeridge, John. *Nurturing Young Disciples*. London: Marshall Pickering, 1995.

Dean, Kenda Creasy. *Almost Christian: What the Faith of Our Teenagers is Telling the American Church*. New York: Oxford University Press, 2010.

———. *Practicing Passion: Youth and the Quest for a Passionate Church*. Grand Rapids: Eerdmans, 2006.

Dean, Kenda Creasy, Chap Clark, and Dave Rahn, eds. *Starting Right: Thinking Theologically about Youth Ministry*. Grand Rapids: Zondervan, 2001.

Dettoni, John M. *Introduction to Youth Ministry*. Grand Rapids: Zondervan, 1993.

Dunn, Richard R., and Mark H. Senter, III, eds. *Reaching a Generation for Christ*. Chicago: Moody Press, 1997.

Emery-Wright, Steven. *Understanding Teenage Sexuality: A Foundation for Christian Relationships*. Singapore: Amour, 2009.

Emery-Wright, Steven, and Ed Mackenzie. *Networks for Faith Formation: Relational Bonds and the Spiritual Growth of Youth*. Eugene: Wipf and Stock, 2017.

Fields, Doug. *Purpose Driven Youth Ministry: 9 Essential Foundations for Healthy Growth*. Manila: OMF Literature, 1998.

Hall, R. Clyde. *Handbook for Youth Discipleship*. Nashville: Broadman, 1988.

Hickford, Andy. *Essential Youth: Why Your Church Needs Young People*. Eastbourne, UK: Kingsway, 1998.

Kelly, Paul G. "A Theology of Youth." *Journal for Baptist Theology and Ministry: Theology of Youth Ministry* 13, no. 1 (Spring 2016): 3–19.

Khoon, Tan Tee. "Youth and the Internet." *Church and Society in Asia Today* 10, no. 2 (August 2007): 89–97.

Kinnaman, David. *You Lost Me: Why Young Christians Are Leaving Church . . . and Rethinking Faith*. Grand Rapids: Baker Books, 2011.

Kinnaman, David, and Mark Matlock. *Faith for Exiles: 5 Ways for a New Generation to Follow Jesus in Digital Babylon*. Grand Rapids: Baker Books, 2019. Kindle.

Koh, Daniel K. S. "Youth and the Internet: A Pastoral Perspective." *Church and Society in Asia Today* 10, no. 2 (August 2007): 98–109.

Marian, Jim. *Growing up Christian*. Wheaton: Victor Books, 1992.

Mercadante, Frank. *Growing Teen Disciples: Strategies for Really Effective Youth Ministry*. Notre Dame, IN: Ave Maria Press, 1998.

Nappa, Mike. *Get Real: Making Core Christian Beliefs Relevant to Teenagers*. Loveland, CO: Group Publishing, 1996.

Ng, David. "Children in the Worshipping Community." *Reformed Liturgy and Music* 31, no. 4 (1997): 233–236.

Nishioka, Rodger. "Preaching and Youth in a Media Culture." *Journal for Preachers* 24, no. 1 (Winter 2000): 39–44.

Olson, G. Keith. *Counselling Teenagers*. Loveland: Group Publishing, 1984.

Parrott III, Les. *Helping the Struggling Adolescent*. Grand Rapids: Zondervan, 1993.

Rice, Wayne, Chap Clark. *New Directions for Youth Ministry*. Loveland: Group Publishing, 1998.

Robbins, Duffy. *The Ministry of Nurture: A Youth Worker's Guide to Discipling Teenagers*. Grand Rapids: Zondervan, 1990.

Root, Andrew. *Bonhoeffer as Youth Worker: A Theological Vision for Discipleship and Life Together*. Ada: Baker Academic, 2015.

———. *Faith Formation in a Secular Age: Responding to the Church's Obsession with Youthfulness*. Ada: Baker Academic, 2017.

Schultz, Thom. *Involving Youth in Youth Ministry*. Loveland: Group Publishing, 1987.

Schultz, Thom, and Joani. *Do It! Active Learning in Youth Ministry*. Loveland: Group Publishing, 1989.

Spotts, Dwight. *Reaching Out to Troubled Youth*. Wheaton: Victor Books, 1987.

Stephens, Larry D. *Your Child's Faith: Building a Foundation*. Grand Rapids: Zondervan, 1996.

Trimmer, Edward A. *Youth Ministry Handbook*. Nashville: Abingdon Press, 1994.

Veerman, David R. *Small Group Ministry with Youth*. Wheaton, IL: Victor Books, 1992.

———. *Youth Evangelism*. Wheaton, IL: Victor Books, 1988.

Vo, Huong Nam. "What is Good about Digital Technology in Discipling Youth." *Religion and Social Communication* 18, no. 2, 2020: 212-238.

———. "Youth Identity in the Digital Age." *Asia Journal of Theology* 35 no. 1 (April 2021): 58-82.

Ward, Pete. *The Church and Youth Ministry*. England: Lynx, 1995.

———. *God at the Mall: Youth Ministry That Meets Kids Where They're At*. Peabody, MA: Hendrickson Publishers, 1999.

———. *Growing up Evangelical: Youthwork and the Making of a Subculture*. London: SPCK, 1996.

———. *Relational Youthwork*. England: Lynx, 1995.

———. *Worship and Youth Culture*. London: Marshall Pickering, 1993.

———. *Youth Culture and the Gospel*. London: Marshall Pickering, 1992.

———. *Youth work and the Mission of God: Frameworks for Relational Outreach*. London: SPCK, 1997.

Youth Specialties. *Camps, Retreats, Missions and Service Ideas for Youth Groups*. Grand Rapids: Zondervan, 1997.

———. *Creative Meetings, Bible Lessons and Worship Ideas for Youth Groups*. Grand Rapids: Zondervan, 1997.

Vietnamese Church Context

Hays, Jeffrey. "Society in Vietnam: Confucianism, History, Social Structures and Communism." *Facts and Details* (website). Accessed October 15, 2020. http://factsanddetails.com/southeast-asia/Vietnam/sub5_9c/entry-3404.html.

Nguyen, Kimson. *Cultural Integration and the Gospel in Vietnamese Mission Theology: A Paradigm Shift*. Carlisle: Langham Monographs, 2019.

Reimer, Reg. *Vietnam's Christians: A Century of Growth in Adversity*. Pasadena, CA: William Carey Library, 2011.

The Alliance. "Beliefs: What Do We Believe?" *The Alliance* (website). Accessed October 14, 2020. Available from https://web.archive.org/web/20201004192010/https://www.cmalliance.org/about/beliefs/.

The Alliance. "History: Then and Now." *The Alliance* (website). Accessed 14, 2020. Available from https://web.archive.org/web/20200702115023/https://cmalliance.org/about/history/.

Van De Walle, Bernie A. *The Heart of the Gospel: A. B. Simpson, the Fourfold Gospel, and Late Nineteenth-Century Evangelical Theology*. Eugene, OR: Pickwick Publications, 2009.

Langham Literature, with its publishing work, is a ministry of Langham Partnership.

Langham Partnership is a global fellowship working in pursuit of the vision God entrusted to its founder John Stott –

> *to facilitate the growth of the church in maturity and Christ-likeness through raising the standards of biblical preaching and teaching.*

Our vision is to see churches in the Majority World equipped for mission and growing to maturity in Christ through the ministry of pastors and leaders who believe, teach and live by the word of God.

Our mission is to strengthen the ministry of the word of God through:
- nurturing national movements for biblical preaching
- fostering the creation and distribution of evangelical literature
- enhancing evangelical theological education

especially in countries where churches are under-resourced.

Our ministry

Langham Preaching partners with national leaders to nurture indigenous biblical preaching movements for pastors and lay preachers all around the world. With the support of a team of trainers from many countries, a multi-level programme of seminars provides practical training, and is followed by a programme for training local facilitators. Local preachers' groups and national and regional networks ensure continuity and ongoing development, seeking to build vigorous movements committed to Bible exposition.

Langham Literature provides Majority World preachers, scholars and seminary libraries with evangelical books and electronic resources through publishing and distribution, grants and discounts. The programme also fosters the creation of indigenous evangelical books in many languages, through writer's grants, strengthening local evangelical publishing houses, and investment in major regional literature projects, such as one volume Bible commentaries like the *Africa Bible Commentary* and the *South Asia Bible Commentary*.

Langham Scholars provides financial support for evangelical doctoral students from the Majority World so that, when they return home, they may train pastors and other Christian leaders with sound, biblical and theological teaching. This programme equips those who equip others. Langham Scholars also works in partnership with Majority World seminaries in strengthening evangelical theological education. A growing number of Langham Scholars study in high quality doctoral programmes in the Majority World itself. As well as teaching the next generation of pastors, graduated Langham Scholars exercise significant influence through their writing and leadership.

To learn more about Langham Partnership and the work we do visit **langham.org**

www.ingramcontent.com/pod-product-compliance
Lightning Source LLC
Chambersburg PA
CBHW070235240426
43673CB00044B/1804